I0213869

THE STUDIA PHILONICA ANNUAL
Studies in Hellenistic Judaism

THE STUDIA PHILONICA ANNUAL

Studies in Hellenistic Judaism

Editors

David T. Runia

Gregory E. Sterling

THE STUDIA PHILONICA ANNUAL

Studies in Hellenistic Judaism

Volume XXI

2009

Society of Biblical Literature
Atlanta

THE STUDIA PHILONICA ANNUAL
Studies in Hellenistic Judaism

The financial support of
C. J. de Vogel Foundation, Utrecht
Queen's College, University of Melbourne
University of Notre Dame
Pepperdine University
is gratefully acknowledged

ISBN: 978-1-58983-443-9
ISSN : 1052-4533

The cover photo, *Ezra Reads the Law,* is from a wall painting in the Dura Europos synagogue and used with permission from Zev Radovan (www.BibleLandPictures.com).

Printed in the United States of America
on acid-free paper

THE STUDIA PHILONICA ANNUAL

STUDIES IN HELLENISTIC JUDAISM

Contributions should be sent to the Editor, Prof. Gregory E. Sterling, Dean of the Graduate School, 408 Main Building, University of Notre Dame, Notre Dame, IN 46556, USA; email: sterling@nd.edu. Please send books for review to the Book Review Editor, Prof. Ronald Cox, Religion Division, Pepperdine University, 24255 Pacific Coast Highway, Malibu, CA 90263-4352, email rcox@pepperdine.edu.

Contributors are requested to observe the "Instructions to Contributors" located at the end of the volume. These can also be consulted on the Annual's website: http://www.nd.edu/~philojud. Articles which do not conform to these instructions cannot be accepted for inclusion.

The Studia Philonica Monograph series accepts monographs in the area of Hellenistic Judaism, with special emphasis on Philo and his *Umwelt*. Proposals for books in this series should be sent to Prof. Gregory E. Sterling, Dean of the Graduate School, 408 Main Building, University of Notre Dame, Notre Dame IN 46556, USA; email sterling.1@nd.edu

CONTENTS*

ARTICLES

REVIEW ARTICLE

BIBLIOGRAPHY SECTION

BOOK REVIEW SECTION

* The editors wish to thank the typesetter Gonni Runia once again for her tireless and meticulous work on this volume. They also wish to thank Tamar Primoratz (Melbourne) for her assistance with the bibliography, Sister Lisa Marie Belz OSU, ABD for proofreading the final manuscript, and Kindalee DeLong for the assistance she has given in maintaining the Annual's website. As in previous years we are deeply grateful to our publisher SBL and to Leigh Andersen and Kathie Klein for making the publication of the Annual possible.

ABBREVIATIONS

For a complete listing of abbreviations used in this volume, please refer to the Instructions to Contributors section, pages 155–161.

The Studia Philonica Annual 21 (2009) 1–24

THE THEME OF FLIGHT AND EXILE IN THE ALLEGORICAL THOUGHT-WORLD OF PHILO OF ALEXANDRIA

DAVID T. RUNIA

1. *A thought-experiment*[*]

Let us begin this paper on the theme of flight and exile in Philo with a thought-experiment. We are to imagine that in the second century of our era a well-schooled reader came across a book-roll with the following title on the outside of the roll:

ΦΙΛΩΝΟΣ ΠΕΡΙ ΦΥΓΗΣ ΚΑΙ ΕΥΡΕΣΕΩΣ
(Of Philo On flight/exile and discovery)

What conclusions would he or she be likely to reach? The first thought that would cross the reader's mind, I suspect, was that he had come across a treatise on the subject of φυγή, exile. He would be well aware, of course, that quite a few philosophers and other writers had written books or speeches with the title Περὶ φυγῆς, for example Plutarch of Chaeronea, Dio of Prusa, Favorinus of Arles, in earlier times Teles of Megara.[1] The name Philo was one of the most common, and he could by no means be sure which Philo was meant.[2] What might be puzzling for him was the combination of

[*] This paper was written at the request of Prof. Christoph Riedweg (Zurich) for a colloqium on the subject of "Exil in der Literatur" which he and his colleague Prof. Elisabeth Bronfen organized at the University of Zurich in the summer of 1999. It was also presented at the École Normale Supérieure, Paris, in 2000, at the University of British Columbia, Vancouver, in 2002, and at the University of Stellenbosch, South Africa, in 2009. I would like to thank all my hosts for their hospitality and my audiences for their constructive responses to the lecture. My thanks too to Ellen Birnbaum for encouraging me to publish it. I have retained some elements of the initial oral presentation.

[1] Plutarch, extant at *Mor.* 599A–607F; Dio Chrysostomus, extant as *Or.* 13; Favorinus, partly preserved as *Vatic. Pap.* 11 (see *DPhA* 3.422); Teles, long excerpt at Stobaeus *Flor.* 3.40.8.

[2] It is possible that Philo's name could have been qualified with Ἑβραίου or Ἰουδαίου, but this was by no means necessarily the case. The Coptos papyrus, which contains the

themes, exile and discovery. What could περὶ εὑρέσεως mean in this title? Surely not, as one might suspect if it were a title on its own, the subject of invention of arguments as part of rhetoric.[3] What could be the connection with exile? The two subjects do not appear to go together at all.

If our reader proceeded to unfold the scroll, the mystery might well not be immediately cleared up. He would read the following:[4]

> καὶ ἐκάκωσεν αὐτὴν Σάρα, καὶ ἀπέδρα ἀπὸ προσώπου αὐτῆς. εὗρε δὲ αὐτὴν ἄγγελος κυρίου ἐπὶ τῆς πηγῆς τοῦ ὕδατος ἐν τῇ ἐρήμῳ, ἐπὶ τῆς πηγῆς ἐν τῇ ὁδῷ Σούρ. καὶ εἶπεν αὐτῇ ὁ ἄγγελος κυρίου· παιδίσκη Σάρας, πόθεν ἔρχῃ, καὶ ποῦ πορεύῃ; καὶ εἶπεν· ἀπὸ προσώπου Σάρας τῆς κυρίας μου ἐγὼ ἀποδιδράσκω. εἶπε δὲ αὐτῇ ὁ ἄγγελος κυρίου· ἀποστράφηθι πρὸς τὴν κυρίαν σου καὶ ταπεινώθητι ὑπὸ τὰς χεῖρας αὐτῆς.
>
> (And Sarah treated her harshly, and she ran away from her face. But Lord's messenger found her at the spring of water in the desert, at the spring on the road to Sur. And Lord's messenger said to her: slave-girl of Sarah, where do you come from and where are you going to? And she said: I am running away from the face of Sarah my mistress. But Lord's messenger said to her: return to your mistress and be humbled under her hands.) (Gen 16:6b–9)

Our imaginary reader would have to be *very* widely read—someone like the author of the treatise *On the Sublime*[5]—to recognize that these words were drawn from the sacred scriptures of the Jewish people. He would of course immediately understand that the title of the work coheres with the opening words of the cited text, the flight of the slave-girl and her discovery by "Lord's messenger" (which by the way he would have found a slightly curious phrase because the word κύριος lacks the article). And if he read on, he would discover that the first half of the treatise deals in broad terms with the theme of flight and exiles (§§1–119), while the second half treats the theme of finding, which the author has combined with the theme of seeking that precedes finding (§§119–213). No matter how learned our reader was, he would have found the treatise *very* heavy going, even if he did come across a couple of familiar quotations from Plato's *Theaetetus* on the way (§63, §82). I imagine his reaction would have been something like this: "What on earth have I got hold of here? This is quite unusual material." And he would have been quite right. It *is* esoteric material. In

---

complete text of two of Philo's allegorical treatises, simply gives as title ΦΙΛΩΝΟΣ ΠΕΡΙ . . .; cf. PCW 1.xlii.

[3] Cf. the extant treatise of the rhetor Hermogenes and the subdivision of rhetoric in the Stoic doxography in D.L. 7.43.

[4] I have given a rather literal translation of the Septuagintal text in order to try to convey the impression its language would have made on an educated Greek reader.

[5] Acquainted with the book of Genesis; see *Subl.* 9.9 and Stern *GLAJJ* 1.361–365.

order to understand what he had in his hands, our reader would have needed an introduction into the allegorical thought-world of the treatise's author, a learned Jew from Alexandria called Philo.

2. *Our subject*

This is precisely the aim of my paper, to introduce the allegorical thought-world of Philo of Alexandria, specifically in relation to the theme of flight and exile. It is a fascinating theme, occupying a central place in Philo's thought, and yet so far little researched.[6] But it is also a theme that could not be more relevant to our own time, when political and economic exigencies are forcing millions of people to leave their homes and seek to live in exile, often in the most desperate and heart-breaking circumstances.

As we shall see, Philo's allegorical treatment of the theme of flight and exile converts it into a spiritual theme, rather than a direct reflection on his own personal situation and the political circumstances of his own time. But it would be wrong to make too sharp a distinction between the two spheres of theory and practice. I will begin, therefore, by examining the theme of flight and exile in Jewish thought and how it relates to Philo's own situation. After this I will first proceed to introduce the method and chief features of Philo's allegorical thought-world. The main part of the lecture will then examine the manner in which our theme is worked out in Philo's allegorical exegesis of the biblical text.[7] This will be followed by a briefer analysis of how the theme works in Philo's thinking in relation to his intellectual background in both Greek and Jewish thought. Finally we will return to Philo's own situation, with which we began.

3. *Flight and exile in Judaism and Philo's situation in the Diaspora*

It can safely be said that the theme of exile (*galuth*) occupies a larger place in Jewish than it does in Greek thought.[8] As almost always, the foundations

[6] I know of no study in Philonic scholarship that deals with this specific theme. There is a valuable overview in the introduction to the commentary on *Fug.* by Esther Starobinski-Safran, PAPM vol. 17 (Paris: Cerf, 1970), 53–77.

[7] This means that most of the texts we will be citing will be from his grand Allegorical Commentary, which survives in 21 books. But allegorical material from the other two commentaries is not excluded; see further n. 25 below.

[8] See James M. Scott, *Exile: Old Testament, Jewish and Christian Conceptions*, (JSJSup 56, Leiden: Brill, 1997) and the brief but excellent article in *ODJ* 243–244.

are laid in the Hebrew Bible, which records two periods of exile, the descent of Jacob and his children into Egypt and, much later, the period of Babylonian captivity. To these a third and much longer period of exile was added. In later Jewish tradition the entire period after the fall of Jerusalem and the destruction of the temple in 70 C.E. up to modern times was conceived as *galuth*. Whether this period came to an end with the founding of the state of Israel in 1948 depends on one's political and religious convictions. There is at any rate a clear difference with the conception of exile as experienced in the Greco-Roman world. It is not just the experience of an individual or a small group. It involves the fate of an entire people. The meanings that can be attached to the experience of exile on this scale are enormous, involving separation and alienation, not only from the homeland, but possibly also from God, which brings along with it the themes of punishment, redemption and the hope of a future conceived in eschatological terms.

As it happens, the main character of our account today was a Jew who lived in one of the periods when Israel was *not* in exile. He himself, however, did not live in the Jewish homeland but in Alexandria, as a leading member of the largest Jewish community of the so-called Diaspora. Philo knows full well what exile meant in the Greco-Roman context of his day. He gives one of the more vivid descriptions of an individual undergoing exile when he describes the fate of the Egyptian governor Flaccus, who after his involvement in the anti-Jewish riots of 38 C.E. in Alexandria, fell out of favour with the Emperor Gaius and was banished to the notorious Aegean island of Andros, only to be executed there as a result of an imperial whim.[9] He will also have known of the Jewish period of exile in Babylonia and the subsequent restoration under Ezra and Nehemiah. But there is no evidence to suggest that he regarded living in the Diaspora as a kind of exile from the Jewish homeland. Indeed he never makes use of this term in the technical sense. [10] Instead he exploits the Greek imagery of a mother-city establishing colonies outside its border to describe the spread of Jewish communities throughout the Greco-Roman world.[11] We know

[9] *Flacc*. 146–191.

[10] Note especially his description of the wider Jewish world at *Flacc*. 45–46. See further the analysis of Willem C. van Unnik, *Das Selbstverständnis der jüdischen Diaspora in der hellenistisch-römischen Zeit: aus dem Nachlaß herausgegeben und bearbeitet von P. W. van der Horst* (AGJU 17; Leiden: Brill, 1993), 127–37.

[11] Philo here adapts a long-standing apologetic theme in the Hellenistic world that formed part of the competitive culture wards. Hecataeus of Abdera had argued that Egypt sent out colonies all over the world as a way to claim that Egypt was the fount of civilization. (I owe this point to Greg Sterling).

from an incidental remark that he visited Jerusalem to join in religious observances in the Temple.[12] It is quite likely that he maintained social and political connections with fellow Jews in Jerusalem.[13]

4. *Philo's "Allegorical thought-world"*

But even if Philo and other members of the Jewish community in Alexandria did not regard themselves as living in exile, they were certainly aware that they had the status of a minority group in a society that had long been governed and dominated by a Hellenized political and cultural elite. In the three centuries before Philo's birth the Jews of Alexandria had adapted themselves well to this situation. It can be convincingly argued that openness to Hellenic culture was one of the defining characteristics of Alexandrian Judaism.[14] These Jews spoke and wrote Greek, and to a considerable degree they also thought in Greek. The entire Hebrew Bible had been translated into the Greek language. A body of literature had developed in which Jewish history and Jewish ideas had been remodelled in Hellenic terms. Philo's extensive allegorical commentaries belong to this movement of cultural adaptation. He himself arrived relatively late on the scene, and could profit from a strong intellectual tradition—both exegetical and literary—that is now almost entirely lost to us. During his lifetime this *modus vivendi* came increasingly under threat, as Roman imperial dominance destroyed the delicate political balance that existed between the city's three main groups, Greeks, Jews and native Egyptians.[15] Soon after Philo's death the world of Hellenized Judaism in Alexandria was to disappear, just

[12] *Prov.* 2.107.

[13] In one text Philo interprets the prophecy of Moses in Deut 30:3–5 known as the "ingathering of the exiles" as involving the future return of οἱ σπόραδες—those scattered throughout Greece and the barbarian world—back to their homeland (*Praem.* 165–166). This text with its undeniable eschatological overtones has been the subject of much discussion in recent years (including the study of Van Unnik cited above in n. 8). I agree with the careful analysis of the Israeli scholar Yehoshua Amir, who argues that, though this text represents a position that Philo can accept and as such should most definitely not be ignored, it is not representative of his usual understanding of the situation of the Jews in the Diaspora; see Yehoshua Amir, *Die hellenistische Gestalt des Judentums bei Philon von Alexandrien* (Forschungen zum jüdisch-christlichen Dialog 5; Neukirchen–Vluyn: Neukirchener Verlag, 1983), 31–37.

[14] As well stated by Gregory E. Sterling, "'Thus are Israel': Jewish Self-Definition in Alexandria," *The Studia Philonica Annual* 7 (1995): 1–18.

[15] Well emphasized by Daniel R. Schwartz, "Philo, His Family, and His Times," in *The Cambridge Companion to Philo*, (ed. Adam Kamesar; New York: Cambridge University Press, 2009), 19–31.

like the cosmopolitan world of Alexandrian life evoked in the poems of Cavafy and the novels of Lawrence Durrell has disappeared in our lifetime.

Because of the theme we have chosen, we will be concentrating on the allegorical treatises of Philo which comprise nearly half his writings. They form an intriguing but enormously sophisticated and complex whole. It is a "world of thought" that one cannot plunge into without some form of introduction. I would like to introduce it by emphasizing the following four points.

(1) Allegory in Philo is in the first place a form of textual hermeneutics. Its basis lies in the authoritative text of the Pentateuch of Five books of Moses (i.e. Philo's Torah). The starting point is always the actual words of the text, whether these are names or concepts or numbers or whatever the case may be. Such words are related to or explained by means of *other* concepts or conceptual frameworks (ἀλληγορία literally means "other-speaking"). Such frameworks, it is claimed, reveal the *deeper* or underlying meaning of the text (ὑπόνοια). But even here, in Philo's practice, the meaning can usually only be teased out by relating the words to other texts in which they also occur. The entire Pentateuch thus forms a complex network of meaning. When we examine the theme of flight and exile, we shall thus need to start with the exegesis of those biblical texts in which these notions occur.

(2) Allegory, as we just saw, involved the relation and application of biblical words to other conceptual frameworks which are not immediately recognizable on the surface of the text. Such frameworks can be of various kinds. Philo is not very systematic in this area. Later divisions into the three-fold or four-fold meaning of the text are not found in his writings. He distinguishes between the literal and the figurative meaning of the text, and the latter is sometimes described as speaking φυσικῶς ("naturally" in the sense of "in conformity with the deeper underlying nature concealed within the text") or ἠθικῶς ("ethically" in the sense of "pertaining to the character or behaviour of the human person or soul'). Although there is some physical or cosmological allegory in Philo, by far the majority of his allegorical explanations involve the nature and fate of the soul. We can subdivide these further into psychological, ethical and anagogic or mystical allegory, but we would then be more specific than Philo himself. The focus is fairly and squarely on the soul, its nature and its progress through life and beyond. Our theme thus centres on flight and exile as it pertains to the life of the soul.

(3) Philo's allegorical exegeses are not interpretations of single texts taken on their own. The thematics of a single text are situated within larger networks of allegorical interpretations which form complete allegorical

systems in their own right. Such systems, I would argue, exhibit a large measure of *coherence*, without being *consistently* applied in all details. What I mean by this is that the various details of the interpretations are rooted in larger conceptual frameworks. These are assumed rather than explicitly spelled out, chiefly because the starting point is always the concrete text being explained. In the working out of the details of the individual exegesis, the aim is never to achieve any kind of far-reaching consistency. This too is because the individual text (and other texts which it is connected with) is the focus of attention. When speaking of allegorical systems and conceptual frameworks, I use the plural on purpose. We have to do here with one of the more controversial aspects of Philonic studies. It is plain that differing frameworks of interpretation which are often not fully consistent with each other lie behind Philo's various allegorical interpretations. Why does he reveal such diversity? The most likely answer is that Philo is an *inclusive* thinker working within an established tradition. He builds on the results of previous allegorists and develops them further. What I would wish to emphasize is that Philo's allegorical interpretations and the conceptual frameworks that they presume, together form what I would like to call an "allegorical thought-world," the term I have used in the title of my paper. It is a like an autonomous world of its own that we can enter by reading and studying Philo's allegorical treatises. In the same way that the trees in paradise as described in Gen 2, when allegorized, are not trees at all, but rather virtues, so the biblical characters in Philo's thought-world are not primarily people, but souls and concepts. But before we can enter this fascinating "thought-world," there is one further aspect we should take into account.

(4) In order to make my point, I want to draw an analogy that you may at first sight find a bit odd. My sons used to spend far too much time playing computer games. I never played them myself, but from time to time I did spend some fascinating hours watching them play. In such games the players are introduced into a virtual world, for example, the mysterious island called Myst.[16] This world is created by the software designer, and is basically fixed, though always with an impressive number of features, for example mountains, caves, harbours, beaches. Within that world you can move around, discover things, confront dangers, eliminate enemies and so on. It is when you are doing this that you are playing a so-called "game" (you can save such a game and continue where you left off after a quick break to do some homework, for example). One can thus make a distinction

[16] A prominent game in the late nineties when I first presented this paper; for more information on the game see the extensive article "Myst" in Wikipedia.

between the artificial world in which the game is played and the game itself. It is a distinction between an established environment and a single performance.

It seems to me that something similar goes on in Philo's allegorical writings. An individual treatise, which gives exegesis of a particular biblical passage—it can sometime be a number of verses—is rather like a performance. It works within the established conceptual frameworks of Philo's allegorical thought-world. He identifies a number of themes to which the biblical text gives rise and then develops these through the course of the treatise. In so doing he draws the reader through those aspects of the allegorical thought-world that he considers necessary for the deeper understanding of the text. For example, in the treatise *De fuga et inventione* Philo starts, as we have already seen, by quoting the biblical text. He then states that the text discusses the subject of fugitives, and informs the reader that Moses speaks about such people on several occasions. There are three reasons for flight, hatred, fear, and shame. Examples of the first two can be found in the case of Jacob, who fled from his father-in-law Laban out of hatred and from his brother Esau out of fear. These examples are working out at great length in §§7–52 of the treatise. Much more is said about Jacob than the subject of the text to be given exegesis, the slave-girl Hagar. This is the performance that Philo chooses to give when he sets out explaining this text. We are thus led through the various connotations of the theme of flight which in actual fact extend well beyond the cited text. These aspects are illustrated by drawing on other features of Philo's allegorical thought-world. This "performance aspect" of Philo's treatises, which the reader *experiences* by reading or listening to them, is one of the reasons that scholars compare them to sermons, even though formally they are presented as biblical commentaries.

I should add that this feature of Philo's allegorical writings confronted me with a dilemma when I was preparing this paper. From the point of view of method it is surely best to follow Philo on his own paths, i.e. to analyse various treatises or passages within them which focus on the theme of flight. The treatise with flight in its title is an obvious candidate for such analysis. Nevertheless I have chosen not to do this because it does not lend itself to presentation within the confines of a scholarly paper. Instead I will give a broad systematically organized depiction of the theme of flight and exile as this is related to the allegorized biblical characters that inhabit Philo's allegorical thought-world. In the process only a limited number of texts can be referred to. Many more could be adduced. If you want to gain acquaintance with Philo's treatment in all its detail, there is no alternative but to read his treatises, i.e. his allegorical performances, for yourself. This is something that is done far too little. I recommend it.

5. *Some final lexical and semantic preliminaries*

It has taken quite some time, but we now have almost all we need to tackle our subject. As has become clear from the previous remarks, our starting-point must be the same as Philo's, the biblical text. The chief term for flight and exile in Greek, as we have already seen, is the noun φυγή, connected to the verb φεύγειν, "to flee," "run away from," "avoid." As it happens, the term φυγή is not found in the Pentateuch at all (although the later translator Aquila does use it in his version of the Hagar episode).[17] The nouns φυγάς ("exiled person") and φυγαδευτήριον ("place of refuge") are used in connection with the cities of refuge in Exodus and Numbers.[18] The verb is more common, with about twenty-five instances in the books of Moses. Philo can also connect the theme of flight and exile to other verbs such as ἐκβάλλειν ("to expel") and ἀποδιδράσκειν ("to run away"). The latter verb is found in the Hagar story quoted at the outset of the paper (Gen 16:6). The relation to further terms such as ἀποδημία ("journey abroad" or "migration") is more problematic, as we shall see directly.

It is clear from this brief inventory that Philo has a basis in the biblical text which allows him to exploit the theme of flight and exile for allegorical purposes. Whether in so doing he gives it an importance that goes beyond what the biblical text warrants is something that will have to become clear in the course of our investigation.

But before we begin, we cannot avoid taking a closer look at the term φυγή itself. It needs to be subjected to a brief semantic analysis. φυγή, as we saw, means in the first instance "flight." Essential to *use* of the term (let us be Wittgenstinians in our methodology) is the notion of fleeing *from* something. This can be meant in quite a weak sense. φυγή can simply mean "avoidance," as in the standard phrase of αἵρεσις καὶ φυγή, "choice and avoidance."[19] But such a weak usage of the term is *not* what we are discussing in this paper. Flight generally involves an element of urgency or pressure. Even if flight is voluntary, in the sense that you flee from something

[17] Edwin Hatch and Henry A. Redpath, *A Concordance to the Septuagint and the Other Greek Versions of the Old Testament (Including the Apocryphal Books)*, 3 vols. (Oxford: Clarendon Press, 1897; repr. in 2 vols. Grand Rapids: Baker, 1987) 1440.

[18] Exod 23:27, Num 35:6–32; see Hatch and Redpath, *Concordance*, 1440.

[19] Numerous examples in Philo; the two terms are used in conjunction at *Cher*. 30, *Plant*. 45, *Mut*. 153, *Spec*. 1.340, 4.108.

because you don't like it or you think it is bad for you, there is still something that is driving you to take this action. Far more often flight is involuntary. It can be dictated by circumstances, such as when refugees have to flee from a war-zone. It can be the consequence of a deliberate act imposed upon a person, as in the case of banishment or expulsion. In the last case the result of the flight is exile, the second major meaning of φυγή. Someone who has suffered this fate is a φυγάς, an exile.

There is, however, a further aspect of φυγή that is particularly relevant for Philo's usage. Although φυγή always means "flight from," it can also entail "flight to" something or someone. A famous example is the final words of the *Enneads* of Plotinus: the life of the gods and divine men is a φυγὴ μόνου πρὸς μόνον, a flight of the alone to the alone.[20] The person who makes this flight is himself or herself a πρόσφυξ, a "refugee."[21] The word φυγή *can* on its own mean where one flees to, i.e. place of refuge, but examples are very rare.[22] Compound words are better suited to this meaning, and especially the noun καταφυγή, "refuge." In German and Dutch the same effect is achieved with the words *Zuflucht* and *toevlucht*. If one is engaged in καταφεύγειν, one makes a successful flight, one reaches a place of refuge, a καταφυγή or a φυγαδευτήριον.[23] This usage is fairly common in the LXX. The best example in the Pentateuch is the altar that Moses erects after defeating Amalek, which he gives the name Κύριός μου καταφυγή (the Lord is my place of refuge, Exod 17:15). Surprisingly Philo only refers to this text once and rather superficially at that (*Mos.* 1.219). But it fits in perfectly with an important aspect of his views on flight and exile, as we shall soon see.

6. *Flight and exile as exegetical theme*

Let us now, then, review the biblical motifs which are relevant for the theme of flight and exile in Philo's allegories. There will be ten in all.

20 *Enn.* 6.9.11.51.

21 The word is rare, but Philo patently uses it in this sense, e.g. *Plant.* 63 and *Her.* 124, where it is used of the Levites and conjoined with ἱκέτις. It is not found in LXX.

22 See LSJ s.v. I 3. I have found no examples in Philo.

23 The second word is only found in the LXX and the tradition depending on it. Philo uses it with reference to Num 35:12 in *Fug.* 100 and *Spec.* 3.123 (this reference is missing in Peder Borgen, Kåre Fuglseth and Roald Skarsten, *The Philo Index: A Complete Greek Word Index to the Writings of Philo of Alexandria*, 2nd ed. (Grand Rapids–Leiden: Brill, 2000) 356). Remarkably he puts the word in Flaccus' mouth when he bewails his place of banishment in *Flacc.* 159.

1. *In the beginning.* We must begin at the very beginning, when the cosmos was created and the first man was formed from the earth. Adam is created the perfect exemplar of manhood and virtue. He is a κοσμοπολίτης, a citizen of the world, that is to say, the cosmos is his *polis* city and *patris* fatherland (*Opif.* 142). Paradise should not be read literally, but interpreted as the garden of virtues (ἀρεταί) in the soul, with the tree of life symbolizing εὐσέβεια (piety) and the tree of good and evil φρόνησις (practical wisdom) (§155). But when the creator saw the soul inclining to evil rather than good, it was banished from the garden with no hope of return (§156). In allegorical terms the incident of Adam, Eve, and the snake is explained in terms of the entrapment of the mind in the snares of pleasure, with a most distressing result:[24]

> *Nous* (intellect) becomes a subject instead of a ruler, a slave instead of a master, an exile instead of a citizen, mortal instead of immortal. (*Opif.* 165)

This is a brief summary of the account of the banishment of Adam and Eve from paradise as given in Philo's exegesis of the creation story in the *De opificio mundi,* a treatise in which allegorical interpretation is rather restricted. [25] The dominant scheme is the presence of goodness or evil in the soul, goodness meaning here the exercise of virtue, with much emphasis placed on the specific virtue of piety. In the *Legum allegoriae* the story of Adam and Eve is told in much more detail. At the beginning of Book 3, Gen 3:8 is expounded: "And Adam and his wife hid themselves from the face of the Lord God in the middle of the wood of the paradise." Philo explains this text as follows:

> Moses introduces a doctrine teaching that the evil man is an exile. For if the city native to wise men is virtue, the person who is unable to partake of this virtue is driven away from the city of which he cannot partake. Therefore the bad person only has been driven away and exiled. But the exile from virtue has by being such immediately hidden himself from God. For if wise persons are revealed to God's sight, because they are his friends, it is apparent that all bad persons hide away and disappear, as one would expect with those who are hostile and bear ill-will to right reason (ὀρθὸς λόγος). (*Leg.* 3.1)

The soul is here already an exile before the banishment from paradise takes place because the alienation from virtue has already occurred. But how can bad people be said to "hide themselves" from God who is everywhere? The explanation can only be that the bad person has a wrong conception of

[24] Translations of Philonic texts are my own.

[25] If should be noted that formally this treatise falls outside the Allegorical Commentary. It does, however, give an allegorical interpretation of the story of Adam and Eve.

God, i.e. he thinks that God is in a place (§6). Where then does he try to hide? According to the text it is in the middle of the wood of the garden, that is in the centre of the intellect. This means that the person who runs away from God takes refuge (καταφεύγει) in himself, whereas he who flees (φεύγει) from his own mind, takes refuge in God, the divine mind (§29).

2. *After the banishment from paradise.* There is, therefore, an alternative for fleeing from virtue and from God. One can also flee back to him. But is this still possible for human beings who have been banished from paradise? We can compare two texts on this issue. At the beginning of *De cherubim* Philo cites Gen 3:24, "And he [God] banished Adam and settled him over against the pleasure-garden . . ." He then immediately goes on to say:

> Now he says "banished" (ἐξέβαλε), whereas earlier (v. 23) he said "sent away" (ἐξαπέστειλεν), not setting down words casually, but knowing their precise and appropriate application to the matters at hand. He who is sent away is not prevented from obtaining a return, but he who is banished by God endures exile forever. For him who is not yet firmly in the grip of evil it is given to repent and return to his fatherland virtue, from which he was thrown out. But the person who is oppressed and overwhelmed by that violent and incurable disease is thrown out into the place of the impious and must endure undying horrors for the rest of time . . . (*Cher.* 2)

We encounter here an allegorical sleight of hand.[26] The text of course talks about the same person, but Philo, by focusing on exact expressions, can make a distinction which gives a ray of hope. One does not have to be banished forever from paradise. There may be a way back.

A similar promise is held out in a later text, but here the two persons *are* distinct. At the beginning of *De posteritate Caini* the biblical text has moved on to Gen 4:16, "And Cain went out from the face of God and he settled in the land of Naid over against Eden." Philo comments:

> So Adam God drives out, whereas Cain goes out voluntarily. Moses is showing us the two kinds of moral failure, that which is voluntary and that which is involuntary. The involuntary act, because it is not the result of our own deliberate judgment, will later obtain the healing that can be achieved, "for God will raise up another seed instead of Abel, whom Cain killed (Gen 4:25)," a masculine offspring for the soul whose failure did not come from itself, Seth . . . But the voluntary act, because it occurred with deliberation and forethought, will obtain everlasting and incurable doom. (*Post.* 10)

Strictly speaking, of course, this interpretation contradicts the previous one, because there banishment was permanent. But this is no problem for the flexible allegorist. Once again it is the distinction that counts. The fall of the

[26] The same technique is used at *Leg.* 1.54.

soul (or of all humankind) is not absolute. Through the birth of Seth there is hope of return from exile for the banished soul. Seth, we should note, is the distant ancestor of the Hebrews.

3. *For a time evil prevails.* But we should not move too fast. From the time of Cain until the Babel-builders it is evil that prevails. A righteous man in the eyes of the Lord such as Noah (Gen 6:8) is the exception. As we just saw, Cain goes out from the face of God. No greater punishment than this can be thought of, to be exiled from the ruler of the universe (*Post.* 9). Cain is the most potent symbol in Philo's thought-world of the irremediably corrupt and wicked mind which asserts itself against God. In his footsteps follow the giants in Gen 6. Among them is Nimrod, whose name means "desertion," "going over to the enemy." Just as the wicked man (φαῦλος) is an exile without a home or city, so he is also a deserter (*Gig.* 67). The actions of the Babel-builders reveal that they stand in the lineage of Cain, succumbing to passions and wicked deeds (*Conf.* 21ff.), exalting the human mind and exhibiting self-love (φιλαυτία, §128). Their fate is to be "scattered" (διέσπειρεν, Gen 11:8), that is to say:

> God puts them to flight, makes them invisible . . . As planter he wishes to sow goodness (καλοκάγαθία) in the universe, but to disperse and drive out from the community of the cosmos the impiety that he loathes, so that the characters who hate virtue will cease building the city of wickedness and the tower of godlessness. (*Conf.* 196)

4. *The first Patriarch.* In Gen 12 the first of the Patriarchs of the Jewish people makes his appearance. Like Cain, Abraham also "goes out," but it is in the opposite direction. God commands him to go out from his land and his kinship and his father's house to the land which He will show him (Gen 12:1). Philo's initial interpretation in *De migratione Abrahami* is radical and appears at first to link up with our theme quite well: "land" means "body, "kinship" means "sense-perception," "father's house" means "spoken word" (§7). These he must leave behind. The language used for the body is very strong:

> Depart, you here, from the earthly matter that surrounds you, escaping (ἐκφυγών) from that foulest prison, the body, and from its pleasures and desires that are like jailers with all your might and strength. (*Migr.* 9)

But here we confront a difficulty. Flight and exile are not the main themes that are used to describe Abraham's journeyings. Abraham is the emigrant (μετανάστης) and sojourner or temporary resident (πάροικος) *par excellence*. He migrates from Chaldea to Haran and from Haran to the promised land. In the classic exegesis presented in *Migr.* 176–197 this is interpreted as leaving behind the doctrine of cosmic autonomy symbolized by the Chaldeans, then examining the characteristics of the human self symbolized by Haran, and from there moving on to knowledge of God as the universal father and first cause. In one text Abraham as emigrant and exile are brought close together:

> Am I not an emigrant (μετανάστης) from my fatherland? And am I not an outcast from my kinship? Am I not alienated from my father's house? Do not all people call me an excommunicate and exile, deserted and disenfranchised? But you, master, are my fatherland, you are my kinship, you my paternal hearth . . . (*Her.* 26)

In general, however, I believe it is better to separate these themes. An emigrant may feel separated from his native land. Perhaps he did not even wish to leave it behind. But there was a goal which he wished to reach by departing, and this goal lies before him, gives him a perspective. In the case of Abraham it was the promise that God set out before him. In one particular text (*Cher.* 121, not connected with Abraham) Philo distinguishes between three categories: (1) the true citizen, (2) the resident alien, and (3) the outcast or exile. The citizen in the true sense is God. All created beings have the status of resident aliens. The wise person is happy to claim this status, when compared with God. The exile is the fool, for him there is no place in the city of God.

In the case of Hagar, Abraham's concubine, sojourning and flight both play a role. Hagar's name in fact means "sojourning" (*Congr.* 20), and this is entirely apposite, for she stays temporarily with the married couple. But there is no doubt that she also flees, as we already saw at the beginning of our paper. In fact she flees twice. The first time, in Gen 16, she returns to her mistress. The second time she is banished for good (Gen 21:10). Philo explains this as follows (*Cher.* 4ff.).[27] Hagar symbolizes preliminary education (the ἐγκύκλιος παιδεία). In the case of her first stay, Abram and Saraï were not yet fully developed as mind and wisdom respectively. This meant that preliminary education could stay with them and even be of use to them (cf. also *Congr.* 22ff.). But later, when they have become Abraham and Sarah, and they have reached perfection, there is no room for inferior learning. Hagar and her son Ishmael, symbolizing sophistry, are expelled for good.

5. *Isaac and Jacob.* The second patriarch Isaac is never associated with migration or flight. In the Bible this does not happen, and in the allegory he represents spiritual perfection. Perfection of course never flees. It is exactly where it wants to be. Not so in the case of the third patriarch. Jacob is in

27 I simplify the complexities of the allegory here somewhat.

many respects the archetypal "man of flight." But in his case fleeing becomes a somewhat more positive activity, even though he is still "fleeing *from*" more than "fleeing *to*." This is hardly surprising because Jacob is the ἀσκητής (practiser), symbolizing the soul progressing to perfection through practice and spiritual exercise. As we saw earlier, he flees twice, once from his brother Esau and later from his father-in-law Laban. In *Fug.* they are discussed at length in reverse order. Jacob flees from Laban because he detests what the latter represents, namely a materialistic world-view—elsewhere associated with Egypt—which fails to recognize the form and order imposed on creation by God (§§7–22). Because he is not yet Israel (he that sees God), he is unable to vanquish this view and so flees away from it (cf. *Leg.* 3.15). The flight from Esau, on the other hand, is on account of fear (§§23–52). Once again this is because he is *en route,* at the stage of the *bios praktikos* (life of action) on his way to the more excellent state of *bios theôrêtikos* (the contemplative life). Even at this stage Esau, the wild man without a city, is a threat (cf. *Fug.* 39, *Leg.* 3.2). But ultimately Jacob will wrestle with the angel, obtains the name Israel because he does see God, and return to his fatherland. The final words of Book I of *De somniis* (in which Jacob's dreams are interpreted) offers a lesson to the reader:[28]

> Why, then, you soul, do not become a pupil of the practiser . . . You too will be able also to return to your father's house, fleeing away from that long and endless wandering in a foreign land. (*Somn.* 1.256)

6. *Joseph.* For various reasons Jacob's son, Joseph, is an ambivalent character in Philo's allegories. Some things he does are admirable, such as fleeing away from passion in the form of Potiphar's wife.[29] He descends into Egypt, which in Philo's allegories is always a negative symbol, representing the body. Joseph can thus be seen as the champion of bodily power. If he had reached perfection, he would have fled from Egypt, but this he did not do (*Sobr.* 13).

7. *The exodus out of Egypt.* Through the intervention of Joseph, as we all know, the children of Israel emigrate to Egypt and stay there for four hundred years. Philo does not, however, dwell on this connection. Rather, just like in the Pentateuch, he takes the book of Exodus as a kind of new beginning, a second round of exile and liberation. Philo's allegorizing of the Exodus story is less systematic than his allegorization of Genesis. But here too the theme of flight and exile is prominent. I shall again indicate the main features, this time a little more compactly.

28 Accepting Colson's emendation to ἄλην.

29 *Leg.* 3.240, with reference to Gen 39:12.

As in the case of Abraham, the Exodus could be seen as an *emigration* or *departure* than a *flight* in the strict sense. The Israelites had once taken refuge as suppliants in the land. They are strangers (ξένοι) who should be free to leave.[30] But the Pharaoh, the mind that lords it over the realm of the body, has enslaved them against their will. Philo certainly regards the Exodus as a flight. For example Moses calls his second son Eliezer, which means "God is my helper." He then quotes Exod 18:4, "for the God of my father is my helper and delivered me from the hand of Pharaoh" and then adds:

> But those who are still companions of the life of blood and sense-perception are attacked by the character who scatters all thoughts of piety, whose name is Pharaoh. It is impossible to flee from (ἐκφυγεῖν) his tyranny full of lawlessness and savagery, unless Eliezer is begotten in the soul and looks in hope to the help that only God the saviour can give. (*Her.* 60)

The crossing of the Red Sea is precisely the flight from the passions symbolized by the rush of the water (*Leg.* 3.172). The Israelites succeed, since for them the water freezes solid. The Egyptians, however, do not flee *from* the water, but, in the words of Exod 14:27, they flee "*under* the water," that is, they sink under the stream of passions and are submerged, throwing away the stability of virtue in exchange for the confusion of vice (*Conf.* 70).

My final text on the Exodus is the most significant. Philo links the final words of the Song of Moses sung in celebration of the victory over Pharaoh and his hosts with theme of the trees in paradise:

> Moses, lamenting over those who had become emigrants from the garden of the virtues, prays to both the absolute power of God and his gracious and gentle powers that the people endowed with spiritual vision may be planted in the spot from where Adam the earthly mind was banished. For he says: "Lead them in and plant them on the mountain of your inheritance." (Exod 15:17)." (*Plant.* 46)

The children of Israel and their leader Moses, in their flight *from* Egypt and their flight *to* God, are the antithesis of Adam, who had been banished from the garden of Eden. Through the grace of God the exile of humankind has been revoked.[31]

[30] Cf. *Mos.* 1.34, but without an allegorical perspective.

[31] Note that "the people endowed with spiritual vision" are not necessarily confined to the Jewish nation. On Philo's characteristic blend of universalism and devotion to Jewish tradition see Ellen Birnbaum, *The Place of Judaism in Philo's Thought: Israel, Jews, and Proselytes*, (Brown Judaic Studies 290; Studia Philonica Monographs 2; Atlanta: Scholars Press, 1996); "Allegorical Interpretation and Jewish Identity among Alexandrian Jewish Writers," in *Neotestamentica et Philonica: Studies in Honor of Peder Borgen*, (ed. David E.

8. *The election of the Levites.* Of all the incidents in the account of the wandering of the Israelites through the desert, by far the most important for our theme is the election of the Levites as the tribe specially devoted to the service of God. The Levites represent those who leave family and possessions behind and become suppliants of God, *taking refuge* in him. To take one text out of many as an example: why are the Levites appointed as a ransom for Israel's first-born (cf. Num 3:12–13)?

> Reason (λόγος) who has taken refuge with God (ὁ καταπεφευγὼς ἐπὶ θεόν) and become his suppliant, is named Levite. This reason God has taken from the middlemost and most sovereign part of the soul, that is to say claiming it and allotting it to himself, and adjudged it worthy of the part of the chief inheritance . . . Just as Jacob is found to be the inheritor of Esau's birthright, so Reuben must yield to Levi, who achieves perfect virtue. The clearest proof of such perfection is that he has become a refuge-seeker (πρόσφυγα) with God, abandoning all dealings with created reality. (*Sacr.* 119–120)

Virtually every text that mentions the Levites emphasizes that they take refuge in God. There is in fact no direct warrant for this in the biblical text, where they are described as receiving an *inheritance* from God (esp. Deut 10:9). Philo is making an extrapolation from a special role that the Levites have in the Mosaic legislation, as we shall now see in the next theme.

9. *The cities of refuge.* In *Fug.* the theme of flight causes Philo to dwell at length on the theme of the six Levitic cities which are designated as "places of refuge" (φευγαδευτήρια).[32] The person who has committed involuntary homicide and is pursued by those bent on revenge can take refuge in these six cities until he obtains amnesty at the death of the high priest (cf. Num 36). This piece of legislation is fitting because the Levites themselves were homicides in their religious zeal during the incident of the Golden calf (cf. *Sacr.* 130). Philo's allegorization of this theme is complex, but one aspect is particularly striking, the association of flight with life.[33] The entire passage *Fug.* 53–86 plays with this theme, as is only natural because the involuntary homicides first take *life*, but are themselves rescued from *death* by means of the refuge they find, whereas those who commit murder deliberately must themselves be *put to death*. In his allegorical explanation Philo links up the theme with the commitment of Israel to God in Deut 4:4:

Aune, Torrey Seland and Jarl H. Ulrichsen; Supplements to Novum Testamentum 106; Leiden–Boston, 2003), 307–29.

[32] On this term see above n. 23.

[33] On the theme of the life and death of the soul in Philo see Dieter Zeller, "The Life and Death of the Soul in Philo of Alexandria: the Use and Origin of a Metaphor," *SPhA* 7 (1995): 19–56; see also now Emma Wasserman, *The Death of the Soul in Romans 7: Sin, Death, and the Law in Light of Hellenistic Moral Psychology*, WUNT 2.256 (Tübingen 2008).

> "You that have attached yourselves to the Lord God, all of you are alive today." For only those who have taken refuge in God (πρόσφυγας again) and have become his suppliants does Moses recognize as living, regarding the others as corpses. To the former, as it appears, he testifies to their immortality through his addition of the words "you shall live today," "today" representing the unlimited and endless entirety of time (αἰών) . . . (*Fug.* 56)
>
> And in another text he says (Deut 19:5), "Whoever flees there, shall also live." But is not life eternal taking refuge with Him who IS, whereas death is to flee away from him. (*Fug.* 78)

Refuge in God, the characteristic act of Levitic spirituality, thus brings not only life, but eternal life to the soul.

10. *Expulsion from the Mosaic polity.* I end with one final, less positive theme. It is part of Philo's interpretation of the Mosaic legislation. In the Law certain groups of people are removed from membership of the holy congregation, the Mosaic πολιτεία, people such as eunuchs and prostitutes and soothsayers. This in fact amounts to more than exile or banishment. It is complete *expulsion,* for there is no way back. Allegorically Philo converts the theme into the banishment of various kinds of wrong thinking, as seen especially in the extensive treatment in *Spec.* 1.319–345. Let us end our lengthy overview with a text—the final words of the treatise *De ebrietate*—in which he subtly links this theme with that of paradise. The soul does not wish to grow the vine of Sodom (cf. Deut 32:32), which is barren of virtue and gladness, but rather,[34]

> let us pray to the all-merciful God that he destroy this wild vine and decree everlasting banishment (φυγή) to the Eunuchs and all those who do not produce virtue, and that he instead of these plant in our souls the trees of right instruction and grant us noble and truly masculine fruits and reasonings that are capable of sowing fine actions and also of increasing our virtues, and are sufficient to hold together and preserve all that has affinity to a life of well-being (εὐδαιμονία) forever. (*Ebr.* 224)

Human well-being or felicity, which amounts to a return to paradise, will be achieved through good deeds and good thoughts, and, as we now recognize, this will take place when the soul returns to God and takes refuge in him.

7. *Analysis of a complex theme*

Although our survey of Philo's exegetical use of the theme of exile and flight has been necessarily selective, we have been able to demonstrate that

[34] Final words paraphrased.

it is a prominent and complex theme. It has also given us a good insight into the breadth and versatility of his allegorical thought-world. The various aspects we have studied show us how he uses a number of recurrent techniques—notably diaeresis, antithesis, and verbal and conceptual association—that allow him to construct complex structures of thinking. Further analysis shows that there are three main lines of thought.

The first is *exile from the city (or garden) of virtue*. It is apparent, when Philo speaks of the fallen Adam or Cain as exile, that he is exploiting the Stoic theme that the sage is the true citizen, and that the bad man is an exile. In his philosophical treatise *Every good man is free* Philo makes much of this paradox, for which he—together with Cicero—is our chief source.[35] The antithesis between the good person and the bad person is absolute. The former possesses all the virtues in his soul and carries out good deeds, the latter succumbs to pleasure, the passions and vice. The fall into wickedness is what constitutes exile from the city, or, in more biblical terms, banishment from the garden of virtues which is paradise. The philosophical metaphor of the cosmos as city, prominent in Philo's interpretation of the creation account,[36] is combined with the plant imagery which occurs so frequently in the Bible, in the story of the garden of Eden, for example, but also in the Song of Moses and in the Psalms.[37] It is a stark antithesis, too stark to be exegetically valuable for very long. As soon as there is spiritual progress, as in the case of the προκόπτων (the "advancer" in Stoic ethics), the antithesis is undermined and there is a chance that the exile may recover his citizenship. The theme of the city is also relevant to Philo's conception of the Mosaic *politeia*,[38] from which certain classes of wrong thinking are expelled. The city of true thinking and virtuous living is Israel in the spiritual sense, the ὁρατικοί, the people who are orientated towards God.

The second line of thought is more complicated. It can be given the title *flight from here to the higher realm*. As soon as we can speak of spiritual

[35] Esp. *Prob.* 6–8; cf. *SVF* 3.677–681 (chiefly Philonic texts), Cicero *Parad.* 18, 27–32, *Tusc.* 5.105–109.

[36] On the image and its source in Greek philosophy see my *Philo of Alexandria and the* Timaeus *of Plato* (2d ed.; Philosophia Antiqua 44; Leiden: Brill, 1986), 168.

[37] On these motifs see especially Marguerite Harl, "Adam et les deux arbres du Paradis (Gen. II-III) ou l'homme milieu entre deux termes (μέσος–μεθόριος) chez Philon d'Alexandrie: pour une histoire de la doctrine du libre-arbitre," *Recherches de Science Religieuse* 50 (1962): 321–88; see also the comments of Monique Alexandre in her note at PAPM 16 (Paris: Cerf, 1967) 239.

[38] On the theme of the Mosaic *politeia* in Philo see now Caroline Carlier, *La Cité de Moïse*, (Monothéismes et Philosophie 11; Turnhout: Brepols, 2008).

progress, the notion of flight becomes double-sided: flight *from* and flight *to*. The very formulation that I have used for this line of thought betrays the influence of Platonic philosophy. As we saw earlier, in *Fug.* Philo quotes verbatim the famous words from the *Theatetus*:

> Therefore we should flee from here to there as fast as we can. This flight is becoming like unto God to the extent possible. (176a8–b1)

The soul must flee *from* its rootedness in earthly existence and its attachment to the body, and seek to flee *to* the higher realm of the heavens and the mind. In its purest Platonic form we find this conception in the following text:

> Other souls, recognizing that mortal life is a lot of nonsense, call the body a jail and a tomb and, fleeing as though from a prison or a grave, they are lifted up on light wings towards the ether and circulate there on high for ever. (*Somn.* 1.139)

But this text is somewhat deceptive. It is taken from an account of the transmigration of souls which is no doubt based on a Middle Platonist handbook, and cannot be considered representative for Philonic thought. Flight from the body certainly is strongly present in the allegories. Egypt symbolizes the body, and it is out of Egypt that the Exodus takes place. The theme should not be understood only in cosmological terms. Jacob's flight from Laban is a flight from materialistic thinking. The quest for virtue and perfection can also be cast in terms of flight from the passions caused by interaction with the body, as in the case of the wildness of Esau that Jacob flees from. The problem lies more in what the soul flees *to*. In the Platonic schema it is the divine heavenly realm where privileged souls dwell, as in the final chapter of Plutarch's treatise on exile (*Mor.* 607E). Metaphorically speaking, these souls can be located in the incorporeal realm, since that is the object of their contemplation. For Philo, however, heaven is only divine at most in a derivative sense.[39] As we have seen, the soul flees—almost always—*beyond* the heavens to God. God can be described as the creator or the ruler of the universe (cf. *Post.* 9 cited above), or as Being (τὸ ὄν). At the same time, however, he is unquestionably the God of Israel.

The paradigm for ascending beyond the heavens and the universe to God is Abraham. The first patriarch, as we saw, is the archetypal emigrant

[39] See now my analysis in "Why Philo of Alexandria Is an Important Writer and Thinker," in *Philon d'Alexandrie. Un penseur à l'intersection des cultures gréco-romaine, orientale, juive et chrétienne,* (ed. Baudouin Decharneux and Sabrina Inowlocki; Monothéismes et philosophie; Turnhout: Brepols, 2009), 13–33, esp. 20–31.

and sojourner (πάροικος). The great Philonic scholar Valentin Nikiprowetzky convincingly argued that the theme of migration was *the* central theme in Philo's thought:[40]

> Migration is the spiritual itinerary which is followed by the soul of the wise individual or by the consecrated people in its entirety, from the flesh to the spirit, from the material world with its darkness and passions, to the light of the intelligible world, from slavery in Egypt to freedom in Canaan, land of virtue or city of God.

As I indicated earlier, I am hesitant to identify migration and flight completely. It seems to me that flight involves greater urgency, a stronger pressure of circumstances. The separation and alienation that it assumes is more profound. This is particularly the case when flight and exile are the result of explusion.

The problem of the relation between migration and flight does not become any easier if the context in the history of ideas is taken into account. Philo's use of the theme of migration is certainly indebted to allegorical interpretations of Homer's *Odyssey* in terms of Platonic philosophy. Odysseus the wanderer is buffeted by the storms and tribulations of earthly and bodily reality until he finds his way to his fatherland, the heavenly and spiritual realm. We do not have an explicit reference to such an allegory until much later (Numenius, as reported by Porphyry). But Philo gives unambiguous evidence that it already existed earlier, when he tells his reader that he should:[41]

> steer clear "of smoke and wave" (*Od.* 12.219) and run away from the ridiculous pursuits of mortal life as from that terrifying Charybdis, not touching it even with the tip of your toe. (*Somn.* 2.70)

Here we see Homeric allegory combined with the Platonic theme of flight. The question that remains is whether there was any use of the theme of flight as exile in the tradition of Homeric interpretation that was at all similar to the theme of expulsion from paradise in the tradition of biblical interpretation. This may rightly be doubted. After all, Odysseus is not forced to leave Ithaca but departs voluntarily.

[40] Valentin Nikiprowetzky, *Le commentaire de l'Écriture chez Philon d'Alexandrie: son caractère et sa portée; observations philologiques*, (ALGHJ 11; Leiden: Brill, 1977), 239 (my translation). In Nikiprowetzky's view the theme is inspired by Plato's text in *Tht.* 176a–b (*ibid.*).

[41] On this text and the link to Numenius fr. 60 (= Porphyry *De antro* 6) see Robert Lamberton, *Homer the Theologian: Neoplatonist Allegorical Reading and the Growth of the Epic Tradition*, (The Transformation of the Classical Heritage 9; Berkeley: University of California Press, 1986) 53.

One central line of thought remains, but it will hardly come as a surprise. It may be entitled *flight as taking refuge in God*. Ultimately flight in Philo's allegories is not just negative, but also—and perhaps primarily—positive. The final goal of the soul is to take or find refuge in God. Here the dominant conception is biblical and Jewish. For the soul, flight has its pendant not just in a *return*, that is return to paradise from which it was banished, but also in a *finding*. This, we recall, was the double title of Philo's treatise, which, as we suggested at the beginning of our paper, a non-Jewish reader might have found hard to decipher.

Philo is in fact advocating a Levitic spirituality.[42] The Levites have been chosen by God and they respond by dedicating themselves to him entirely. How is such refuge in God attained? Not just through virtue and good living, though that is certainly a requisite. Also not just through piety in the primarily religious sense of loving and worshipping the Lord. It is characteristic for Philo that there is an extra, philosophical dimension. Piety also involves right thinking about the relation between human beings and God. Humanity must understand its own nothingness (οὐδένεια) over against its creator. The Levites recognize this gulf between creator and creature and have chosen to dedicate themselves entirely to God. It is a matter of life and death, as Philo can show by making the link to the theme of the Levitic cities of refuge. Taking refuge in God means salvation, flight from him means separation, alienation, death. This is an authentically biblical and Jewish voice.

8. *Philo, Jew and Hellene*

I end with some concluding words. The first and easiest conclusion is that the exploration of the theme of flight in Philo's allegorical thought-world leads the reader into the very centre of his thought. But it would seem that that the theme is no less complex than the thought-world in which it is located.

We may be tempted to conclude that, in the final analysis, Judaism triumphs over Hellenism in Philo's thought. The Levitic spirituality that I have just outlined is genuinely Jewish: it belongs to the biblical tradition as it is worked out in both Jewish and Christian thought. Philo's ideal is perhaps best seen in the community of the Therapeutae, a group of Jewish ascetics living just outside Alexandria, who spend their days engaged in

[42] See the magnificent treatment of this theme by Marguerite Harl in her Introduction to PAPM 15 on *Quis Heres* (Paris: Cerf, 1967), 130–150.

spiritual contemplation. Their name, from the verb θεραπεύειν, indicates that they are both worshippers of God and healers of the soul (*Contempl.* 2).

Nevertheless, if this certainly is Judaism, it is Judaism of a particular kind, differing from other Judaisms, contemporary and subsequent. Israel for Philo—in his standard, though dubious etymology—is "he who sees God."[43] This seems to be about the individual, but it can also be taken in a wider sense. As stressed by Nikiprowetzky in the passage I quoted earlier,[44] at its widest it represents the collective body that is the Jewish nation. There are moments when Philo is not without a form of eschatological hope. There may come a day when Israel leads the way to peace and felicity in the world. There may even come a day on which the "ingathering of the exiles" takes place, when Jews scattered throughout the world will return to their homeland.[45] But I would argue with some insistence that this is not the main thrust of Philo's thought, and certainly not of his allegories.

We should note here a peculiar and somewhat paradoxical characteristic of the allegorical process of interpretation. The whole idea of allegory is to make the text directly relevant to the reader. It is not primarily about those ancient patriarchs, it bears directly on the soul of someone living in contemporary Alexandria. But what *happens* is that, because the interpretation has become profoundly ahistorical, it also causes the text to become less concrete for the actual situation of Jews in Alexandria. The prime thrust of allegory lies in the area of character and thought. Eschatology gives way to spirituality. If the allegorical interpretation yields the deeper signifycance, as is Philo's conviction, then this is the level that counts most.

To conclude, in Philo's Judaism obedience to the Law and eschatology (the fate of the Jewish nation) are not the determinative components, but rather a contemplative spirituality which aims at ultimately gaining knowledge of God. God is conceived as belonging to the intelligible realm, or at least to be approached via that realm (ultimately, Philo emphasizes, God's essence is beyond human knowledge). Exile and separation from God can be undone through flight from evil and flight to God. The *terms* in which this itinerary are cast, with the emphasis on the soul, the role of virtue and contemplation, belong—as we have seen—to Hellenic thought and are inspired by philosophy, particularly by Platonism.

My position can be stated as follows. There are two poles in Philo's thought, his Judaism and his Hellenism. In the final analysis it is impossible to privilege one of them at the expense of the other. Allow me to use once

43 See above n. 31.

44 See text above to n. 40.

45 See n. 13 on exegesis Deut 30:3–5.

again the image of the ellipse to illustrate this as seen in the following diagram:[46]

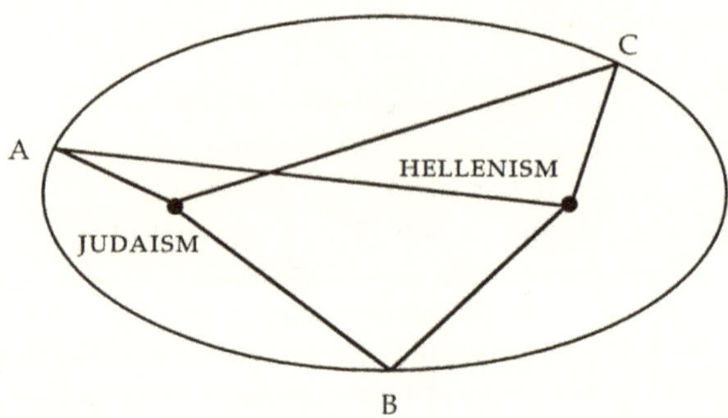

We see how the path of Philo's thought that can be traced out is always connected to the two main poles of Hellenism and Judaism. The diagram illustrates various situations. Even when you are far away from Hellenism on the Jewish side (as is the case in A), the connection with Hellenism is still there. The same also applies in the case of Judaism when you are on the side of Hellenism (as in C). And very often the two poles contribute in roughly equal measure (as in B).

I would argue that it is precisely this double aspect of Philo's thought—his Judaism in the biblical tradition and his Hellenism in the tradition of Greek philosophy—that makes him such a fascinating object of study. It has been well illustrated in the specific case of the theme of flight and exile, both in his allegorical thought-world, and also in the broader context of his situation as a Jew in a world in which Hellenism was the dominant cultural force.

[46] Reproduced from *SPhA* 5(1993): 130.

The Studia Philonica Annual 21 (2009) 25–47

SEEING GOD IN PHILO OF ALEXANDRIA: THE LOGOS, THE POWERS, OR THE EXISTENT ONE?

SCOTT D. MACKIE

1. *Introduction*

For Philo, seeing God represents the greatest experience a human can hope for. It is the "crowning point of happiness" (*Abr.* 58), and the "most precious of all possessions" (*Legat.* 4). Throughout his works, in numerous circumstances and in a variety of contexts, one finds Philo lauding the mystical ascent to the Ideal world, the "noetic realm" (κόσμος νοητός), which more often than not has as its goal the vision of God. The call of Abraham is transformed into a noetic ascent (*Abr.* 70–71), as is Jacob's encounter with God at Bethel (*Praem.* 36–40). Moses' receipt of the law is recast in the shape of a mystical noetic ascent, and not surprisingly, study of that same law can engender a similar experience (*Mos.* 1.158–159; *Spec.* 3.6). The true meaning and task of "philosophy" is defined as "nothing other than the earnest desire to see" God and his Logos (*Conf.* 97). And as one might then expect, Philo's autobiographical accounts of his own philosophical and exegetical study are imbued with noetic visual experiences (*Spec.* 3.1–6; *Migr.* 34–35). Even the name of the historic people of God, "Israel," is etymologically extended beyond ethnic borders, as Philo identifies "those who see God" as "all respected philosophers, whether Jewish or not."[1]

Despite a wealth of material, determining the content and nature of Philo's *visio Dei* experience is often extremely difficult. Because he touches on the topic in numerous contexts, while discussing a variety of topics, or in the process of interpreting LXX texts, his thoughts appear to be "filled with contradictions and inconsistencies."[2] Most significantly, the identity of the

[1] Ellen Birnbaum, *The Place of Judaism in Philo's Thought: Israel, Jews, and Proselytes* (BJS 290; SPhM 2; Atlanta: Scholars Press, 1996), 116.

[2] Ellen Birnbaum, "What Does Philo Mean by 'Seeing God'? Some Methodological Considerations," SBLSPS (1995): 545. A slightly condensed version of this paper appears in her monograph, *The Place of Judaism in Philo's Thought*, 77–90.

object of sight in Philo's *visio Dei* accounts is somewhat ambiguous. Though in many contexts God himself is seen, in other places the vision appears to be restricted to divine intermediaries, such as the Powers or the Logos. One even occasionally encounters a blanket statement declaring the *visio Dei* an utter impossibility (*Post.* 167–168), even for Moses (*Mut.* 7–9).

When the most significant *visio Dei* passages are examined, it becomes obvious that Philo's individual discussions are largely conditioned by the goals of his immediate rhetorical context, and thus they resist any easy systematization.[3] That he felt no compulsion to perform rote recitals of his "doctrine" of mystical, visual practice is apparent as well. Therefore it is essential to be attentive to the immediate context and be willing to allow ambiguities to stand unresolved; one must also resist the urge to impose synthetic assumptions. Our discussion will demonstrate that a perfectly consistent synthesis is neither possible, nor is it desirable. Nevertheless, as the full range of Philo's views on the identity of the object of sight in his *visio Dei* accounts are presented and allowed to stand on their own, it will become apparent that he is, in broad terms, generally consistent, and certainly coherent.

2. *Transcendence and invisibility*

Some of the apparent inconsistencies and difficulties derive from Philo's strict adherence to the notion of God's utter transcendence.[4] In fact, the role of divine transcendence in Philo's thought can scarcely be overestimated, as Peter Frick has observed:

> In Philo's thought, the idea of transcendence functions as the hermeneutic key that determines the shape of the doctrine of God which in turn determines the

[3] See David T. Runia, "The Beginnings of the End: Philo of Alexandria and Hellenistic Theology," in *Traditions of Theology: Studies in Hellenistic Theology, Its Background and Aftermath* (ed. Dorothea Frede and André Laks; Philosophia Antiqua 89; Leiden: Brill, 2002), 287: "I believe that Philo has a clear rationale for what he is doing. In his commentaries he takes the scriptural text as his starting-point, to which he as a commentator is subordinate. The exegetical context thus determines the perspective from which he employs philosophical doctrines. If grand attempts are made to make a synthesis of all these passages, the perspective from which they are written soon becomes lost, and the results cannot fail to be unsatisfactory."

[4] Occasionally one comes across an assertion of immanence, such as in *Somn.* 1.149: "Be zealous, O Soul, to become a house of God, a holy temple, a most beautiful abiding place." The Logos is also occasionally portrayed as indwelling an individual (*Conf.* 134).

idea of immanence and establishes the proper place of other features of his thought.[5]

With regard to the *visio Dei*, one of the most pertinent aspects of Philo's articulation of transcendence is his commonly made claim that God's existence may be ascertained, but his essence (οὐσία), or qualified nature (ποιότης), is unknowable.[6]

Also relevant to our discussion are the unqualified assertions of God's invisibility that one occasionally encounters. If even Moses was incapable of seeing God (*Mut*. 7–9), then only the most arrogant person "will boast of seeing the invisible God" (*QE* 2.37). Moreover, an ontological gulf separates humans from God: "By his very nature he cannot be seen" by created beings (*Mut*. 9; *Post*. 168). Occupants of an entirely different order of existence, humans are ontologically and biologically incapable of perceiving God, "for we have in us no organ by which we can envisage the Existent One, neither in sense . . . nor in mind" (*Mut*. 7; cf. also *Det*. 86–87). In *Opif*. 70–71, the problem is not the lack of an organ of perception, but the shortcomings of that apparatus in the presence of an overwhelmingly radiant God. The philosopher's mind, drawn aloft "on soaring wing," "reaches out to the noetic realm." And though "it seems to be on its way to the Great King himself . . . pure and unmixed beams of concentrated light stream forth like a torrent, so that the eyes of the mind are overwhelmed by the brightness and suffer from vertigo" (see also *Abr*. 76; *Spec*. 1.36–50).[7] Philo also conjectures that "perhaps it is contrary to holiness that the mortal should touch (ψαύω) the eternal" with the "eyes of the body" (*Abr*. 76).[8]

[5] Peter Frick, *Divine Providence in Philo of Alexandria* (TSAJ 77; Tübingen: J.C.B. Mohr; [Paul Siebeck], 1999), 26. On transcendence, cf. David Winston, "Was Philo a Mystic?" in *Studies in Jewish Mysticism* (ed. Joseph Dan and Frank Talmadge; Cambridge, Mass: Association for Jewish Studies, 1982), 16–18.

[6] This assertion is made in a number of *visio Dei* accounts, including: *Praem*. 39; *Post*. 15–16, 167–169; *Fug*. 141, 164–165; *Spec*. 1.40; *Virt*. 215.

[7] The Platonic theory of vision may inform this failed *visio Dei*. Because of their essential similarity, the eye's fire and the fire of daylight form a "single homogenous body" that extends from the eye to the visible object (*Tim*. 45B–D). A key principle of Plato's theory, "like is known by like," informs and conditions the act of seeing. The attempted *visio Dei* in *Opif*. 70–71 may then have failed because of the essential differences in God's radiant light and the less powerful light rays emanating from the mind's eyes of the noetic mystic. On Plato's theory of vision, see David C. Lindberg, *Theories of Vision from Al-Kindi to Kepler* (Chicago: University of Chicago Press, 1976), 3–6.

[8] The verb "touch" (ψαύω) may be used literally here to represent the tactility associated with the extramission theory of vision. To reach out and touch God is an act of irreverent indecency, "contrary to piety/holiness" (ὁσιότης). The verb can be used figuratively in similar contexts, as in Sophocles, *Ant*. 961: "He learned at last it was madness to attack (ψαύω) the god with insults."

Finally, in *Post.* 167–168, Philo employs the "allegorical defense" in what appears to be an attempt to backpedal away from any prior claims he may have made about the possibility of seeing God: "When we say that the Existent One (τὸ ὄν) is visible, we are not using words in their literal sense . . . it is impossible that the God who Is (τὸν κατὰ τὸ εἶναι θεόν) should be perceived at all by created beings."

These unequivocal denials of the possibility of seeing God are relatively rare, however. Philo more commonly portrays the great goal of the contemplative life as attainable. "For the beginning and end of happiness is to be able to see God" (*QE* 2.51), he exclaims, and such perfect and complete happiness he regularly commends to all who are serious and virtuous lovers of wisdom.[9] Nevertheless, the presence of the aforementioned denials reveals that Philo is somewhat conflicted about the matter. Perhaps this conflicted, ambivalent testimony about the possibility of seeing God is deliberate, appropriately reflecting the complexity and uncertainty of the enterprise.[10]

3. *The object of the vision: God or his intermediaries?*

As mentioned before, the identity of the object of sight in Philo's *visio Dei* accounts varies, and making a precise determination can sometimes be difficult. Occasionally Philo's commitment to divine transcendence causes him to represent the Logos and/or Powers as the means by which the transcendent God relates to the world. In many instances, however, God himself appears to be the object of sight.

[9] The term for happiness here is εὐδαιμονία, which according to almost all schools of Greek philosophy is the ultimate goal of human existence. On its usage in Philo and Hellenistic Judaism see David T. Runia, "Eudaimonism in Hellenistic-Jewish Literature," in *Shem in the Tents of Japheth: Essays on the Encounter of Judaism and Hellenism,* (ed. James L. Kugel; JSJSup 74; Leiden: Brill, 2002), 131–157.

[10] Wilhelm Michaelis comes to the conclusion that Philo, controlled by his allegiance to transcendence, is ultimately convinced of God's absolute invisibility, even to the "eyes of the soul/mind" ("ὁράω," *TDNT* 5:336–338). John Dillon, taking into account Philo's commitment to the traditional Jewish "personal God," arrives at the opposite conclusion: "When one has established a totally transcendent God, there straightway arises in an acute form the problem of his relations with the universe . . . in this situation, . . . a kind of mystical vision is the only thing that can connect us to any extent with God" (*The Middle Platonists, 80 B.C. to A.D. 220,* rev. ed. [Ithaca, N.Y.: Cornell University Press, 1996], 157).

3.1. *The Logos*

The Logos is of inestimable importance to Philo's thought.[11] Occupying a crucial intermediary role between the transcendent God and his creation, the Logos, as divine "Reason," or "Intellect," is

> that aspect of God that is directed towards creation, whether conceptually (e.g., in the formation of the intelligible cosmos) or in terms of active participation in the ordering of physical reality and its administration (in conjunction with God's powers).[12]

Thus the Logos both provided the *pattern* according to which the universe was ordered, and operated as the *instrument* through which it was created (*Opif.* 20–25; *Leg.* 3.96; *Cher.* 127; *Spec.* 1.81). The Logos continues to uphold the universe (*Somn.* 1.241), and represent that created order to humanity, in the form of rational thought (*Opif.* 146; *Praem.* 163; *Det.* 86–90). Further connecting God and humanity is the Logos' role as the "image of God," as well as humanity's creation in the image of the Logos, "the image of an image" (*Her.* 231; *Conf.* 147). Finally, the Logos functions anagogically, employed by God "to lead up (ἀνάγω) the perfect person from earthly things to himself" (*Sacr.* 8).

3.2. *The Powers*

The Powers occupy a similar mediatorial role in Philo's thought, though they are not nearly as prominent as the Logos.[13] Philo typically identifies the two Powers as "God," representing the deity's generative capacity, as well as his goodness, and "Lord," which denotes both his sovereignty and right to issue punitive judgment.[14] These Powers stand beside God like the cherubim over the mercy seat (*Her.* 166). An inspired allegorical reading of the expulsion of Adam from the Garden of Eden, in *Cher.* 27–30, also

[11] On Philo's Logos, see David Winston, *Logos and Mystical Theology in Philo of Alexandra* (Cincinnati: Hebrew Union College Press, 1985), 15–25; David T. Runia, *Philo of Alexandria and the* Timaeus *of Plato* (Philosophia Antiqua 44; Leiden: Brill, 1986), 446–451; idem. "Logos," in *Dictionary of Deities and Demons in the Bible*, 2nd ed. (ed. Karel van der Toorn, Bob Becking, Pieter W. van der Horst; Leiden: Brill / Grand Rapids: Eerdmans, 1999), 528; Thomas H. Tobin, "Logos," *ABD* 4:350–351; Dillon, *The Middle Platonists, 80 B.C. to A.D. 220*, 158–161; Kenneth Schenck, *A Brief Guide to Philo* (Louisville: Westminster John Knox, 2005), 58–62.

[12] David T. Runia, *Philo of Alexandria: On the Creation of the Cosmos according to Moses. Introduction, Translation and Commentary* (PACS 1; Atlanta: Society of Biblical Literature, 2001), 142.

[13] On the Powers, see Dillon, *The Middle Platonists, 80 B.C. to A.D. 220*, 161–163.

[14] Cf. *Fug.* 94–105; *Abr.* 119–132; *QG* 2.16, 51, 75; 3.39; 4.2–8; 30; *QE* 2.62, 68; *Legat.* 6.

identifies the Powers with the cherubim, while the Logos represents the flaming sword that stands in between the two and "unites them, for it is through the Logos that God is both ruler and good." Philo prioritizes the Logos again in *QE* 2.68, describing the Powers as emanating from the Logos: "like from a spring," they "divide and break forth." [15] Though here and in *Cher.* 28 Philo clearly defines the status and roles of the three intermediaries, usually his presentation lacks such careful definition. As Alan Segal has noted:

> How the powers relate to the *logos* is ambiguous. Since the *logos* can also signify the sum of all the powers, it logically stands above the two powers in the ascent from concrete to abstract. Yet sometimes Philo uses *kyrios* and *theos* to refer to the two powers of God and at other times to refer to the *logos* and the highest God, being-in-itself. Basically he uses whatever exegesis makes most sense in the allegorical context.[16]

It is particularly the title θεός, "God," that complicates our discussion. Because of its frequent application to the Powers, and occasionally the Logos, it can nowhere be assumed to refer to the most high God, the Existent One (τὸ ὄν). Instead, the individual context is determinative.

3.3. *Recent interpreters*

After expending such effort to systematically distance humanity from God, via the Logos and Powers, we might expect Philo to accordingly restrict the scope of the *visio Dei* to these mediators. And it is perhaps the comprehensive mediatorial presence of the Logos in Philo's thought that leads David Winston to repeatedly assert that humanity's "highest union with God, according to Philo, is limited to the Deity's manifestation as Logos."[17]

[15] On the background of Philo's equation of the cherubim and the Powers, see Fred Strickert, "On the Cherubim," *SPhA* 8 (1996): 40–57.

[16] Alan F. Segal, *Two Powers in Heaven: Early Rabbinic Reports About Christianity and Gnosticism* (SJLA 25; Leiden: Brill, 1977), 175.

[17] David Winston, *Philo of Alexandria: The Contemplative Life, The Giants, and Selections* (CWS; New York: Paulist Press, 1981), 21. This statement is repeated in his "Was Philo a Mystic?" 15. Similar statements appear throughout his works on the subject: "For Philo, it is through the Logos and the Logos alone" that humans are "capable of participating in the divine" (*Logos and Mystical Theology in Philo of Alexandra*, 25); "He probably conceived of a mystical contact that was limited only to an aspect of the Deity, namely, his manifestation as Logos" ("Philo's Mysticism," *SPhA* 8 [1996], 74); "Since Philo's mystical theology bars a direct approach to God's essence, we must seek it out through the oblique traces disclosed by its noetic aspect, the Logos" (*Logos and Mystical Theology in Philo of Alexandra*, 15); "The highest divine level with which mystical experience is associated by Philo is of the Intelligible World, or God qua Logos" ("Philo's Mysticism," 82). Winston is joined in this

Thus the noetic ascent "that carries the soul to the uttermost bounds of the universe" issues not in a vision of the Existent One (τὸ ὄν), rather, it enables the mystic "to gaze on the Divine Logos."[18] In his support, Winston cites just two passages: *Conf.* 95 and *Ebr.* 152.[19]

In her detailed consideration of the *visio Dei* theme in Philo, Ellen Birnbaum offers a more comprehensive assessment of the issue: "Although Philo occasionally seems to speak without qualification about the possibility of seeing God, at other times he claims that God can be seen only through apprehension of His various intermediaries."[20] Birnbaum's discussion primarily focuses on *visio Dei* passages involving intermediaries. And in addition to *Conf.* 95–97, she appeals to *Somn.* 1.64–67 and *QG* 4.2 in support of her claim that the *visio Dei* is occasionally restricted to intermediaries. Furthermore, Birnbaum has demonstrated the necessity of analyzing the various *visio Dei* passages with respect to their location in the three commentary series (the Allegory, Exposition, and *QGE*), since they were written for different audiences who presumably possessed varying levels of biblical knowledge as well as spiritual and philosophical sophistication.[21]

3.4. Visio Dei *passages in the Allegorical Commentary*

The complex and nuanced content of the treatises in the Allegory series indicates they were written for an audience reasonably aware of both biblical traditions and Greco-Roman philosophy.[22] David M. Hay has

---

opinion by others, including: Erwin R. Goodenough, *By Light, Light: The Mystic Gospel of Hellenistic Judaism* (New Haven: Yale University Press, 1935), 22–47; Burton L. Mack, "Moses on the Mountain Top: A Philonic View," in *The School of Moses: Studies in Philo and Hellenistic Religion in Memory of Horst R. Moehring* (ed. John Peter Kenney; BJS 304; SPhM 1; Atlanta: Scholars Press, 1995), 24. David M. Hay, "The Psychology of Faith in Hellenistic Judaism," *ANRW* 2.20.2 (1987), 904–905, 921, contends "it is not clear" whether Philo considers God visible.

18 Winston, *Logos and Mystical Theology in Philo of Alexandra*, 54.

19 This same claim and citations are found in his *Philo of Alexandria: The Contemplative Life, The Giants, and Selections*, 33–34; "Philo and the Contemplative Life," in *Jewish Spirituality: From the Bible through the Middle Ages* (ed. Arthur Green; New York: Crossroad, 1986), 225; and "Was Philo a Mystic?" 31.

20 Birnbaum, "What Does Philo Mean by 'Seeing God'? Some Methodological Considerations," 540; eadem. *The Place of Judaism in Philo's Thought*, 80.

21 Birnbaum, "What Does Philo Mean by 'Seeing God'? Some Methodological Considerations," 549–550; eadem. *The Place of Judaism in Philo's Thought*, 17–21, 89–90.

22 See the remarks of Gregory E. Sterling, "'The School of Sacred Laws': The Social Setting of Philo's Treatises," *VC* 53.2 (1999): 159: the implied audience of the Allegorical Commentary knew the "biblical text exceptionally well" and were "capable of appreciating extended philosophical expositions of it."

characterized the implied audience as "persons committed to the Jewish religion," and aspiring to a "deeper religious experience."[23] Therefore the "main theme" of Philo's "preaching" in the Allegory is "the means of turning to God, the barriers people encounter when they try to grow closer to God, and the stages of spiritual progress."[24]

3.4.1. *Conf.* 95 and *Somn.* 1.64–67: God's transcendence of "place"

In the first passage cited by David Winston, *Conf.* 95–97, Philo interrupts a discussion of Israel's enslavement in Egypt to briefly touch upon the topic of noetic ascent. Like the Israelites who followed Moses out of Egypt, all "those who serve the Existent One" (τὸ ὄν) will similarly follow Moses into the noetic realm, "ascending in their thoughts to the heavenly height." It is there, according to Philo, that "they will behold the place which in fact is the Logos, where God stands." This allusion to the appearance of God at Sinai to Moses, Aaron, Nadab, Abihu, and seventy of Israel's elders (Exod 24:9–11), is developed at length elsewhere (cf. *QE* 2.37, 39). Philo perhaps assumed the familiarity of his readers with this allegory, which is largely dependent on an LXX translation that refocuses the object of sight from God to the "place" where he stood.[25] Thus, it is the *place* where God stood that was visible at Sinai, not God himself (as in the MT), and Philo allegorically identifies that "place" as the Logos. Philo concludes this digression with a further qualification: noetic philosophers

> desire to see the Existent One (τὸ ὄν) if they may, but, if they cannot, to see his image, the most holy Logos, and after the Logos its most perfect work of all that our senses know, that is the world. For by philosophy nothing else has ever been meant, than the earnest desire to see these things exactly as they are (*Conf.* 97).

Rather than precluding the possibility of seeing τὸ ὄν, this passage merely states that some noetic mystics may be restricted to seeing only the Logos.[26] It also infers the existence of a third group, whose experience is limited to

[23] David M. Hay, "Philo of Alexandria," in *Justification and Variegated Nomism. Volume 1: The Complexities of Second Temple Judaism* (ed. D. A. Carson, Peter T. O'Brien, and Mark A. Siefrid; WUNT 2.140; Tübingen: Mohr Siebeck / Grand Rapids: Baker Academic, 2001), 365.

[24] Ibid. Erwin R. Goodenough, *An Introduction to Philo Judaeus*, 2nd ed. (Oxford: Blackwell, 1962), 13, notes that the Allegory is the most speculative and mystical of the three commentary series.

[25] Exod 24:10 (LXX): καὶ εἶδον τὸν τόπον οὗ εἱστήκει ἐκεῖ ὁ θεὸς τοῦ Ισραηλ.

[26] A similar sentiment is expressed in *Somn.* 1.117: "To meet a 'place' or 'word' (λόγος) is an all-sufficient gift to those who are unable to see God who is prior to 'place' and 'word.'"

insights about creation. As we will soon see, such a hierarchy of mystical experience, typically involving three grades of accomplishment, is commonly encountered in Philo's writings.

In *Somn.* 1.64–67, a passage Birnbaum appeals to in support of her claim that Philo occasionally restricts the *visio Dei* to intermediaries, Philo once again plays on the concept of "place" in an attempt to solve a dilemma he finds in Gen 22:3–4: how was Abraham able to "come to a place" and at the same time "see it from afar." As in *Conf.* 95–97, the "place" Abraham came to, Moriah, is interpreted as the Logos, and the person

> who has their place in the divine Logos does not actually reach him who is in very essence God, but sees him from afar; or rather, not even from a distance is one capable of contemplating Him; all one sees is the bare fact that God is far away from all creation, and that the apprehension of him is removed to a very great distance from all human power of thought (1.66).

This passage nowhere states that the Logos is seen instead of God. It instead makes an assertion of divine transcendence: "all one sees is the bare fact that God is far away from all creation" (1.66).

The notion that God cannot be confined to a place, "but rather contains all things within himself," is a recurring topic in Philo's oeuvre.[27] The Yahwist's anthropomorphic Gardener (Gen 2:8) provokes Philo to engage in some "pruning" of his own: "For not even the whole world would be a fit place for God to make his abode, since God is his own place, and he is filled by himself, . . . filling and containing all other things . . . but himself contained by nothing else" (*Leg.* 1.44).[28] Philo's focus on "place" in his discussions of Gen 2, 11, 22, 28 and Exod 24, and the careful assignation of the Logos, or Powers, to that place, is typically the result of his larger preoccupation with God's transcendence of place, not his invisibility to eyesight.[29] The larger conceptuality, God's transcendence of place, steers the discussion, even when it is not immediately apparent.[30] The Logos only

27 Cf. Ronald Williamson, *Philo and the Epistle to the Hebrews* (ALGHJ 4; Leiden: Brill, 1970), 217; Harry A. Wolfson, *Philo: Foundation of Religious Philosophy in Judaism, Christianity, and Islam*, 2nd ed. (2 vols.; Cambridge, Mass.: Harvard University Press, 1947), 1:240–252.

28 Cf. also *Sobr.* 63; *Conf.* 136–139; *Migr.* 182–183; *Somn.* 1.184–185.

29 Cf. *Somn.* 1.62: Space is defined as the Divine Logos, "which God himself has completely filled throughout with incorporeal powers"; and *Opif.* 20: Just as the plans of a city initially exist solely in the mind of the architect, so also the noetic realm has its place in the Logos "who gives the ideas their ordered disposition." See Runia, *On the Creation of the Cosmos*, 143.

30 Though the discussions appear at times to be occasioned by an anti-anthropomorphic apologetic, they more often than not lead to elaborate defenses of divine transcendence of "place."

enters this discussion as a secondary consideration, drawn into the conversation at the bidding of the more pertinent agenda. Transcendence, not vision and the object of sight, is the controlling consideration.

3.4.2. *Ebr.* 152: The Uncreated (ἀγένητος): the Logos or God?

The second passage cited by Winston, *Ebr.* 152, is also problematic. Philo discusses the "sober intoxication" of the "God-possessed," who, like Samuel's mother Hannah, will "pour out their souls before the Lord" (1 Sam 1:15), and thus soar "to the bounds of the All, hastening to that most glorious and loveliest of visions — the vision of the Uncreated" (ἀγένητος). Winston appears to assume that ἀγένητος, "the Uncreated One," refers to the Logos, though there is nothing in the surrounding context that can be appealed to in support of that identification.

The word ἀγένητος appears 101 times in the Philonic corpus, and in almost half these occurrences, ἀγένητος would seem to refer to the most high God, τὸ ὄν.[31] Perhaps even more important are the five passages in which God the Uncreated One is the object of sight (*Sacr.* 60; *Det.* 158; *Post.* 63; *Plant.* 22; *QG* 4.1).[32] In only two instances is the Logos possibly called ἀγένητος. The first possible occurrence, *Leg.* 3.100–103, is somewhat convoluted, and must be read within its larger context. Philo compares two

[31] (1) Contexts that explicitly identify the "Existent One" (τὸ ὄν) as ἀγένητος: *Det.* 158; *Deus* 56, 60; *Plant.* 22; *Ebr.* 84; *Somn.* 1.184; *Spec.* 2.166; *Virt.* 180, 213, 218; *QG* 4.1.

(2) Contexts that identify θεός as ἀγένητος, and which lack the presence of intermediaries: *Leg.* 1.51; *Cher.* 44; *Sacr.* 57, 63, 101; *Post.* 63; *Gig.* 14; *Plant.* 64, 66; *Ebr.* 94; *Migr.* 157; *Her.* 98; *Congr.* 48, 107, 134; *Somn.* 1.249; *Ios.* 265; *Mos.* 2.171; *Decal.* 41, 120; *Praem.* 46, 87.

(3) Contexts where intermediaries are present, but ἀγένητος undoubtedly refers to τὸ ὄν: *Leg.* 3.208; *Sacr.* 60, 66; *Det.* 124; *Plant.* 31; *Conf.* 98; *Migr.* 91, 192; *Her.* 206; *Somn.* 1.94; *Decal.* 60, 64.

(4) Contexts where it may be inferred that ἀγένητος refers to τὸ ὄν: *Her.* 14; *Somn.* 1.77; *Legat.* 5.

(5) Contexts that are inconclusive: *Leg.* 3.31; *Cher.* 52; *Gig.* 42; *Deus* 160.

[32] Cf. esp. *Sacr.* 60: While discussing the three divine visitors in Gen 18, Philo remarks, "God who overtops his powers in that He is visible apart from them, yet is revealed in them." The word ἀγένητος appears with some frequency in three other contexts:

(1) In the debate over whether the earth is eternal, i.e., "uncreated" (*Opif.* 7, 9, 54, 171; *Plant.* 50; *Ebr.* 199; *Her.* 246; *Somn.* 2.283; cf. also *Aet.* 7, 10, 12, 20, 27 [2X]; 52, 69, 75, 93).

(2) When comparing the created and "uncreated" realms/spheres (*Opif.* 12; *Post.* 172; *Fug.* 59; *Her.* 181; *Mut.* 45; *Somn.* 2.231, 234, 253; *Abr.* 162). Though in his treatment of *Opif.* 12, Runia argues against the notion that the noetic realm is being referred to, rather ἀγένητος "more likely refers to God" (*On the Creation of the Cosmos*, 120).

(3) To denote something "false," that is "without basis," that "never happened," or "lacks real existence" (*Abr.* 192; *Ios.* 167; *Spec.* 3.45; 4.48; *Flacc.* 139).

types of minds: the first infers God's existence through the deity's causal relationship to creation, while the second mind is

> more perfect and more thoroughly cleansed, having undergone initiation into the great mysteries, and it gains its knowledge of the First Cause not from created things, . . . but in lifting its eyes above and beyond creation it obtains a clear vision of the Uncreated (ἔμφασιν ἐναργῆ τοῦ ἀγενήτοῦ), so as to apprehend both himself and his shadow. To apprehend that, as we saw, was to apprehend both the Logos and this world (ὅπερ ἦν τόν τε λόγον καὶ τόνδε τὸν κόσμον) (3.100).

It initially seems that the final sentence defines the content of the "clear vision of the Uncreated" as involving both "himself and his shadow," immediately thereafter defined as "the Logos and this world." However, in previous sections—which Philo calls to our attention with his reminder, "as we saw" (ὅπερ ἦν)—Philo first defined God's "shadow" (σκιά) as the Logos (3.96), and then his works, his creation (3.99). Therefore, "the Logos and this world" in 3.100 do not correspond in parallel to "himself and his shadow," they refer instead to "his shadow(s)." Thus the "palpable vision of the Uncreated" involves three realities: τὸ ὄν, and his shadow(s): i.e., the Logos and creation. In reiterating the contrast in 3.102, Philo insists the second type of mind, exemplified by Moses, "receives the vision of God (τὴν ἔμφασιν τοῦ θεοῦ) from the First Cause himself." And in contrast to prophets, God speaks to Moses "mouth to mouth in manifest form" (εἶδος, 3.103).

On only one occasion, in *Cher.* 86, does Philo appear to describe the Logos as ἀγένητος:

> For the good and beautiful things in the world could never have been what they are, unless they were made in the image of the archetype, which is truly beautiful and good, the Uncreated (ἀγένητος), the blessed, the imperishable.

Interestingly, Philo once defines the Logos as "neither uncreated as God, nor created as humans," but occupying a middle point between the two (*Her.* 206).[33] Philo also conceives of the Logos as God's first-born son (πρωτόγονος υἱός, *Agr.* 51; *Conf.* 146; *Somn.* 1.215).[34] Finally, there are three occasions in which the Powers might possibly be called ἀγένητος (*Deus* 78;

[33] Wolfson describes the Logos as having three stages of existence: (1) as the "mind of God," identical with his essence and therefore eternal; (2) as "an incorporeal mind created by God, having existence outside of God's essence"; (3) as immanent in the world (*Philo,* 1:232, 327).

[34] In his essay, "Was Philo a Mystic?" Winston defines the Logos as "the first-begotten Son of the Uncreated Father" (20).

Mut. 22; *QG* 2.16). Thus, given the evidence, *Ebr.* 152 is most likely referring to a vision of God himself, τὸ ὄν, not his Logos or Powers.

3.4.3. *Mut.* 15–24: *"The Lord (not 'The Existent One') was seen by Abraham"*

Awareness of the larger context is decisive in *Mut.* 15–24, in which Philo conclusively limits the object of sight to the Powers. The first thirty sections of *Mut.* respond to the two assertions of Gen 17:1, that the Lord "appeared to Abraham," and declared, "I am your God." Philo severely qualifies these two statements, emphatically asserting God's invisibility (1–10), "unnamedability" (11–15), transcendence (15–17), and non-relational nature (18–30). In fact it is the Powers who are visible, nameable, imminent, and relationally oriented toward creation and humanity. The primary purpose of this extended section, then, is to demonstrate God's distance from creation and humanity, and establish the role of the Powers as intermediaries.[35]

In the midst of this larger program, in *Mut.* 15–17, Philo treats the claim of Gen 17:1: "The Lord was seen of Abraham." He conclusively dismisses the idea that "the Cause of all" appeared to him. Rather, Abraham saw only the Power "Lord," the world's "charioteer, pilot," and ruler: "Therefore the words are, 'The Lord (not "the Existent One") was seen by him'" (διὸ λέγεται "ὤφθη" οὐ τὸ ὄν, ἀλλὰ κύριος, *Mut.* 17).

The discussion then shifts focus in *Mut.* 18–24: when the Power "God" is also revealed to Abraham, Philo calls this "a still higher gift." The various manifestations of the Powers are then arranged in a hierarchy of mystical experience: (1) the "wicked person" experiences the Power "Lord," and thus "with awe and groaning feels the fear of the Master hanging over them." (2) The "person of progress" reaches perfection through their relations with the Power "God." (3) Like Abraham, the "perfect person" experiences both Powers, "God" and "Lord." This hierarchy motif is quite common in Philo, and is typically represented as involving three stages of initiatory progress. And as we will see in our discussions of *QG* 4.2, 4–5, 8 and *Abr.* 107, 119–132, it most often accords the highest category the privilege of seeing the Existent One.[36]

[35] See the thorough treatment of this passage in David T. Runia, "Naming and Knowing: Themes in Philonic Theology with Special Reference to the *De mutatione nominum*," in *Knowledge of God in the Graeco-Roman World* (ed. R. van den Broek, T. Maarda, and J. Mansfield; Leiden: Brill, 1988), 69–91. He notes that the main purpose of *Mut.* is to compare the steadfast and unchanging God, whose "diverse improper names" are not subject to change, and humans, whose names change as their natures change, for better (Abraham and Sarah) or worse (Joseph) (81–82).

[36] On *Mut.* 15–18, cf. Segal, *Two Powers in Heaven*, 177–178.

3.4.4. *Migr.* 168–175, *Leg.* 3.169–178, *Sacr.* 8: The Logos' role as ἀναγωγός, the means and guide of the noetic ascent

Throughout Philo's writings there is some ambiguity as to whether the Powers and the Logos are autonomous ontological realities (i.e., hypostases), or merely theophanic manifestations (i.e., projections of God's being and/or activity). David T. Runia has aptly summarized the issue:

> It cannot be denied that Philo personifies the Logos when talking about him, but it remains difficult to interpret the extent to which he accords him separate existence. In many texts the Logos represents God's presence or activity in the world, so that the distinction between God and Logos is more conceptual than real. There are other texts, however, in which the Logos is presented as an *hypostasis* separate from and ontologically inferior to God himself.[37]

In at least three passages in the Allegory the Logos appears to operate autonomously in its capacity as the ἀναγωγός, the means and guide of the noetic ascent. This role is unnecessary, and even incoherent, if the Logos is conceptually indistinct from τὸ ὄν. The Logos' autonomy is explicitly indicated in *Migr.* 168–175, where Philo appeals to two scriptural examples, the elders who accompanied Moses to Sinai in Exod 24, and Moses' request for God to accompany the people in the wilderness (Exod 33:12–17), to establish the necessity of the Logos' guidance in the noetic ascent. However, the "divine Logos" is only necessary as long as the contemplative person "falls short of perfection" (τελειόω). Once the state of "full knowledge" (ἄκρος ἐπιστήμη) is reached, the philosopher will ascend at a "pace equal to him who formerly led the way," i.e., the Logos, "and they will both become attendants (ὀπαδοί) of the All-leading God" (τοῦ πανηγεμόνος θεοῦ). That the noetic mystic and the Logos are together identified as both ascending at an equal pace and functioning as "attendants of the All-leading God" further reinforces the distinction between τὸ ὄν and the Logos.

In *Leg.* 3.169–178, Philo describes the Logos as communing with and "summoning the soul to itself," so as to effect a "congealment" (πῆξις) of the "earthly, bodily, and sense-bound" (3.171–172). This work of the Logos is essential if one hopes to attain a vision of τὸ ὄν: "the person who sees God is studying flight from the passions . . . in order that those who see the Existent One (ὁ βλέπων τὸν ὄντα) might pass beyond passion" (3.172). Philo then clearly distinguishes between the Logos and τὸ ὄν: like the manna that fed the Israelites in the wilderness, so also "the soul of the most perfect is fed by the Logos" (3.176). However Jacob "looks even higher than the

[37] Runia, "Logos," 528.

Logos, and says he is fed by God himself. He looks on God as feeding him, not his Logos" (3.177).

Finally, in *Sacr*. 8, Philo discusses those noetic philosophers of the highest order, who, like Moses, "God has advanced even higher, training them to soar above species and genus alike, and stationing them beside himself." Philo then notes that "God prizes" this "wise person as the whole world, for that same Logos, by which he made the cosmos, is used by God to lead up (ἀνάγω) the perfect person from earthly things to himself."

3.4.5. Seeing the Existent One in the Allegory

Though *Mut*. 15–24 unequivocally insists God is visible solely through his intermediaries, the force of this passage is mitigated somewhat when the entire treatise is taken into consideration. Thus, we find Philo asserting in *Mut*. 81–82 that the *visio Dei* is attainable, if pursued with unstinting philosophic athleticism. Those who do so will "be endowed with eyes" and receive the power "to behold the Existent One with sharp vision" (τὸν ὄντα δυνήσεται θεωρεῖν ὀξυδερκῶς).[38] And then in *Mut*. 203, Philo contrasts Balaam, "the dealer in augury" and "soothsaying," with Israel, "the soul's best eye that alone has been trained to see God" (θεός).

Finally, a direct visual encounter with τὸ ὄν is documented in two other notable passages in the Allegory. In both, Jacob/Israel, "the one who sees God," is said to have seen τὸ ὄν. Representing the "person of practice," he experienced the "most perfect blessing," the "sight of the Absolutely Existent" (τὸ ὄντως ὄν, *Ebr*. 82–83). And as *Praem*. 37–39 recounts, when his "continuous striving" and "unutterable longing" were met with divine mercy, he saw the "Father and Savior" (see also *Praem*. 27).

3.5. Visio Dei *in* QG *4.2, 4–5, 8: The wavering vision*

Like the implied audience of the Allegory, we can assume those addressed in *QGE* were quite conversant in both scripture and philosophy, though a wider Jewish audience may also be envisioned. The format followed in *QGE* differs from the Allegory, as individual passages in Genesis and

[38] Runia, "Naming and Knowing: Themes in Philonic Theology with Special Reference to the *De mutatione nominum*," 80, argues that Philo probably intended to use θεός here in *Mut*. 82, thus with reference to the Power "God." Runia therefore believes the reference to τὸν ὄντα is relatively insignificant, since Philo "finds it quite impossible and quite unnecessary to achieve consistency and correctness in the use and non-use of God's names."

Exodus are treated atomistically, with both literal and allegorical interpretations occasionally appearing side by side.[39] Birnbaum has therefore characterized *QGE* as a "collocation or digest of interpretations reflecting the opinions of a broader community of Alexandrian Jews."[40] According to Hay, in *QGE*, Philo "conceives of exegesis as a kind of dialogical enterprise that involves many debate partners and opponents."[41]

What is perhaps one of Philo's most important, and complicated discussions of *visio Dei* is found in *QG* 4.2, 4–5, 8.[42] This lengthy treatment of the theophany of Gen 18:2–7 is primarily focused on an apparent discrepancy found in both the MT and LXX. Abraham and the narrator waver back and forth concerning the number of visitors: a single visitor is assumed in Gen 18:3, 10, 13–15, and "three men" are spoken of and addressed in 18:2, 4–5, 8–9, 16. This ambivalence is especially pronounced in the varying pronouns used in 18:2–5. Philo clearly notes these changes in *QG* 4.2, quoting all the pertinent passages and dividing them into two respective groupings. He concludes the first group, which assumes a single visitor, with the observation, "all these passages point to his appearance as God." The second grouping he prefaces by saying: "The following indicate an appearance as of strange men."

This same awareness is evident in other comments made in *QG* 4.2. Philo initially indicates that God "cannot be seen in his oneness without something (else), the chief Powers that exist immediately with him, the creative, which is called God, and the kingly, which is called Lord." Near the end of the passage, Philo deviates from this stance: "Seeing the vision before his eyes, which was not constant, being at one time God, at another time that of the strangers, . . ." Thus the vision does not always include three divine beings, rather it oscillates back and forth from one to three. Abraham, and presumably Philo himself, are experiencing at the height of their mystic vision of God an oscillating vision, one where God is seen through his creation, and in his creative capacity, as well as his lordship

[39] In *QGE* Philo's responses to these assorted exegetical interpretations varies: at times he approves of the literalist interpretations, while other interpretations he critiques, particularly those of the "critics," literalist exegetes who demean the scriptures. And in some instances, Philo fails to respond to a literalist interpretation (*QG* 1.32, 81; 3.52; 4.64, 121, 123, 145, 196). See David M. Hay, "References to Other Exegetes," in *Both Literal and Allegorical Studies in Philo of Alexandria's* Questions and Answers on Genesis and Exodus (ed. David M. Hay; BJS 232; Atlanta: Scholars Press, 1991), 81–97.

[40] Birnbaum, *The Place of Judaism in Philo's Thought*, 19.

[41] Hay, "References to Other Exegetes," 97.

[42] Given the Armenian text, the exact names of the divine characters are sometimes uncertain. However, as we will see, the flow and logic of the argument allow for a fairly precise delineation of the characters involved.

over creation, and then occasionally, but only momentarily, are they able to soar above these aspects of God's actions and gain a fleeting glimpse of the truly Existent One.

In *QG* 4.4 Philo again makes this oscillating pattern explicit while commenting on Gen 18:3, wherein Abraham addresses a single "Lord." Philo says that this change was predicated on a transformation of Abraham's "mind"; it "now more clearly forms an impression with more open eyes and more lucid vision, and not roaming about nor wandering off with the triad." Thus Abraham's mind "runs towards the one," since God has "manifested himself without the Powers that belong to him." In the next passage, *QG* 4.5, Philo notes the change back to plural address that occurs in Gen 18:4, and most remarkably, he identifies God as "him who had made himself directly visible."

Finally, towards the end of *QG* 4.8, Philo attributes the triadic vision to the weakness of human sight: "He in his oneness is likened to a triad because of the weakness of the beholders." Just as the eyes of the body will sometimes see two lights glaring from a single light source, so also is the case with the "eyes of the soul." They cannot see God in his singular "Oneness"; instead they "receive an impression of the triad." Philo then places the whole discussion under the rubric of a mystery initiation. The three measures of flour used by Sarah to make "ash-cakes" for the visitor(s) cryptically triggers the claim that the "knowledge and understanding of the wisdom of the Father and his two highest Powers are hidden from many."[43] This is appropriate, for "revealing mysteries to uninitiated and unworthy people is the act of one who destroys, sacks, and undermines the laws of the mysteries of divine perfection."

Ellen Birnbaum attributes Philo's vacillation in *QG* 4.2, 4 to his careful exegetical technique. Philo handles each verse of Gen 18 separately, and in what amounts to a charge of near-sightedness, she alleges he is "so verse-focused that he may contradict himself from one moment to the next, without acknowledging the inconsistency either in the Bible or in his own discussion."[44] However, although Philo's discussion in *QG* 4.2, 4–5, 8 is lengthy and not easy to follow, if one pays careful attention it becomes clear that Philo's discussion is, in fact, predicated on the "inconsistency" of the biblical narrative as it progresses. As mentioned above, his awareness of,

[43] As Ralph Marcus points out in a footnote to his translation, this unexpected exegetical turn may have been inspired by wordplay between ἐγκρυφίας, "ash-cakes," and κρυπτός, "hidden" (PLCL, 282).

[44] Birnbaum, "What Does Philo Mean by 'Seeing God'? Some Methodological Considerations," 547; eadem. *The Place of Judaism in Philo's Thought*, 87.

and attention towards, the nuances of the entire biblical narrative is explicit in 4.2, when he lists both the single and plural subject addresses and phrases, and in 4.5, where he notes the unexpected return back to plural address in Gen 18:4. Moreover, it is implicit throughout the discussion, as Philo attempts to explain why the text vacillates back and forth between the singular and plural.

Decisive to understanding the whole discussion, in fact, are Philo's repeated claims that the change is attributable to the state of the viewing subject. In contrast to the "ignoble and idle soul," whose sight is "in a deep sleep" and "always blocked," Abraham is the "virtuous person," whose "spiritual eyes" "are awake and see" (4.2). Abraham, the model philosopher, also overcomes the weakness of sight that typically causes the "lucid and bright" eyes of the soul to become "dimmed" in the presence of the deity (4.8). His "mind" is able to "clearly form an impression with more open eyes and more lucid vision, and not roaming about nor wandering off with the triad." His "fully opened" mind then "runs towards the one," and he sees God as one, clearly manifest, "directly visible" (4.4). Philo's concluding remarks in 4.8, on the necessity of initiation, functions as a cautionary: only an adept would fully fathom this subtle and nuanced conversation. Abraham Terian considers *QG* 4.8 to be "one of Philo's most profound explanations of the mystical apprehension of God," and most likely reflecting his "personal experience."[45] Thus, *QG* 4.2, 4–5, 8, with its claim that Abraham is apparently able to achieve a depth of vision attainable by few others, hints once again at Philo's propensity towards establishing quantifiable levels of philosophic achievement, or "spiritual consciousness."[46]

[45] Abraham Terian, "Inspiration and Originality: Philo's Distinctive Exclamations," *SPhA* 7 (1995): 79. Recognition of both the meticulous care with which the passage is exegeted, and the well charted flow of logic, also precludes the possibility that *QG* 4.2, 4–5, 8 contains unassimilated and unreconciled earlier traditions. Though the work of his exegetical predecessors is probably present in *QG* 4.2, 4–5, 8, Philo has apparently shaped and conformed the entire passage to reflect his own views and *visio Dei* experiences.

[46] See also the detailed consideration of Philo's various three-tiered schema in David M. Hay, "The Psychology of Faith in Hellenistic Judaism," 902–907. Two accounts pertinent to our present discussion are *Gig.* 60–61 and *QG* 3.34. In *Gig.* 60–61, Philo identifies the three classes as (1) the "earth-born" who indulge in the pleasures of the flesh; (2) the "heaven-born" who love to learn; (3) and the "people of God" who refuse citizenship in the world, and "who have risen wholly above the sphere of sense-perception and have been translated into the noetic realm and who dwell there as registered citizens of the commonwealth of Ideas, which are imperishable and incorporeal." On this passage, see David Winston and John Dillon's "Commentary on *De Gigantibus*," in *Two Treatises of Philo of Alexandria: A Commentary on* De Gigantibus *and* Quod Deus Sit Immutabilis (ed. David Winston and John Dillon; BJS 25; Chico, Calif.: Scholars Press, 1983), 269–270. In *QG* 3.34, Philo's interpretation of Hagar's visionary encounter with God (Gen 16:13) also

And this hierarchical, gradational thinking is crucial to Philo's conception of the vision of God.[47]

3.6. Visio Dei *passages in the Exposition*

The Exposition of the Law is the "most systematic and thematically unified" of the three commentary series, and in its ten individual treatises[48] Philo most commonly operates at the literal level of the biblical tradition, though symbolic and allegorical interpretations occasionally surface.[49] This "rewritten Bible" would then appear to be directed to a general audience of Jews, and possibly some non-Jews, possessed of minimal acquaintance with either scripture or philosophy.[50]

3.6.1. *Abr.* 107, 119–132: The three stages of initiatory progress

A hierarchical ordering of visionary accomplishment reappears in *Abr.* 107, 119–132, while treating the same passage as *QG* 4.2, 4–5, 8: Gen 18:2–7. This time, however, Philo explicitly divides noetic philosophers into three stages of initiatory progress, or spiritual development. Though the "mind that is highly purified," the "visionary mind" (τῇ ὁρατικῇ διανοίᾳ), will sometimes see God as three, it will occasionally be able to see him as one, the Existent One (τὸ ὄν). Those who are "not yet initiated into the higher mysteries," however, are "unable to see the Existent One alone by himself." This lower class of philosopher will instead only see God as Three. They will see God not as he exists, but as he acts, through his Powers (*Abr.* 122). In *Abr.* 124–125, Philo further delineates the object of vision experienced by each level

---

promotes a hierarchy of visionary experience, this time based on the social status of the visionary. Though Hagar believed she saw God directly, she was mistaken. As a servant, she was capable only of seeing God's servant, his Logos (referred to in Genesis as the "angel of Yahweh"). Philo further denigrates Hagar, comparing her experience to that of an ignorant and inexperienced rural person mistaking a small village for a metropolis. She mistook a "satrap" for the "Great King." Throughout the same passage Philo implies that Sarah, here referred to as "Wisdom," actually did see God himself.

[47] See also *QE* 2.51: The "worthily initiated" are promised their "closed eyes" will be opened, and they will see "the First (Cause)." They will be roused from "deep sleep" and in "wakefulness" there will "appear to them that manifest One, who causes incorporeal rays to shine."

[48] Or twelve if you include the two books of *Mos.*; cf. the discussion of this issue below, in footnote 52.

[49] Runia, *On the Creation of the Cosmos*, 6.

[50] The sole exception being *Opif.*, which assumes on the part of its readership a fair level of philosophical knowledge. On the place of *Opif.* within the Exposition, see Runia, *On the Creation of the Cosmos*, 1–4.

of noetic philosopher: (1) the "best class" sees the "essentially Existent One" (τὸ ὄντως ὄν). (2) The second class sees the beneficent Power "God." (3) The third sees the governing Power "Lord."[51]

Furthermore, we can assume on the basis of his careful delineation of the various levels of attainment, and the divine characters encountered therein, that Philo has not, at least in *Abr.* 107, 119–132 and *QG* 4.2, 4–5, 8, collapsed his various intermediaries into manifestations of a single deity. Like the passages in the Allegory that present the Logos functioning as the ἀναγωγός of the noetic ascent, in these two passages the intermediaries also appear to operate as autonomous realities.

3.6.2. *Spec.* 1.41–50: Existence and essence

Despite its presumably less sophisticated audience, the Exposition contains one of the most complicated *visio Dei* accounts in the Philonic corpus: *Spec.* 1.41–50. In the middle of this passage Philo seems to imply that the Powers are all one can see of the deity. His discussion of Exod 33:12–23 begins with Moses' "inspired cry" to God: "Reveal yourself to me!" There then follows the record of a lengthy conversation between Moses and God. Moses admits only God can reveal himself, to which God replies that created beings are incapable of apprehending (κατάληψις) him. Moses humbly acknowledges the wisdom of God's response, admitting,

> I never could have received the vision of you clearly manifested, but I beg that you would show me the glory that surrounds you, and by that I mean the Powers that guard you, of whom I would love to gain apprehension (κατάληψις) . . . the thought of which creates in me a mighty longing to have knowledge of them (1.45).

God responds that the Powers are "not discerned by sight but by the mind even as I, whose they are, am discerned by mind and not by sight" (1.46). These Powers, "while in their essence they are beyond your apprehension, they present to your sight (παραφαίνω) a sort of impress and copy of their active working" (1.47). Further qualifications are then made:

> Do not hope to ever be able to apprehend me or any of my Powers in our essence. But I will readily allow you a share of what is attainable. That means I welcome you to come and contemplate the universe and its contents, a spectacle apprehended not by the eyes of the body but by the unsleeping eyes of the mind (1.49).

[51] While discussing this passage in his essay, "Was Philo a Mystic?" Winston accurately reproduces the argument of *Abr.* 119–123, yet fails to allow it to influence his conviction that only the Logos is seen (21).

Though 1.49 initially appears to be making the common distinction between God's existence and essence, it immediately and severely qualifies the grasp of even divine existence, ultimately allowing only an inferential relationship: it is solely in "contemplating the universe and its contents" that one can see the creator God. Thus *Spec.* 1.41–50 charts a course that moves in the opposite direction of many other *visio Dei* passages. Though mid-passage it appears to propose that at least the Powers are seen, it quickly moves to disallow even that, and ultimately argues for the utter invisibility of both God and his Powers. *Spec.* 1.41–50 demonstrates again the necessity of following a unit from its beginning to its end.

3.6.3. *Abr.* 79–80, *Opif.* 69–71, *Mos.* 1.158: "Intermediary-free" *visio Dei* passages

The Exposition also contains a number of passages where Philo portrays the vision of God as occurring without the intervention or presence of intermediaries. Of Abraham it is said that he

> received a vision of him who so long lay hidden and invisible. . . . God did not turn away his face, but came forward to meet Abraham, and revealed his nature, so far as the beholder's power of sight allowed. That is why we are told not that the Sage saw God, but that God was seen by him. For it is impossible that anyone should by themselves apprehend the truly Existent One (τὸ ἀλήθειαν ὄν), if he did not reveal and manifest himself (*Abr.* 79–80).

The creaturely limitations of the "beholder's power of sight" are decisive also in *Opif.* 69–71, which describes a noetic philosopher soaring into the heavens, only to be repelled by the blinding radiance of the "Great King himself."

One of the more remarkable instances of an "intermediary-free" *visio Dei* is found in *Mos.* 1.158,[52] which elaborates on Moses' receipt of the torah on Sinai. Philo reports that Moses, the "god and king of the whole nation, entered into the darkness where God was, that is into the unseen, invisible, incorporeal and archetypical essence of existing things." That Moses "beheld what was hidden from the sight of mortal nature" indicates, with all probability, the Existent One (τὸ ὄν) was the object of Moses' sight.

[52] Scholars are divided on whether *Mos.* is an integral part of the Exposition of the Law or related to it as a general introductory treatise. See Jenny Morris, "Philo the Jewish Philosopher," in *The History of the Jewish People in the Age of Jesus Christ (175 B.C. – A.D. 135)*, (ed. E. Schürer, G. Vermes et al., vol. 3 part 2; Edinburgh: T&T Clark, 1987), 854; Albert C. Geljon, *Philonic Exegesis in Gregory of Nyssa's* De vita Moysis, (BJS 333: SPhM 5; Providence R. I.: Brown Judaic Studies, 2002), 7–30.

4. *Conclusion*

Our survey of selected *visio Dei* passages has demonstrated the presence of four recurring elements in all three of the commentary series. (1) The identity of the object of sight varies, not only from passage to passage in a treatise, but even within the same passage. Nevertheless, in all three commentary series there are clear statements of the visibility of τὸ ὄν. (2) A hierarchy of visionary accomplishment, based on the spiritual advancement of the noetic philosopher, often determines who is seen, and quite often it is τὸ ὄν who is seen by the highest category of mystic philosopher. (3) The intermediaries operate as autonomous agents, conceptually distinct from τὸ ὄν, both in passages promoting a hierarchy of visionary accomplishment, as well as those depicting the Logos as the ἀναγωγός, the means and guide of the noetic ascent. (4) Philo occasionally allows his allegiance to divine transcendence to direct the discussion, and τὸ ὄν is then said to be absolutely "non-visible." It is also apparent that "intermediary-free" *visio Dei* passages are not as commonly encountered as those populated by intermediaries, and are most prevalent in the Exposition.

Ellen Birnbaum has provided a convincing explanation for some of these phenomena that is based on a treatise's intended audience. Since the Exposition is directed towards a less sophisticated audience, who would be both unaware of the intermediaries and somewhat unprepared to discuss seeing God, the *visio Dei* is therefore rarely mentioned in these treatises, and when it is, a simple, unmediated visual encounter with God is described. In the much larger Allegorical Commentary, with its more mature audience, Philo not only speaks more often of seeing God, but it is a much more nuanced conversation, frequently involving intermediaries.[53] There are some complications, however. As our survey has shown, the question of audiences, and their relative sophistication, is not an entirely reliable predictor of the manner in which Philo presents his *visio Dei* accounts. *Spec.* 1.41–50, in the Exposition, offers one of the most detailed defenses for God's invisibility, one involving not only mediators, but also the subtle distinction between essence and existence. And perhaps Philo's most advanced discussion of the *visio Dei* appears in *QG* 4.2, 4–5, 8, whose audience would also have undoubtedly included novices.[54] Even more

53 Birnbaum, "What Does Philo Mean by 'Seeing God'? Some Methodological Considerations," 549–550; eadem. *The Place of Judaism in Philo's Thought*, 89–90.

54 Gregory E. Sterling considers the "pedagogical character of the format and the listing of multiple interpretations" in *QGE* proof they "were written for beginning students in his school" ("General Introduction," in Runia, *On the Creation of the Cosmos*, xi. See also idem. "'The School of Sacred Laws': The Social Setting of Philo's Treatises," 159–160).

confounding is the presence of a similarly complex treatment of Gen 18:2–7 in the Exposition, in *Abr.* 107, 119–132. In the case of this particular piece of recurring exegesis, we may perhaps assume that all Philo's students were aware of his various three-stage hierarchies of spiritual development, and the novices in particular would want to know the nature and contents of the hierarchical order. Or perhaps Philo simply lost himself, and like so many of us, temporarily allowed his exegetical interests to overrun his pedagogical program!

Although the issue of a treatise's implied audience is generally instructive, it is incapable of accounting for all the variances in Philo's *visio Dei* accounts. At least some of the ambiguities and apparent inconsistencies may be attributed to three other factors. (1) Perhaps the foremost of these factors are the exegetical traditions that Philo occasionally draws upon in commentaries, particularly the Allegory and *QGE*. These "conversation partners" are quoted for the sake of completeness but not completely assimilated into, or coherently harmonized, with Philo's own views. As Sterling notes:

> The inconcinnities and tensions which annoy modern readers are marks of a school tradition. Philo offers various interpretations as a matter of preserving the traditions. Since he is working within a tradition there is no need to impose his own views on all of his predecessors; he is content to allow them a voice as well as to make his own heard in matters of importance. Philo presents multiple views as a means of illustrating the range of meanings of a text to the students.[55]

(2) The varying views may also reflect Philo's own spiritual growth and philosophical development over the course of his lifetime. A trace of such development might be evident in the admission made in *Post.* 167: "When we say that the Existent One (τὸ ὄν) is visible, we are not using words in their literal sense." This severe qualification of prior claims of God's visibility does not square with the vivid and emotional texture of the *visio Dei* accounts we find throughout Philo's writings, which would most naturally lead one to take them quite literally. (3) Finally, as we have earlier suggested, Philo may well have been conflicted about the whole matter. His ambivalence about the possibility of seeing God would then be a deliberate effort to appropriately represent both the complexity and uncertainty of a

[55] Sterling, "'The School of Sacred Laws': The Social Setting of Philo's Treatises," 160.

mystical experience that is ultimately inscrutable.[56] Furthermore, this mystical experience, perhaps more so than any other aspect of Philo's thought and experience, created an irreconcilable tension between his philosophical commitment to transcendence and his religious commitment to the often-imminent God of Israel, as revealed in the writings of Moses. In addition to the issue of audience, these three factors, when taken into account, help to mitigate the effect of the ambiguities and apparent inconsistencies.

As we have seen, Philo's views about the object of the *visio Dei* are varied and often highly nuanced. More often than not his commitment to divine transcendence seems to necessitate the inclusion of intermediaries in the discussion. Nevertheless, in his semi-ubiquitous schema of stages of initiatory progress, perhaps evidence of an essential pedagogical orientation, he more often than not accords those in the highest class a glimpse of the transcendent Existent One. In both these passages and those where the Logos functions anagogically, as well as those remarkable instances which are "intermediary-free," the noetic mystic is portrayed as soaring into the κόσμος νοητός and enjoying the "beginning and end of human happiness" (*QE* 2.51), the "most precious of all possessions" (*Legat.* 4), a vision of the Existent One.[57]

[56] The issue of agency is similarly characterized by ambivalence, and will be discussed in a forthcoming paper, tentatively entitled: "Seeing God in Philo of Alexandria: Methods and Means." I intend to demonstrate that in some passages divine initiative is solely responsible for the vision of God, while in many others Philo emphasizes the role of vigorous human striving. And in at least two passages, *Mut.* 81–82 and *Praem.* 37–39, Philo achieves a perfect synergistic balance between human effort and divine grace.

[57] This article is dedicated to the memory of David M. Scholer (1938–2008). Ten years ago in a graduate seminar on Second Temple Literature, David's contagious passion for Philo opened my eyes to the joys of studying the "Alexandrian Exegete."

The Studia Philonica Annual 21 (2009) 49–62

PERSPECTIVE, PAIDEIA, AND ACCOMMODATION IN PHILO

TZVI NOVICK

Perspectival exegesis may be defined as exegesis that attends to the point of view represented by a given proposition in a text. It appreciates the possibility that the proposition does not provide a transparent, disembodied window onto the text's world, but instead reflects the viewpoint—the knowledge, character, rhetorical style, etc.—of a specific figure in that world. Perspectival exegesis rests upon an awareness of the differing perspectives of the text's characters, and, more fundamentally, of the difference between characters' perspectives and that of the narrator. It also discerns cases of interpenetration, where texts formally marked as character speech in fact represent the narrator's point of view, or, inversely, where speech attributed to the narrator reflects the perspective of (or, is "focalized" through) a character.

While perspectival exegesis is a hallmark of contemporary narratology, it is well known that ancient literary critics, too, made use of this tool.[1] The principle of the λύσις ἐκ τοῦ προσώπου "solution from the character" describes a particularly well-developed mode of perspectival exegesis. Under this principle, an apparent contradiction between two texts is solved through the observation that the speakers of the two texts differ.[2] One

* A different version of this paper was delivered before the Philo of Alexandria group at the 2008 Society of Biblical Literature Annual Meeting. I thank the group's chairs for the opportunity to present it, and the participants for their feedback. Yonatan Moss and the journal's anonymous readers also provided very helpful comments.

1 For an excellent introduction to narratology see Mieke Bal, *Narratology: Introduction to the Theory of Narrative* (2nd ed.; Toronto: University of Toronto Press, 1997). From the recent survey of literary criticism in the Greek scholia by René Nünlist (*The Ancient Critic at Work: Terms and Concepts of Literary Criticism in Greek Scholia* [Cambridge: Cambridge University Press, 2009]), much of the material analyzed in the chapters on "Narrative and Speech" (94–115), "Characters" (238–56), and especially "Focalisation" (116–34), would fall under the rubric of perspectival exegesis.

2 On the λύσις ἐκ τοῦ προσώπου, see most recently Nünlist, *Ancient Critic*, 116; *idem*, "The Homeric Scholia on Focalization," *Mnemosyne* 56 (2003): 62–64.

example concerns the apparently inconsistent descriptions of Menelaos' military prowess in the *Iliad*: Apollo, disguised as Phainops, calls him a soft warrior (*Il.* 17.588), but the narrator elsewhere describes him as dear to Ares (*Il.* 3.21 *et passim*). Aristonikos (Erbse ed., schol. A *Il.* 17.588) offers this solution:

> One must not understand that Menelaos is indeed a soft warrior, but the character speaking, being an enemy, says it slanderously. For the poet calls him dear to Ares.[3]

While the poet characterizes Menelaos accurately, "Phainops" describes him not as he is, but as he would have him viewed.

A similar example of "solution from the character" occurs in *Mekilta R. Ishmael,* a rabbinic commentary on the book of Exodus edited in the third century C.E.

> "[And it was told to the king of Egypt] that the people were fleeing" (Exod 14:5). But were they fleeing? Does it not already say, "On the morrow of the Passover, the children of Israel left with upraised hand [before the eyes of all Egypt]" (Num 33:3)? What is meant, then, by "that the people were fleeing"? Because the Israelites had struck their guards, the latter went and told Pharaoh, saying: see, the Israelites struck some of us, injured some of us, killed some of us, and none protested; they have no ruler or leader, as it says, "The locust have no king." (Prov 30:27)[4]

The midrash poses a contradiction between Exod 14:5, wherein it is asserted that the Israelites "fled" Egypt, evidently as a disorderly, furtive mass, and Num 33:3, which implies that they departed in a stately, public fashion. The solution is that the characterization of the Israelites in Exod 14:5 represents the view of the guards who (according to the midrash) had accompanied the people out of Egypt. When the Israelites injured and killed some of these guards, the latter formed the impression that they were a leaderless mob.[5]

[3] I follow the translation in Nünlist, "Homeric Scholia," 63.

[4] *Mek. R. Ish. Beshalaḥ* 2 (Horowitz-Rabin ed., 86). The translation is mine.

[5] The logic of the midrash is not altogether clear. I take the apparent contradiction between Exod 14:5 and Num 33:3 as involving the *manner* of Israel's departure. This interpretation seems to me the only way to make sense of the solution proposed in the continuation. Another reading of the apparent contradiction, possibly more natural in itself, is as involving the *legal status* of Israel's departure, with Exod 14:5 implying that Israel departed without Egypt's consent, and Num 33:3 implying the opposite. Cf. *Mek. R. Ish. Beshalaḥ* 1 (Horowitz-Rabin ed., 83–84), where the Israelites, in conversation with their guards, indeed cite Num 33:3 as evidence of the legal status of their departure, albeit as proof that their departure did *not* depend on Pharaoh's consent. But this approach seems unable to account for the continuation of the midrash. On the Israelites' interaction with

The topic of this essay is perspectival exegesis in the Philonic corpus. I aim not to provide a comprehensive catalogue of cases in which Philo resorts to perspectival exegesis, but instead to identify the peculiar features of this technique within the larger framework of Philo's exegetical poetics. The first part of the essay surveys some examples of perspectival exegesis in Philo. The second part, building off the final example, focuses on the intersection of perspectival exegesis with Philo's view that the mythic aspects of the biblical narrative have a paedeutic function. In the third part of the essay I analyze one example of perspectival exegesis in Philo that illustrates how it can bridge between literal and allegorical reading. I do not dwell in this essay on the question of influence. While the extensive and varied manifestations of perspectival exegesis among contemporary critics of classical Greek literature may have been known to and partially have inspired Philo, the absence of explicit acknowledgment and of pronounced terminological continuity, coupled with the existence of other, independent pressures toward perspectival exegesis, makes influence difficult to prove, even if such influence is inevitably more likely in the case of the Alexandrian philosopher than in that of the rabbis of Palestine.[6]

---

their guards in *Mekilta R. Ishmael* (but expressing no position on the above problem) see Gerald J. Blidstein, "Prayer, Rescue, and Redemption in the Mekilta," *JSJ* 39 (2008): 74–76. For a survey of a set of formulae through which classical rabbinic literature distinguishes among different speakers within brief, continuous stretches of biblical text, see Gershon Brin, '**הנוסחה**: "כל מה שאמר זה לא אמר זה"-הפרשה עירובי דברים' *Beit Mikra* 163 (2000): 329–49. As the above example suggests, a comprehensive portrait of perspectival exegesis in the classical rabbinic corpus cannot rest exclusively on its exegetical formulae; most cases of perspectival exegesis are *ad hoc*. In the post-classical period, perspectival exegesis becomes more self-conscious, especially among Karaite commentators. See Meira Polliack, "The 'Voice' of the Narrator and the 'Voice' of the Characters in the Biblical Commentaries of Yefet ben 'Eli," in *Birkat Shalom: Studies in the Bible, Ancient Near Eastern Literature, and Postbiblical Judaism, Presented to Shalom M. Paul on the Occasion of his Seventieth Birthday*, ed. Chaim Cohen et al.; (Winona Lake, Ind.: Eisenbrauns, 2008), 891–915; and see also the reflections of Jacob al-Qirqisānī in the passage immediately following the one referenced *infra* at n. 19.

6 Even if Philo was unfamiliar with perspectival exegesis as practiced by critics of Homer and other pagan authors, the existence of numerous contemporary Homeric papyri from Oxyrhynchos with marginal glosses indicating speaker (the "poet" or a specific character) and addressee suggests that the basic narratological insights of interest here enjoyed rather widespread circulation. For the papyri, and a survey of the cultural contexts in which these marginal glosses might have proved useful, see Joseph Spooner, ed., *Nine Homeric Papyri from Oxyrhynchos* (Studi e Testi di Papirologia n.s. 1; Firenze: Instituto Papirologico G. Vitelli, 2002), 147–56, 171–78. Philo employs πρόσωπον as a technical term most extensively in his remarks on the categories of divine speech in Scripture, where he distinguishes between utterances spoken by God in his own person (ἐκ προσώπου τοῦ θεοῦ), cases in which Moses asks and God responds, and oracles delivered by an "ecstatic" Moses in his own person (ἐκ προσώπου Μωυσέως) (*Mos.* 2.158). On this and related passages see

1. *Perspectival Exegesis in Philo: Some Examples*

In *Migr.* 155–63, Philo observes that when Joseph leaves the land of Egypt for Canaan, the Egyptians who accompany him proceed in an honorably well-organized fashion: Pharaoh's servants, the elders of his house, the elders of Egypt, and all his household (after Gen 50:7). When, by contrast, the nation of Israel departs from Egypt, the Egyptians who join themselves to it are characterized as a "mixed multitude" (Exod 12:38). At the literal level, of course, there is no contradiction, but at the allegorical level, where Egypt has a single network of correlates—the body, vanity, all that is the opposite of virtue—we should expect it to be consistently described. Philo solves this "problem" by suggesting that the text represents the different perspectives of the Israel soul ("the man whose vision is quite perfect") and the Joseph soul ("the man who still cherishes low aims") on vice.

> For whereas in the view of the man whose vision is quite perfect and who is a lover of virtue, all that is not virtue and virtue's doing seems to be mixed up and to be in confusion, in the eyes of the man who still cherishes low aims, earth's prizes are deemed to be in themselves worthy of love and worthy of honor.[7]

Thus the contradiction is only apparent, because the two verses offer not an impartial description of Egypt/vice, but different characters' viewpoints: Israel correctly sees vice as a confused mass, while Joseph incorrectly discerns an order within it. Though Gen 50:8 is narrator speech, Philo reads the text as focalized through the Joseph soul.[8]

Philo again has resort to perspectival exegesis in his allegorical exposition of Gen 24:63-65 (*Det.* 29–30). According to Gen 24:63, Isaac goes out to the field to "talk" (ἀδολεσχῆσαι). With whom does he speak? On Philo's

---

Helmut Burkhardt, *Die Inspiration heiliger Schriften bei Philo von Alexandrien* (Giessen: Brunnen Verlag, 1988), especially 150–56; Reinhard Weber, *Das "Gesetz" bei Philon von Alexandrien und Flavius Josephus: Studien zum Verständnis und zur Funktion der Thora bei den beiden Hauptzeugen des hellenistischen Judentums* (Frankfurt: Lang, 2001), 42–67.

[7] Translations of Philo in this essay follow the PLCL, with occasional modification.

[8] My interpretation accords with Colson's note *ad loc.* On "secondary focalisation within the narrator-text" in the Greek scholia see Nünlist, *Ancient Critic*, 126–27. The substance of Philo's exegesis (but not, in any straightforward sense, its perspectival dimension) recollects a statement in *Lev. Rab.* 4:6 (Margulies ed., 93) attributed to R. Joshua b. Qorḥa: "Esau had only six souls, and of him it uses 'souls,' in the plural, as it says, 'and Esau took his wives and sons and daughters and all the souls of his house' (Gen 36:3). Yet Jacob was seventy souls, and of him it uses 'soul,' in the singular, as it says, 'with seventy soul your forefathers descended to Egypt' (Deut 10:22)! [The solution:] Because Esau worshipped many gods, it uses of him 'souls,' in the plural, whereas because Jacob worshipped only one God, it uses of him 'soul,' in the singular."

approach, Isaac is the superior, self-taught mind, whose interlocutor can be none other than God.[9] That Isaac's interlocutor is no mere mortal is proven, for Philo, from the continuation of the narrative (Gen 24:64–65), where Rebecca spots Isaac, and questions the servant who accompanies her about him. Philo remarks on the fact that Rebecca seems to see Isaac alone, and not his conversation partner.

> Rebecca, who is persistence, will presently inquire of the servant as seeing one and receiving an impression of one only, "Who is this man who is coming to meet us?" For the soul that persists in noble courses is indeed capable of apprehending self-taught wisdom, which is represented by the title "Isaac," but is unable as yet to see God the Ruler of wisdom.

The tension between the narrator's report, which implies the presence of two figures in the field, and Rebecca's question, which refers only to one, is resolved by privileging the first as the fact of the matter, and characterizing the second as the product of the Rebeccan soul's circumscribed, deficient point of view.

Another instance of perspectival exegesis in Philo involves Gen 3:8, which I divide for analytical purposes into two halves: "(a)And they heard the sound of the Lord God walking in the garden in the afternoon, (b) and Adam and his wife hid themselves from the presence of the Lord God in the trees of the garden." Philo rejects the assumption of Gen 3:8b on its literal interpretation, that a person can in fact conceal himself from God: "were one not to take the language allegorically (εἰ δὲ μὴ ἀλληγορήσειέ τις), it would be impossible to accept the statement, for God fills and penetrates all things" (*Leg.* 3.4). Philo offers two allegorical solutions. One is conventional: "in the bad man (τῷ φαύλῳ), the true opinion concerning God is hidden in obscurity," and appropriately, he is "in banishment from the divine company" (*Leg.* 3.7). Philo's other solution is perspectival (*Leg.* 3.6):

> The bad man (ὁ φαῦλος) thinks that he can hide from Him, fancying that God, the Author of all things, is not in that part, which he has chosen for his lurking place.

According to both solutions, Adam is the bad man, who entertains an incorrect view of God. But there is a significant narratological difference. The former approach, that of *Leg.* 3.7, which I have characterized as conventional, assumes that Gen 3:8b, as narrator speech, is straightforwardly

[9] See *Mek. R. Ish. Beshalaḥ* 2 (Horowitz-Rabin ed., 92): "'And Isaac went out *laśuaḥ* in the field' (Gen 24:63): *śiḥah* is nothing other than prayer." For a review of modern scholarship on Isaac's activity in the field, see Gregory Vall, "What Was Isaac Doing in the Field (Genesis XXIV 63)?" *VT* 44 (1994): 513–23.

"true," or authoritative. To validate the text, despite its patently mythical character, Philo allegorizes: the first couple, having eaten of the forbidden fruit, can properly be said to have "hidden" themselves from God insofar as the true conception of God is not available to the bad person. "Hiding" signifies epistemological inaccessibility. The other, perspectival approach, takes Gen 3:8b as representing the characters' perspective. Philo can thus leave the literal meaning of the text more or less intact, for it now describes not an event, but a bad person's interpretation of an event: Adam and Eve really did hide from God, albeit only in their imagination. David Dawson has observed, in a different context, that Philo attempts, even in his allegorical exposition, "to protect the integrity of the literal textuality of scripture."[10] Perspectival allegoresis represents an extreme form of this tendency.

Philo's perspectival approach to Gen 3:8b is presumably encouraged by the first half of the verse (Gen 3:8a), which asserts not that God was walking in the garden, but that the couple *heard* God walking in the garden. Because this text, like the one involving Rebecca in the above example from *Det.* 29–30, is marked as a perception scene, the reader is primed to understand it as representing the point of view of the perceiving subject, here Adam and Eve, rather than as the fact of the matter.[11] Indeed, Philo elsewhere (*QG* 1.42) subjects the first half of Gen 3:8 to perspectival exegesis. Philo is, of course, troubled by the text's anthropomorphic representation of God as walking. His response:

> Whatever sensible gods are in heaven—that is the stars—all move in a circle and proceed in revolutions. But the highest and eldest cause is stable and immobile, as the theory of the ancients holds. For He gives an indication and impression as though He wished to give the appearance of moving; for though no voice is given forth, prophets hear through a certain power a divine voice sounding what is said to them. Accordingly, as He is heard without speaking, so also He gives the impression of walking without actually walking, indeed without moving at all. And you see that before there was any tasting of evil, (men) were stable, constant, immobile, peaceful and eternal; similarly and in the same way they believed God to be, just as He is in truth. But after they had come into association with deceit, they moved of themselves, and changed from being immobile, and believed that there was alteration and change in Him.

[10] *Allegorical Readers and Cultural Revision in Ancient Alexandria* (Berkeley: University of California Press, 1992), 101.

[11] Cf. Nünlist, *Ancient Critic*, 127, observing that certain ancient Greek critics "took it for granted that a scene of perception ... ought to be presented in 'secondary focalisation,'" i.e., from the perceiving character's perspective, not from that of the narrator. Of course, in having the perception verb in Gen 3:8a govern not only the first half of the verse but the second, Philo violates the text's plain sense.

By focalizing God's walking through Adam and Eve's perceptive act, the verse means to convey their "fallen" perspective, a perspective at variance with the truth.[12] In contrast with his perspectival analysis of Gen 3:8b in *Leg.* 3.6, which situates the notion that one might hide from God wholly in the misguided mind of the "bad man," and allows it no basis in fact, Philo seems to concede in this passage that God did, in a certain sense, walk, or at least that the fallen couple's mistaken impression of God was to some extent God's own doing.

Taken together, Philo's comments on Gen 3:8 in *Leg.* 3.6-7 and *QG* 1.42 suggest a spectrum of approaches to mythic passages that portray God in anthropomorphic terms. At the allegorical extreme is the "conventional" allegoresis of Gen 3:8b in *Leg.* 3.7, which reads the first couple's "hiding" from God as their inability to appreciate the true character of God. The perspectival allegoresis of Gen 3:8b in *Leg.* 3.6, because it attributes the mythical description to the perceiving character rather than to the narrator, ends up considerably more literalist: the man and woman indeed hide from God, if only according to their mistaken impression. Still more protective of the literal surface of Scripture is the perspectival interpretation of Gen 3:8a in *QG* 1.42, which finds some truth in the character's myth-like imaginings. True, God does not walk, but He can give the impression of walking.

2. *Perspectival Exegesis and Paedeutic Myth*

Another point on this spectrum emerges from Philo's remarks about two principles to which he occasionally adverts in his exegesis of biblical myth: that God both is, and is not, "as a man." Thus, for example, in Exod 24:10, Moses and the elders see brick-like sapphire work beneath God's feet. According to *Conf.* 98, the brick-like work is the perceptible world. In putting the world under God's feet, Moses means to say, *inter alia,* that God guides it. But the feet, *per se,* are illusory:

> [T]o say that He uses hands or feet or any created part at all is not the true account. For God is not as man (Num 23:19). It is but the form employed merely for our instruction (ἕνεκα διδασκαλίας) because we cannot get outside ourselves, but frame our conceptions of the Uncreated from our own experience.[13]

[12] For another case of Adamic error see *Cher.* 124; *QG* 1.58.

[13] One might have expected Philo to identify God's feet as his powers, just as elsewhere (*Plant.* 50) he renders God's "hands," in Exod 15:17, as his "world-creating powers," which fashion the "sanctuary" of the verse, i.e., the world of sense-perception. But feet pre-

At other points in the corpus, Philo roots the principle of "instruction," contrasted here with Num 23:19, in Deut 8:5. While Num 23:19 insists that God is not a man, Deut 8:5 appears to insist on some similarity between them. In the LXX it reads thus: "As a man chastens (παιδεύσαι) his son, so the Lord your God will chasten you." For Philo, Deut 8:5 indicates that God accommodates, by means of anthropomorphic representation, those who cannot conceive of him in the proper, far more abstract manner.[14]

A similar example occurs in *Sacr.* 94. Here Philo undertakes to explain why Moses, according to Exod 13:11, depicts God as binding himself by an oath.

> It was so that he might expose the weakness of created man, and, having exposed, might at the same time console. ... We cannot get outside ourselves in forming our ideas .... And therefore we invent for Him hands and feet, incomings and outgoings, enmities, aversions, estrangements, anger, in fact such parts and passions as can never belong to the Cause. And of such is the oath—a mere crutch for our weakness.

Thus the assertion that God took an oath, the literal claim of the biblical text, is a falsehood intended for lesser mortals, or, for mortals insofar as they are mortal.[15]

It is often supposed that Philo uses the two κεφάλαια "principles" or ὁδοί, "ways"—so (*Deus* 53; *Somn.* 1.237) he characterizes the propositions for which Num 23:19 and Deut 8:5 stand—to justify his allegorical hermeneutic. On this account, the notion that "God is not as a man" (Num 23:19) refers to texts in which God is represented in terms appropriate to the divine, and so may be taken literally, while "God is as a man" (Deut 8:5) refers to texts in which God is represented in human terms. The latter may be justified in their literal sense insofar as they serve to instruct lesser souls,

---

sumably lend themselves less easily to this allegorical equation than do hands. Moreover, this strategy is arguably blocked in *Conf.* 98 by the fact that in this context Philo has already (*Conf.* 96) identified the Logos with the "place" of Exod 24:10 (a pious addition in the LXX, absent from the MT).

14 See John Dillon, "The Nature of God in the 'Quod Deus,'" in *Two Treatises of Philo of Alexandria: A Commentary on* De Gigantibus *and* Quod Deus Sit Immutabilis, eds. David Winston and John Dillon; (BJS 25; Chico, California: Scholars Press, 1983), 220.

15 Aside from *Conf.* 98 and *Sacr.* 94, the contrast between Num 23:19 and Deut 8:5 occurs explicitly in five other places in the Philonic corpus: *Deus* 53-54; *Somn.* 1.237; *QG* 1.55, 2.54; and a fragment from the fourth book of the *Legum allegoriae*, published in J.R. Harris, *Fragments of Philo Judaeus* (Cambridge: Cambridge University Press, 1886), 8. A translation of the latter is given in David Winston, "Philo's Ethical Theory", in *Aufstieg und Niedergang der römischen Welt* II.21.1, ed. Wolfgang Haase; (Berlin: de Gruyter, 1984), 378.

but the better approach to such texts is allegorical interpretation.[16] Adam Kamesar has argued instead that the principles originate in an entirely literalist exegetical tradition. The mythic, anthropomorphic texts to which Deut 8:5 refers are justified, on this view, solely insofar as they serve a pedagogic purpose. The view more "characteristic" of Philo, that myth must be "healed" by allegorical interpretation, is foreign to this scheme.[17]

As Kamesar observes, his theory neatly accounts for the fact that in most cases where Philo employs the two principles, such as *Conf.* 98 and *Sacr.* 94, analyzed above, there is no reference to allegoresis. But Kamesar's approach naturally raises the question: if the two principles originated in a literalist approach to myth, how did they manage to insinuate themselves into Philo's system, where the allegorical approach looms so large? A close examination of one case where allegorical interpretation does occur in connection with the two principles offers an explanation. In *Somn.* 1.227 ff., Philo interprets Gen 31:13, where God tells Jacob: "I am the God who was seen by you in the place of God." Philo is struck by the two occurrences of the word *God* (θεός) in this passage. On his account, the first instance, with the definite article, represents God proper, τὸ ὄν, and the second, which is undefined, the Logos. Jacob, the practicing soul, has so far progressed that he discovers that the "God" with whom he had interacted earlier was not in fact God himself, but only an angel, whom Jacob had mistaken for God.[18] Such misapprehensions, suggests Philo, are a regular result of divine accommodation (*Somn.* 1.232):

> Accordingly, to the incorporeal souls which are occupied in his service, it is natural for him to appear as he is, conversing with them as a friend with his friends; but to those souls which are still in the body he must appear in the

[16] This view is summarized in Adam Kamesar, "Philo, the Presence of 'Paideutic' Myth in the Pentateuch, and the 'Principles' or *Kephalaia* of Mosaic Discourse," *SPhA* 10 (1998); 47. Kamesar also describes and refutes a different and less popular version of this traditional account.

[17] Kamesar, "Philo," 48. In addition to the paedeutic and allegorical approaches to myth, Philo evinces a third, philosophical one, drawn from Plato and most prevalent in his comments on Genesis. The latter approach is isolated in Maren R. Niehoff, "Philo's Views on Paganism," in *Tolerance and Intolerance in Early Judaism and Christianity,* eds. Graham N. Stanton and Guy G. Stroumsa; (Cambridge: Cambridge University Press, 1998), 141–51. Compare the not altogether dissimilar suggestion by Adam Kamesar ("The Literary Genres of the Pentateuch as Seen from the Greek Perspective," *SPhA* 9 [1997]; 177–80) that Judaeo-Hellenistic literalists—and to the limited extent that he endorsed their views, Philo himself—saw biblical cosmology as analogous to the myths of the Presocratics, which contemporary literary critics classified as transitional forms that gestured toward "modern" philosophy while retaining mythic elements characteristic of Homer.

[18] A structurally similar account of the Abrahamic soul's progress is given in *Somn.* 1.64-67, in that case dependent on two occurrences of the word "place" (τόπος).

> resemblance of the angels, though without changing his nature (for he is unchangeable), but merely implanting in those who behold him an idea of his having another form, so that they fancy that it is his image, not an imitation of him, but the very archetypal appearance itself.

Philo draws a direct line between this phenomenon and the tendency of Scripture to attribute various human features to God, "not indeed using these expressions with strict truth (πρὸς ἀλήθειαν), but having regard to the advantage (τὸ λυσιτελές) of those who are to learn from it," i.e., the naturally dull (*Somn.* 1.235). In proof Philo cites the two theological principles, Num 23:19 ("God is not as a man") and Deut 8:5 ("God is as a man"). He then returns to Gen 31:13 (*Somn.* 1.238–39):

> Why, then, do we wonder any longer at His assuming the likeness of angels, seeing that for the succor of those that are in need He assumes that of men? Accordingly, when He says "I am the God who was seen of thee in the place of God" (Gen 31:13), understand that He occupied the place of an angel only so far as appeared, without changing, with a view to the profit of him who was not yet capable of seeing the true God. For just as those who are unable to see the sun itself see the gleam of the parhelion and take it for the sun, and take the halo round the moon for the luminary itself, so some regard the image of God, His angel the Word, as His very self.

In this remarkable extended passage, Philo appears to perceive a continuity, indeed almost an equivalence, between the notion of paedeutic myth, i.e., that Scripture depicts God "as a man" so as to educate or instill fear in the vulgar *reader*, and the kind of perspectival hermeneutic of accommodation traced above in connection with Gen 3:8a, wherein God appears other than he is to a *character in the biblical text* for the sake of the latter's profit. The two concepts are, in fact, very much alike; indeed, the latter is, in essence, a text-immanent realization of the former. On the model of paedeutic myth, Scripture serves (*qua* text) as a *tool* in the educative process, while on the model of perspectival accommodation, it *illustrates* this process.[19]

[19] Ephrem the Syrian, too, in a *madrasha* from the cycle *On Faith* that bears close comparison with *Mek. R. Ish. Shirah* 4 (Horowitz-Rabin ed., 129–30), with which it shares the same prooftexts, makes no categorical distinction between, on the one hand, the representation of the divine in human terms to the reader of Scripture, and, on the other, the manifestation of the divine in human form to characters in Scripture. For the text, with translation and brief commentary, see Sebastian P. Brock and George A. Kiraz, eds., *Ephrem the Syrian: Select Poems* (Provo, Utah: Brigham Young University Press, 2006), 16–27. A similar juxtaposition of paedeutic myth and perspectival accommodation occurs in remarks on anthropomorphism by Jacob al-Qirqisānī (Leon Nemoy, *Karaite Anthology: Excerpts from the Early Literature* [YJS 7; New Haven: Yale University Press, 1952], 63–64) and Maimonides (Isadore Twersky, ed., *A Maimonides Reader* [New York: Behrman House,

Insofar as Philo's allegoresis depends on a notion of perspectival accommodation, it is thus conceptually continuous, on Philo's own understanding, with the approach that upholds biblical myth as paedeutic. Philonic allegoresis indeed very typically has this character, as the programmatic discussion in *Abr.* 119–32 suggests. This passage, which we shall examine in broader context below, allegorically interprets Abraham's encounter with the three "men" in Gen 18. For Philo, the three represent God and his two powers. In terms quite similar to those employed in the passage from *Somn.* 1.238–39 quoted above, the relationship among the three is described in terms of light and shadow: "the single object presents to [the mind] a triple vision, one representing the reality, the other two the shadows reflected from it" (*Abr.* 119). Philo contends that "there are three classes of human temperaments, each of them so constituted that the vision presents itself in one of the three ways above-mentioned" (*Abr.* 124). To the best, God appears as he is, and to the two inferior grades of soul, whose worship is sullied by the crass motives of hope of gain and fear of punishment, he appears in the guise of one of the powers. That God deigns to become manifest other than as he is, for the benefit of lesser minds (*Abr.* 129: "for I [i.e., God] know well that they will not only not be worsened, but actually bettered"), is understood by Philo as a distinctively divine kindness (*Abr.* 126–27):

> [M]en, when they see others approaching them under profession of friendship, in quest of advantages to be gained from them, look askance and turn away; they fear that counterfeited adulation and suavity which they regard as exceedingly pernicious. But God cannot suffer injury, and therefore He gladly invites all who set themselves to honor Him under any form whatsoever, and in His eyes none such deserves rejection.[20]

On this account, the ethical and spiritual progress of the soul, which animates much of Philo's allegorical interpretation, is not a lonely struggle; it occurs under God's gracious guidance, by means of perspectival accom-

Inc., 1972], 44–45 [*Mishneh Torah, Book of Knowledge, Basic Principles of the Torah,* 1:9]). For the possibility that al-Qirqisānī's thought on accommodation influenced Maimonides (albeit without comment on this juxtaposition in particular) see Stephen D. Benin, *The Footprints of God: Divine Accommodation in Jewish and Christian Thought* (Albany: State University of New York Press, 1993), 141.

[20] The contrastive rhetoric (ἄνθρωποι μὲν … ὁ δὲ θεὸς) recollects rabbinic midrash, e.g., *Sifre Num.* 133 (Horowitz ed., 176): "The mercies of flesh and blood are unlike the Place's mercies. The mercies of flesh and blood extend more to men than to women. But the One-who-spoke-and-the-world-was is not so: his mercies extend to all."

modation.[21] Philo succeeds in holding together two distinctive responses to biblical myth—the paedeutic, which assigns myth a role in educating/ governing inferior readers, and the allegorical, which interprets it out of existence—because the latter, insofar as it rests upon the notion that God condescends to "appear" to the variety of souls in the form appropriate to them, is in fact structurally and theologically continuous with the former.

3. *Perspectival Exegesis and the Literal/Allegorical Divide*

We turn now to examine a passage that illustrates another way in which perspectival exegesis allows Philo to bridge between literalist and allegorical reading practices. In *Abr.* 107–32, Philo sharply distinguishes between his allegorical exposition of the angels' visit to Abraham, which we analyzed in the previous section, and the literal. On the literal exposition (*Abr.* 107–18), Abraham, manifesting exemplary hospitality, expends great effort in serving his visitors, whose angelic nature he does not perceive. The allegorical exegesis (*Abr.* 119–30), as already noted, views the three visitors as God, the essential τὸ ὄν, shadowed on either side by what are in fact mere reflections, his two powers.[22] Philo points (*Abr.* 131–32) to the alteration in Gen 18 between the singular and the plural in references to the visitors as evidence that the three share a common allegorical referent. He appears to interpret the Abrahamic character as wavering between a vision of the one, when his mind is "highly purified," and of the three, when it is "still a votary only of the minor rites and unable to apprehend the Existent alone by Itself" (*Abr.* 122).

In his treatment of the same biblical passage in *QG* 4.1–20, Philo merges into a single exposition the approaches that, in *Abr.* 107–32, he distinguishes as literal and allegorical. While the wavering between singular and plural carries meaning, in *Abr.* 107–32, only *within* the allegorical exegesis, in *QG* 4.1–20 it conveys nothing less than the alteration *in Abraham's mind* between the interpretations classified in *Abr.* 107–32 as literal and allegorical. When the visitors appear in the plural, Abraham is imagining them as strangers, to whom he extends kindness, and when they appear in the singular, he sees them as manifestations of the divine, toward which he acts with piety.

[21] For a recent discussion of the soul's progress as a central dimension of Philonic allegory see Adam Kamesar, "Biblical Interpretation in Philo," in *idem*, ed., *The Cambridge Companion to Philo* (Cambridge: Cambridge University Press, 2009), 85–91.

[22] See also the fragment *De Deo*, translated with commentary in Folker Siegert, "The Philonian Fragment *De Deo*: First English Translation," in *SPhA* 10 (1998): 1–33.

> Seeing the vision before his eyes, which was not constant, being at one time that of God, at another time that of strangers, he decided to show piety as toward God, and equal oneness and love of man toward strangers.[23]

Likewise, in his remarks on Gen 18:5 (*QG* 4.6), Philo observes that Abraham politely says "I will take bread," rather than using the imperative "take bread," but then immediately follows with the imperative, "and eat."

> Here again he shows his doubt and his inclination toward either appearance. For when it is said, "I will take," he imagines it to be God, to Whom he does not dare to say, "take food." But when (he says) "eat," he imagines it to be the strange men.

Abraham wavers between misperception of the men as mortals, and true perception of the vision's divine character. In the same pericope, Philo characterizes this explanation as the literal meaning of the text.[24] This tour de force of perspectival exegesis in *QG* 4.1–20 manages to smuggle the exegetical alteration between what Philo elsewhere divides between literal and allegorical expositions into the literal narrative itself.

Conclusion

I have attempted in this essay, first and most basically, to provide examples from within the Philonic corpus of the sort of perspectival exegesis that contemporary critics of the Greek canon employed. More ambitiously, I have sought to describe some of the ways in which perspectival exegesis interacts with other dimensions of Philo's poetics. First, perspectival exegesis, even when allegorical, is especially faithful to the shape of the literal

[23] *QG* 4.2. It is likely no coincidence that while *Abr.* 107–18 characterizes the virtue exemplified by Abraham's ministrations on his guests' behalf in specific terms, as hospitality, *QG* 4.1–20 describes it in more general terms, as love of man. Because *QG* 4.1–20 combines the literal and allegorical expositions of *Abr.* 107–32 into a single narrative, it encourages the pairing of piety toward God (the virtue exemplified insofar as Abraham perceives the divine character of his visitors) with its typical counterpart, love of man. On this pairing in Philo and his contemporaries see David Flusser, "The Ten Commandments and the New Testament," in *The Ten Commandments in History and Tradition*, eds. Ben-Zion Segal and Gershon Levi; (Jerusalem: Magnes, 1990), 219–46. By contrast, *Abr.* 107–32, because it distributes the two virtues across two different expositions, is under no pressure to make the pairing, and so can identify Abraham's "literal" virtue more precisely, in accord with the scriptural context, as hospitality. At the same time, Philo's curious parenthetical remarks about piety at *Abr.* 114–16, in the midst of the literal exposition of Gen 18, seem to depend on an awareness of the exegesis of *QG* 4.1–20, wherein kindness toward man and piety toward God belong to the same exposition.

[24] "That is the literal meaning. But as for the deeper meaning ..."

narrative. Indeed, on at least one occasion, Philo manages, through perspectival exegesis, to incorporate what he elsewhere characterizes as the allegorical exposition into the biblical text's literal fabric. Second, and perhaps more importantly, the perspectival approach, when applied to interaction with the divine, mediates between, and draws together, two different approaches to myth in the Philonic corpus, a literalist one that justifies myth in terms of its paedeutic effect, and one that banishes it through allegory. Insofar as Philo's allegoresis partakes of perspectival accommodation, where God is understood as manifesting himself to souls to the degree that they can perceive him, paedeutic myth and allegory merge as two expressions of divine kindness. Conceived of in relation to its readers, the scriptural portrayal of God as other than he is, is an educational *tool*, but, conceived of as representing the perspective of biblical characters, it constitutes a *depiction* of the educational process.

The Studia Philonica Annual 21 (2009) 63–72

REVIEW ARTICLE

HOW DO YOU INTRODUCE PHILO OF ALEXANDRIA? THE CAMBRIDGE COMPANION TO PHILO*

GREGORY E. STERLING

The first modern scholar to write an introduction to the study of Philo was the great historian of religion E. R. Goodenough.[1] Goodenough's introduction was comprehensive in scope and pedagogical in aim. His work helped to set out the basic pattern of subsequent introductions. He treated Philo's life, introduced his writings, and dealt with his major areas of thought. Goodenough devoted the bulk of his pedagogical aide to Philo's thought by summarizing his politics,[2] emphasizing his Judaism in a way that he had not done previously, and expounding the heart of the Philonic enterprise as he understood it in Philo's metaphysics, ethics, and mysticism.[3] Goodenough understood Philo as an example of a thoroughly hellenized Jew who represented a form of marginal Judaism as opposed to the normative Judaism described by his teacher George Foot Moore.[4]

* Adam Kamesar, ed. *The Cambridge Companion to Philo*. Cambridge etc.: Cambridge University Press, 2009. xv + 301 pages. ISBN 978-0-521-86090-1 hb, 978-0-521-67802-5 pb. Price $85 hb, $29.99 pb. (For titles of individual articles see Bibliography section Supplement below.)

[1] E. R. Goodenough, *An Introduction to Philo Judaeus* (New Haven: Yale Univesity Press, 1940; 3rd ed.; Lanham, Md.: University Press of America, 1985).

[2] Goodenough, *An Introduction to Philo Judaeus*, 52–74, is a summary of his *The Politics of Philo Judaeus: Practice and Theory* (New Haven: Yale University Press, 1938).

[3] Goodenough's full statement of Philo's mysticism is in his *By Light, Light: The Mystic Gospel of Hellenistic Judaism* (New Haven: Yale University Press, 1935). He worked this out through symbols in his *Jewish Symbols in the Greco-Roman World* (13 vols.; Bollingen Series 37; New York: Princeton University Press, 1953–68).

[4] G. F. Moore, *Judaism in the First Centuries of the Christian Era: The Age of the Tannaim* (3 vols.; Cambridge, Mass.: Harvard University Press, 1927–30).

Four decades later, one of Goodenough's distinguished students, Samuel Sandmel, published his own introduction.[5] He followed the same basic sequence of his teacher, but divided his work into two parts, separating out the place of Philo in the history of religions as a second part. Like Goodenough he thought that Philo was hellenized, only he thought that his teacher pushed this too far. Unlike his teacher, he did not understand Philo to represent a larger movement, but thought of him as an isolated example of a Jewish intellectual.[6] More recently, Kenneth Schenk has added a helpful introduction that summarizes the *opinio communis* in Philonic studies, but does not make a distinct case for Philo's place in the development of religion as Goodenough and Sandmel had done.[7]

There have been other substantial introductions to Philo within larger works.[8] Perhaps the most noteworthy is that of Jenny Morris whose section in the Revised Schürer has been the best single introduction.[9] The recently released *Cambridge Companion to Philo* edited by Adam Kamesar now deserves that sobriquet. It does not replace Morris who provides fuller detail on a number of technical aspects, but serves as a more inviting introduction for an intelligent but inexperienced reader of Philo. Written by an international team of nine scholars, it represents a selection of the best scholarship on Philo in the world today. Kamesar grouped the essays into three parts with three essays apiece: Philo's Life and Writings, Philo's Thought, and Philo's Influence and Significance. The structure thus stands in the Goodenough–Sandmel tradition, although it has clearly evolved from a series of chapters to two parts and now three parts. We will explore each part. Since a major function of the work is to introduce Philo through the *status quaestionis* of Philonic research, I will indicate the areas in Philonic study that still need additional work. I do not offer these as criticisms of the volume that is the occasion for these reflections, but with the hope that my comments will stimulate others to undertake specific projects.

[5] S. Sandmel, *Philo of Alexandria: An Introduction* (New York: Oxford University Press, 1979).

[6] See Sandmel, *Philo of Alexandria*, 140–47. Cf. also idem, "Philo's Place in Judaism: a Study of Conceptions of Abraham in Jewish Literature," *HUCA* 25 (1954): 209–37; 26 (1955): 151–332, that were both reprinted as a monograph with the same name (New York: Ktav, 1972).

[7] Kenneth Schenk, *A Brief Guide to Philo* (Louisville: Westminster John Knox, 2005).

[8] One worth mentioning is P. Borgen, "Philo of Alexandria," in *Jewish Writings of the Second Temple Period* (ed. M. Stone; CRINT 2.2; Assen: Van Gorcum//Philadelphia: Fortress, 1984), 233–82.

[9] J. Morris, "The Jewish Philosopher Philo," in E. Schürer, *The Literature of the Jewish People in the Age of Jesus Christ* (3 vols.; revised and edited by G. Vermes, F. Millar, and M. Goodman; Edinburgh: T.&T. Clark, 1973–86), 3.2:809–89.

Philo's Life and Writings

Many find a biography of a significant thinker useful as a way to introduce the thinker, especially if the biography relates the intellectual world of the thinker.[10] It helps to contextualize the thought of the individual and to clarify not only the forces against which the thinker reacted, but also the bases from which the thinker attempted to make advances. The humanization of a body or system of thought does not impoverish it, but enriches it. The first three essays provide us with such an introduction to Philo and his corpus.

Daniel R. Schwartz, "Philo: His Family and His Times," contextualizes Philo's world in a helpful way by emphasizing Philo's family about whom we know more than we do about Philo himself and contextualizing the place of the Jewish community in the trouble that exploded in the late thirties in Alexandria. The contribution is a model of careful scholarship and sober judgments.

There is still a good deal that could be done with Philo's family. The most pressing need is to provide a full study of Philo's brother Gaius Julius Alexander.[11] There is also some inscriptional evidence that has not been incorporated in discussions of Philo's family that is worth noting. There are two second century figures mentioned primarily in Roman inscriptions that bear the same name as Tiberius Julius Alexander, Philo's famous nephew: Tiberius Julius Alexander Julianus and Tiberius Julius Alexander. The former served as a legate on Trajan's campaign against Parthia (116–17 C.E.),[12] a chief magistrate in Rome in 117,[13] and among the *Fratres Arvales* in 118,[14] 119(?),[15] 140,[16] 145,[17] and 155.[18] There are some variations in the order

[10] Cambridge University Press has published a number of biographies of significant philosophers that are very useful. For example, consider the orientation of Steven Nadler, *Spinoza: A Life* (Cambridge: Cambridge University Press, 1999), xiii: "The question that lies at the heart of this biography is how did the various aspects of Spinoza's life—his ethnic and social background, his place in exile between two such different cultures as the Amsterdam Portuguese–Jewish community and Dutch society, his intellectual development, and his social and political relationships—come together to produce one of history's most radical thinkers? But there is another, more general question that interests me as well: what did it mean to be a philosopher and a Jew in the Dutch Golden Age?"

[11] The best treatment to date is K. G. Evans, "Alexander the Alabarch: Roman and Jew," *SBLSPS* 34 (1995): 576–94.

[12] Dio Cassius 68.30.2, who mentions a Julius Alexander.

[13] So T. Mommsen, *Chronica minora: Saec. IV, V, VI, VII* (3 vols.; Monumenta Germaniae Historica 9, 11, 13; Berlin: Weidmann, 1892–98), 1:255.

[14] *CIL* 6.32374.

[15] *CIL* 6.2079. Cf. also 6.32378. The year of the service is uncertain.

[16] A. Pasoli, *Acta Fratrum Arvalium* (Bologna: Cesare Zuffi, 1950), no. 68.

of the names in the inscriptions, but the inscriptions all appear to refer to the same individual. He may have been Tiberius Julius Alexander's grandson who followed in the family tradition with a successful public career. The latter is a former magistrate of Alexandria who served as commander of the *Cohors Prima Flavia*.[19] Unlike Tiberius Julius Alexander Julianus who apparently spent his life in Rome, Tiberius Julius Alexander must have spent some time in Alexandria and may reflect a branch of the family that survived the destruction of the Alexandrian Jewish community in 115–17 C.E. This evidence confirms the role of Philo's family as one of the most distinguished Jewish families in first century Egypt and second century Rome, although members of the family in the second century may have had only tenuous ties with Judaism.

Eusebius wrote that "Philo was prolific in expression and broad in thought: he was lofty and elevated in his perspectives on the divine writings and wrote his exposition of the sacred works in varied and diverse ways."[20] It is essential for every introduction to provide an overview of his massive corpus. James R. Royse does just this and in a masterful way. As is well known Philo organized his exegetical works into three major commentary series: *the Questions and Answers on Genesis and Exodus*, the Allegorical Commentary, and the Exposition of the Law. Modern scholars add two other categories to group Philo's other treatises: apologetic or historical and philosophical. Royse follows suit. He also treats lost works and fragments as well as spurious works and points out the difficulties in determining the sequence of works. The most helpful aspect of his treatment is his summary of each treatise.

An area that still needs attention is the presence of cross-references to other works within Philo's treatises.[21] Let me give one example of how these might help. Philo provided a secondary preface for every treatise in the Exposition of the Law except the first, *On the Creation of the Cosmos*.[22] The prefaces link the works together into an organic whole. There may be another example of a work that belongs to the Exposition but lacks a secondary preface. Philo's two-volume work on *The Life of Moses* lacks a

[17] *CIL* 6.32379.

[18] Pasoli, *Acta Fratrum Arvalium*, no. 70.

[19] *OGIS* 705.

[20] Eusebius, *Hist. eccl.* 2.18.1.

[21] For a summary of past work see V. Nikiprowetzky, *Le commentaire de l'Écriture chez Philon d'Alexandrie* (ALGHJ 11; Leiden: Brill, 1977), 192–202.

[22] Philo, *Abr.* 1–6; *Ios.* 1; *Decal.* 1; *Spec.* 1.1; 2.1; 3.7; 4.1, 132–135; *Praem.* 1–3.

secondary preface except for the secondary preface that opens book 2.[23] The secondary preface that opens *On Joseph* mentions the treatments of four ancestors—Abraham, Isaac, Jacob, and Joseph—but does not refer to Moses. We might have expected Philo to deal with Moses as a means of covering the first half of Exodus, although Moses is not an embodiment of the law but the lawgiver. These facts suggest that *The Life of Moses* was not part of the Exposition of the Law. There are, however, some reasons to associate it with this series. First, Philo provided an outline of the Exposition of the Law in the *bios*.[24] Second, Philo referred to the work twice in the following treatises. In *On the Virtues* he wrote: "The things that he did from his early years to old age for the attention and care of each person and for all people have been shown earlier in two treatises that I wrote about the life of Moses (δεδήλωται πρότερον ἐν δυσὶ συντάξεσιν, ἃς ἀνέγραψα περὶ τοῦ βίου Μωυσέως)."[25] He has a similar reference in the next treatise *On Rewards and Punishments*: "All the virtues are virgins, but the one of the greatest beauty, the leading place—as if in a dance—is piety with which the theologian Moses was especially filled and for which, along with other virtues that are mentioned in the writings about his life (ἐν ταῖς γραφεῖσι περὶ τοῦ κατ᾽ αὐτὸν βίου), he obtained four special roles: king, legislator, prophet, and high priest."[26] The roles are an echo of Philo's outline of Moses' life at the outset of the second book.[27] The explicit reference to the work in *On the Virtues* and *On Rewards and Punishments* makes it clear that Philo wrote *The Life of Moses* prior to these works. The fact that the two treatises are part of the Exposition suggests that he may have written *The Life of Moses* at approximately the same time that he wrote the Exposition, since he kept most of his internal references in the Exposition to other works in the same commentary series. How should we explain these conflicting signals? Albert Geljon has recently suggested that the work is an introductory philosophical *bios*, written to introduce the reader to Moses' works in much the same way that Porphyry wrote a *Life of Plotinus* to introduce the *Enneads*.[28] While I agree with his conclusion about the genre of the work, I find it hard to divorce it from the Exposition. I suggest that it was an

23 Philo, *Mos*. 2.1: "The former treatise (ἡ μὲν προτέρα σύνταξις) was about the birth and upbringing of Moses, as well as his education and role as ruler . . . We have arranged the present treatise around the subsequent and following matters."

24 Philo, *Mos*. 2.45–47.

25 Philo, *Virt*. 52.

26 Philo, *Praem*. 53.

27 Philo, *Mos*. 2.3.

28 A. C. Geljon, *Philonic Exegesis in Gregory of Nyssa's* De vita Moysis (BJS 333/SPhM 5; Providence: Brown Judaic Studies, 2002), 7–46.

introduction to the Exposition in particular. I offer this as an example of the need for a thorough and systematic investigation of all cross-references in the Philonic corpus.[29]

The heart of Philo's method is allegorical exegesis. Adam Kamesar tackles this in the third essay of Part One. Kamesar uses ancient literary theory and practice to explain Philo's understanding of the Pentateuch and the rationale for his allegorical exegesis. He suggests that Philo had two bases for his allegorical interpretations: the *defectus litterae* of the biblical text forced him to move beyond literal readings and his understanding of the Pentateuch as inspired created a "pan-Scriptural didacticism" that accepts the literal but moves beyond it by recognizing that even when the text is not defective it may offer instruction at an allegorical level.

An area that Kamesar does not address but that needs additional work is the nature of Philo's commentaries *qua* commentary. There have been some recent efforts to explore the parallels to Philo's commentaries. John Dillon and David T. Runia have both investigated possible parallels to Philo's enterprise, e.g., the Platonic *Anonymous Theatetus Commentary*, Plutarch's *On the Generation of the Soul in the Timaeus*, and Porphyry's *On the Cave of the Nymphs*.[30] There are, however, some differences. The most notable is Philo's tendency to write thematic treatises and to connect them into a whole. This is still an area that needs additional work.

Philo's Thought

If consistency is the hobgoblin of a small mind, Philo had a great mind. Anyone who reads him quickly realizes that he is not thoroughly consistent. The result is that modern scholars often reach different judgments on key points. So, for example, Christina Termini, who described Philo's thought within the context of "Middle Judaism" or what many of us would call Second Temple Judaism, wrote: "Philo's theology cannot be understood

[29] I have made a tentative start in a paper that I delivered this May to the University of Lisbon, "'Prolific in Expression and Broad in Thought': an Introduction to the Writings of Philo of Alexandria."

[30] J. Dillon, "The Formal Structure of Philo's Allegorical Exegesis," in *Two Treatises of Philo of Alexandria* (ed. J. Dillon and D. Winston; BJS 25; Chico, Calif.: Scholars Press, 1983), 77–87; D. T. Runia, "The Structure of Philo's Allegorical Treatises: A Review of Two Recent Studies and Some Additional Comments," *VC* 38 (1984): 209–56; and idem, "Further Observations on the Structure of Philo's Allegorical Treatises," *VC* 41 (1987): 105–38. Runia's essays are reproduced in idem, *Exegesis and Philosophy: Studies on Philo of Alexandria* (Collected Studies Series 332; Aldershot: Variorum, 1990), nos. 4 and 5.

by reference to a scheme whereby an ever more extreme divine transcendence requires the presence of lower intermediaries to bridge the growing distance that separates God from the world."[31] On the other hand, Roberto Radice, who wrote about Philo's theology and understanding of creation by situating him within the context of philosophical traditions, said: "The themes discussed in the preceding paragraphs are also attested in Middle Platonic sources from the period after Philo: the problem of having to safeguard the transcendence of God and obviate His contact with matter; the insertion of intermediary beings between the first principle and the cosmos; and the philosophical terms employed, like God, Ideas as the thoughts of God, matter."[32] How can such divergent judgments spring from reading the same texts?

There are several factors that can explain this. First, Philo did not write systematically but exegetically.[33] The biblical text exercised some control over his thought and led him to take different positions in different contexts. Second, in my judgment, Philo also preserves different traditions at times. He does not always feel the need to harmonize these traditions as long as the differences do not challenge a major principle that he holds.[34] Third, the background against which Philo is read also has a direct bearing on how we understand him, as the citations from Termini and Radice demonstrate. He must be read against both his Jewish context and his Hellenistic philosophical context. Termini does a good job of laying out some of the positions taken by Jewish authors of the Second Temple period and then situating Philo within them. Radice does the same for the Hellenistic world. The world that we privilege will have an impact on our understanding. In the case above, I think that Radice has a better grasp of Philo's understanding of the powers. While Philo's understanding is directly tied to the biblical text, it is also shaped by his Platonism. Radice's analysis of Philo's understanding of God, creation, and the powers and the Logos is a first rate piece of work.

[31] C. Termini, "Philo's Thought within the Context of Middle Judaism," in *The Cambridge Companion to Philo*, 101.

[32] R. Radice, "Philo's Theology and Theory of Creation," in *The Cambridge Companion to Philo*, 137 n. 20; cf. also p. 129.

[33] The basic nature of Philo's enterprise was emphasized by V. Nikiprowetzky, *Le commentaire de l'Écriture chez Philon d'Alexandrie,* and P. Borgen, *Philo of Alexandria, An Exegete for His Time* (NovTSup86; Leiden: Brill, 1997).

[34] The most important treatment of this is T. Tobin, *The Creation of Man: Philo and the History of Interpretation* (CBQMS 14; Washington, D. C.: The Catholic Biblical Association of America, 1983).

Similarly, Carlos Levy explains Philo's ethics primarily—but not exclusively—against the background of Hellenistic philosophy. He suggests that Philo followed the Middle Platonic principle of ὁμοίωσις θεῷ as the basis for his ethic.[35] He knew the Socratic–Stoic tradition of virtue, but brought his understanding into line with the biblical tradition as his treatment of εὐσέβεια[36] and μετάνοια[37] demonstrate. He does something similar with the passions, only in this instance he accepted Platonic and Peripatetic modifications of the standard Stoic scheme of his day. He did adopt the Stoic sense of progression as well as their sense of a natural community and natural law.

The three essays are a good introduction to the interplay between Judaism and Hellenism within Philo. The challenge for a modern reader is that Philo did not see these as opposing forces but looked for the unity between them. From his perspective he did not need to read Platonism and Stoicism into Moses, but out of Moses. Philo did not create a synthesis between two different systems of thought as much as he grasped the unity that existed between different systems. Moses made the definitive articulation of the understanding of reality, but others saw the same reality. So, Philo wrote: "For what comes to adherents of the most esteemed philosophy, comes to the Jews through their laws and customs, namely the knowledge of the highest and most ancient Cause of all and the rejection of the deception of created gods."[38]

Philo's Influence and Significance

Not many people read Philo for Philo. He is typically read as a source or influence for other movements. While this is a shame in many ways—Philo is worth reading in his own right—it is the reality. The three last essays attempt to trace Philo's influence on three major corpora. Folker Siegert explores the relevance and importance of Philo for the study of the New Testament. In an impressive collection of texts, he surveys the possible

[35] See Plato, *Tht.* 176b–c cited by Philo, *Fug.* 63. See W. E. Helleman, "Philo of Alexandria on Deification and Assimilation to God," *SPhA* 2 (1990): 51–71.

[36] On this see now G. E. Sterling, "The Queen of the Virtues: Piety in Philo of Alexandria," *SPhA* 18 (2006): 103–24.

[37] On this see now G. E. Sterling, "'Turning to God': Conversion in Greek-Speaking Judaism and Early Christianity," in *Scripture and Traditions: Essays on Early Judaism and Christianity in Honor of Carl R. Holladay* (ed. P. Gray and G. O'Day; NovTSup; Leiden: Brill, 2008), 69–95.

[38] Philo, *Virt.* 65.

parallels between Philo and the New Testament. He does not argue for direct dependence, but for the importance of Philo as a source for traditions that also surface in the New Testament. In my judgment he is right on target. The days of Ceslas Spicq who argued that the author of Hebrews was a former student of Philo are over.[39] At the same time, the days when New Testament scholars suggest that Philo is irrelevant to the study of a text like Hebrews should also be over.[40] The value of the works of Philo for a student of the New Testament is twofold. First, the same exegetical traditions that we find in Philo also appear in numerous New Testament texts. Philo often provides a fuller exposition of these traditions than New Testament authors and permits us to understand the larger context of a tradition. Second, Philo also offers analogies to the genres and positions in New Testament texts. Readers can use Siegert's essay as an entry into the possibilities: it provides one of the richest collections of material in the short amount of space that is available at the present time. The downside of his collection is that he does not develop his examples and it may be difficult for an inexperienced reader of Philo to appreciate the specifics.

The importance of Philo's influence on Christianity becomes undisputed as we move into the second century. David T. Runia offers a summary and update of his indispensable monograph on the reception of Philo among early Christians.[41] He opens by asking the provocative question: why did early Christians preserve this proud Jewish author? He surveys twelve major early Christian writers who may have used Philo's works—Clement of Alexandria, Theophilus' *Ad Autolycum*, Origen, Arius, Didymus the Blind, Isidore, Eusebius, Basil, Gregory of Nyssa, Theodore of Mopsuestia, Ambrose, Augustine—and mentions a number of other Christians who used his treatises. He suggests that it was Philo's work as a historian and apologist, as an exegete and interpreter, and as a theologian and philosopher that led early Christians to preserve him.

David Winston asks the opposite question: Why did Jews fail to preserve Philo? He suggests that it was because Philo worked and wrote in an exclusively Greek world. This does not mean that there are no overlaps. Winston suggests that Philo knew the basic themes of rabbinic midrash. He compares Philo's treatment of select issues with the rabbis and notes both the similarities and the differences. For example, he thinks that Philo knew

39 C. Spicq, *L'epître aux Hebreux* (2 vols.; Paris: J. Gabalda, 1952), 1:39.

40 E.g., L. D. Hurst, *The Background of Hebrews: Its Background of Thought* (SNTSMS 65; Cambridge: Cambridge University Press, 1990), 67–75.

41 D. T. Runia, *Philo in Early Christian Lierature: A Survey* (CRINT 3.3; Assen: Van Gorcum / / Minneapolis: Fortress, 1993).

early *halakhoth*, but points out that unlike the rabbis who held that there were 613 commandments, Philo thought that the Ten Words were basic principles under which the other commandments could be subsumed. Winston concludes by saying that Philo would have been pleased to be known as either Philo *Judaeus* or Philo *philosophico-mysticus*.

There is another group of authors that need to be studied, pagan authors.[42] While some have recognized the possible influence of Philo on pagan authors, we lack a systematic effort to explore his impact on non-Christian and non-Jewish authors as a whole. In Rome there is some evidence that Pseudo-Longinus and Plotinus knew the works of Philo. In Syria it is likely that Numenius of Apamea and Heliodorus knew the works of Philo. There needs to be further study of whether Plutarch knew some of Philo's treatises. It is also the case that Celsus and Calcidius likely knew Philo's works. We need a careful and full analysis of all of these authors.

Conclusion

How do you introduce an author like Philo? The task is not simple, but would this not be the case for any significant figure who has influenced the history of thought in a profound way. If a student reads Kamesar's edited collection, he or she will have a framework in which to read Philo intelligently. This will now be the text that I will recommend to doctoral students or scholars from other fields who want an introduction to Philo. It sets the standard. At the same time, we should all remember that it is a companion to Philo. Reading this volume is not a substitute for reading Philo directly. One useful way to read this volume would be to read Part One and then read the Exposition of the Law, beginning with the two-volume *Life of Moses*. After reading Part Two, it would be helpful to read the Allegorical Commentary. A person could read the remainder of the corpus after reading Part Three. The greatest test of this volume will be whether it will open the world of Philo up to readers. I am convinced that it will.

University of Notre Dame

42 For earlier surveys see Runia, *Philo in Early Christian Literature*, 8–12; G. E. Sterling, "Recluse or Representative? Philo in Greek-Speaking Judaism Beyond Alexandria," *SBLSPS* 34 (1995): 595–616; and idem, "Recherché or Representative? What is the Relationship between Philo's Treatises and Greek-Speaking Judaism?," *SPhA* 11 (1999): 1–30.

The Studia Philonica Annual 21 (2009) 73–107

BIBLIOGRAPHY SECTION

PHILO OF ALEXANDRIA
AN ANNOTATED BIBLIOGRAPHY 2006

D. T. RUNIA, E. BIRNBAUM, A. C. GELJON, H. M. KEIZER,
J. P. MARTÍN, M. R. NIEHOFF, J. RIAUD, G. SCHIMANOWSKI, T. SELAND

2006*

M. ALEXANDRE Jr, 'O feminino na alegorese filoniana,' *Euphrosyne* N. S. 34 (2006) 259–268.

Discusses the figures of women in some Philonic treaties. In *Leg.* the woman Eva symbolizes sensitivity in front of Adam, the intellect, and receives a subordinate but necessary place in the anthropological vision of Philo. In other treaties of the Allegorical Commentary the figures of Sarah and Hagar have subordinate functions in the acquisition of wisdom, which is proper to Abraham. In *Contempl.* Jewish women, called the Therapeutrides,

* This bibliography has been prepared by the members of the International Philo Bibliography Project, under the leadership of D. T. Runia (Melbourne). The principles on which the annotated bibliography is based have been outlined in *SPhA* 2 (1990) 141–142, and are largely based on those used to compile the "mother works,"; R-R and RRS. The general division of the work this year has been as follows: material in English (and Dutch) by D. T. Runia (DTR), E. Birnbaum (EB), A. C. Geljon (ACG); in French by J. Riaud (JR); in Italian by H. M. Keizer (HMK); in German by G. Schimanowski (GS); in Spanish and Portuguese by J. P. Martín (JPM); in Scandinavian languages (and by Scandinavian scholars) by T. Seland (TS); in Hebrew (and by Israeli scholars) by Maren Niehoff (MSN). Once again this year much benefit has been derived from the related bibliographical labours of L. Perrone (Bologna) and his team in the journal *Adamantius* (Origen studies). Other scholars not (or formerly) in the team who have given assistance this year are Giovanni Benedetto, Gohei Hata, Joseph O'Leary, Tazuko Tago, Sze-Kar Wan, Dieter Zeller. My research assistant in Melbourne, Tamar Primoratz, again helped me with various tasks. This year too I am extremely grateful to my former Leiden colleague M. R. J. Hofstede for laying a secure foundation for the bibliography through his extremely thorough electronic searches. However, the bibliography remains inevitably incomplete because much work on Philo is tucked away in monographs and articles, the titles of which do not mention his name. Scholars are encouraged to get in touch with members of the team if they spot omissions (addresses below in Notes on Contributors). In order to preserve continuity with previous years, the bibliography retains its own customary stylistic conventions and has not changed to those of the Society of Biblical Literature used in the remainder of the Annual. Because of the differing provenance of contributors, some fluctuation of spelling styles occurs.

accompany the male Therapeutai. They reach the state of *eudaimonia* by leaving the female characteristics and acquiring virtues of a man. In general it is concluded that Philo has a positive view of women, but always in a role that is subordinate and complementary in relation to the man striving for perfection. It is only through identification with the male that the woman can embody virtue. (JPM)

J. E. ATKINSON, 'Ethnic cleansing in Roman Alexandria in 38,' *Acta Classica (South Africa)* 49 (2006) 31–54.

The riots against the Jews in Alexandria in 38 were caused by a deep-seated anti-Semitism which had a long history. The visit of King Agrippa I worked like a catalyst and was the immediate cause of the pogrom, as can been seen from Philo's attempt to exculpate him. Philo emphasizes that it was not Agrippa's plan to visit to city. In addition, political circumstances played a role because Gaius was more prepared to promote a ruler cult than Tiberius had been. There were also tensions between Alexandrian Greeks and Egyptians. (ACG)

J. M. G. BARCLAY, ''By the Grace of God I am what I am': Grace and Agency in Philo and Paul,' in J. M. G. BARCLAY and S. GATHERCOLE (eds.), *Divine and Human Agency in Paul and His Cultural Environment* (Edinburgh 2006) 140–157.

The place of grace in the works of Philo is discussed under the main heading given as: 'Philo on divine grace and human virtue', with subheadings as 'Grace in creation and causation'; 'Virtue as a gift', and 'The ascent of the soul'. In his comparisons the author finds that both Philo and Paul emphasize the priority of divine grace, as the originating cause of salvation, including human virtue, but that there is a substantial difference in the theological framework in which they place this grace. For Philo grace is the creative energy of God; for Paul it is revealed and enacted in the Christ-event, and as such is an eschatological event of a new creation. (TS)

A. BIRKAN-SHEAR, ''Does a Serpent Give Life?' Understanding the Brazen Serpent according to Philo and Early Rabbinic Literature,' in I. H. HENDERSON and G. S. OEGEMA (eds.), *The Changing Face of Judaism, Christianity, and Other Greco-Roman Religions in Antiquity (= FS Charlesworth),* Studien zu den jüdischen Schriften aus hellenistisch-römischer Zeit 2 (Gütersloh 2006) 416–426.

The paper discusses interpretations of Num 21:4–9 given by Jewish writers in the first centuries C.E. (Philo, Mishnah, Mekilta of Rabbi Yishmael, Targumim). In Philo's reading, the serpents that bite the Israelites represent pleasure: the people wish to go back to Egypt, the incorporeal mass, and they die in a spiritual sense. Beholding the bronze serpent of Moses heals them. In Philo's view, looking to the serpent means that they observe God Himself. The author concludes that most sources deviate from the literal interpretation of Num 21:4–9. (ACG)

E. BIRNBAUM, 'Two Millennia Later: General Resources and Particular Perspectives on Philo the Jew,' *Currents in Biblical Research* 4 (2006) 241–276.

This bibliographic essay, which focuses more or less on the past two decades, begins with a brief survey of general resources on Philo, including bibliographies, journals, series, monographs, and internet sites. After a consideration of some research trends, the discussion turns to studies of Philo as a Jew. In contrast to the mid-twentieth century, when the center of scholarly concern was whether Philo was more fundamentally a Jew or a Greek, the more recent studies approach him from several different perspectives. These include describing Philo's Judaism ('the descriptive approach'); studying how he balances Jewish and universal elements ('the thematic approach'); comparing his writings with other traditions ('the comparative approach'); observing how he shapes his presentations of Jews and Judaism to impress his readers ('the presentational approach'); and considering Philo's attitudes toward others and examining the relationship between his exegetical and historical writings ('the socio-political approach'). The essay concludes with a discussion of studies of Philo within broader historical contexts, a summary of current trends, and suggestions for future directions. (EB)

P. BORGEN, 'Crucified for His Own Sins—Crucified for Our Sins: Observations on a Pauline Perspective,' in J. FOTOPOULOS (ed.), *The New Testament and Early Christian Literature in Greco-Roman Context: Studies in Honor of David E. Aune,* Novum Testamentum Supplements 122 (Leiden–Boston 2006) 17–36.

In this article Borgen focuses on Romans 1:18–32 and 7:7–8:3 in order to show that it was part of the aim of Paul to document that although Jesus Christ was executed as a criminal, he did not die for his own crimes, but for ours. Both Rom 1:22–23 and Rev 18:4–8 are seen as a crime-and-punishment list, comparable to Philo's *Flacc.* 170–175. Rom 7:7–8:4 is another way of reporting on crime and punishment in the form of a story. Thus this passage is studied in light of Sophocles' *Antigone,* Philo's *In Flaccum,* Joseph and Asenath and Genesis 2–3. Borgen argues that both Rom 1:18–32 and 7:7–8:3 reveal how Paul transforms traditional Jewish understanding of the relationship between Jews and non-Jews: Jesus Christ did not die for his own sins but for 'our sins'. The passages thus expound the crime story of humankind in texts having the form of crime-and-punishment reports about Jesus Christ. (TS)

P. BORGEN, 'Some Crime-and-Punishment Reports,' in J. NEUSNER, A. J. AVERY PECK, A. LAATO, R. NURMELA and K.-G. SANDELIN (eds.), *Ancient Israel, Judaism, and Christianity in Contemporary Perspective: Essays in Memory of Karl-Johan Illman* (Lanham, MD 2006) 67–80.

In setting out to analyse some crime-and-punishment reports, the author chooses to discuss first the Philonic example *Flacc.* 171–175; then further examples follow in Josephus *War* 7.437–453, 2 Macc 7:7–9:29, and Acts 12:1–24. His main points of focus are on what is seen as the basic principles for evaluating the crimes committed: is the perspective extra-mural, concerning the relations between Jews and non-Jews? Or are there intra-mural aspects present? Based upon his findings he suggests that there are reasons to ask whether the form of crime-and-punishment reports should be classified as a genre of its own, distinct from biographies. Furthermore, if so, one might ask whether the Gospel of John as well as the Gospel of Mark follows the structure of crime-and-punishment reports. (TS)

P. R. BOSMAN, 'Conscience and Free Speech in Philo,' *The Studia Philonica Annual* 18 (2006) 33–47.

The word συνειδός (conscience), which occurs 32 times in Philo's writings, has a predominantly negative connotation: having a 'conscience' means having a 'guilty awareness'. The conscience, which is a component of the soul, can be regarded as the inner court of law and acts as a prosecutor and admonisher. Philo combines 'conscience' with 'free speech' (παρρησία). It is only possible to speak freely if one has a clear conscience. Both a pure conscience and freedom of speech result from living virtuously. (ACG)

D. BRAKKE, 'Origins and Authenticity: Studying the Reception of Greek and Roman Spiritual Traditions in Early Christian Monasticism,' in D. BRAKKE, A.-C. JACOBSEN and J. ULRICH (eds.), *Beyond Reception. Mutual Influences between Antique Religion, Judaism, and Early Christinanity*, Early Christianity in the Context of Antiquity (Bern 2006) 175–189.

In asking 'how did early Christian monasticism receive the ascetic and spiritual traditions of Judaism and their wider Greco-Roman world,' the author deals with Philo's Therapeutae as portrayed in *Contempl.* on pp. 176–178. He himself is of the opinion that the Therapeutae did not actually exist; hence there is no possibility of a continuous ascetic or monastic tradition in Egypt from the first to the fourth century. He is also skeptical about any influence of Philo's literary portrait of the Therapeutae on early Christian monasticism. (TS)

M. BRÄNDLE, *Der Agon bei Paulus. Herkunft und Profil paulinischer Agonmetaphorik*, Wissenschaftliche Untersuchungen zum Neuen Testament 2.222 (Tübingen 2006), esp. 85–115, 133–137.

Philon is the main source for technical terms in the whole ancient Greek literature. His writings feature the largest collection of *agon* metaphors of all Greek authors. Indeed, many metaphors are so detailed and precise that they provide a detailed reconstruction of the rules and practices of the competitions. On the presumption that he and his family did indeed hold full civil rights, Philo would have passed through the ephebe education himself, which in turn fits the description in *Spec.* 2.230. In this way he could address his writings to both Jews and non-Jews, for he hoped that the non-Jewish would follow the superior laws of Israel in the future (see *Mos.* 2.43f). Philon picks up Cynic motifs and integrates them with Stoic elements in a worldview which is marked by Platonic ideas. This is the way that Philo presents his 'conquest' of Hellenistic culture, which is regarded as being based on Jewish writings and is counted as its heritage. This is the reason that the Israelite 'athletes of virtue' are able to accomplish typical Greek ideals. On the other hand, the theocentric worldview which shows the ἀγὼν εὐσεβείας as the service for God links Philon to Stoic conceptions. He acknowledges the idea that humans depend on God's grace (see *Deus* 75). Making reference to Plato, Philon differs from Paul's use of the metaphor crown and prize of victory (ἄφθαρτος/φθαρτὸς στέφανος, 1 Cor 9:25). (GS)

M. BRINKSCHRÖDER, *Sodom als Sympton. Gleichgeschlechtliche Sexualität im christlichen Imaginären—eine religionsgeschichtliche Anamnese*, Religionsgeschichtliche Versuche und Vorarbeiten 55 (Berlin–New York 2006), esp. 334–388.

Following on from his earlier article (cf. *SPhA* 2008 p. 192), the author gives a survey of the Philonic verdict on pederasty. In addition he surveys the Philonic system of gender, the reproaches of pederasty as a feminization and annihilation of the sperm, and the symbols of psychic androgyny, namely virtue, wisdom and virginity. Fictive sexuality is an important point of reference in the relationship between man and God, corresponding to sensuous and physical love in asceticism. Nevertheless this asceticism opposes the principle of so-called pro-creationism. Sexual reproduction becomes compulsory and provides a kind of residuum for lust and desire. Here the author sees the essential roots of future Christian ideas of sexuality. (GS)

M. BROZE, 'Les Enseignement de Sylvanos et la parole tranchante. Jeux de mots et assonances plurilinguistiques,' *Apocrypha* 17 (2006) 79–86.

The author argues that the Philonic concept of the *logos tomeus* was also found in pagan Egyptian circles and that this encouraged the author of the *Teachings of Sylvanus* to exploit the same theme. (DTR)

R. BRUCKER, 'Observations of the Wirkungsgeschichte of the Septuagint Psalms in Ancient Judaism and Early Christianity,' in W. KRAUS and R. G. WOODEN (eds.), *Septuagint Research: Issues and Challenges in the Study of the Greek Jewish Scriptures*, Society of Biblical Literature Septuagint and Cognate Studies 53 (Leiden–Boston 2006) 355–369, esp. 358–360.

To study the Wirkungsgeschichte (reception history) of LXX Psalms in Jewish and Christian sources, the author devotes sections to 1 Maccabees, Philo (358–360), Josephus, Greco-Roman writings (in an excursus), Gospels, Paul, other NT writings, Apostolic Fathers, Apologists, and Greek Fathers. The focus is on quotations and indirect allusions to Psalms and questions of author, genre, and canonicity. Philo includes several Psalm quotations as well as references to other biblical songs. As for authors of Psalms, Philo speaks of associates of Moses, employs locutions like 'the divine man' or 'a prophetic man,' and uses the passive voice, as in 'it is said.' Because of the traditional ascription of Psalmic authorship to David, of which Philo is aware (*Conf.* 149), it is striking that he associates the Psalter with associates of Moses instead of with David. This association can be understood when one recalls that Moses is Philo's hero. (EB)

S. Y. CHAN, *1 Timothy 2:13–15 in the Light of Views concerning Eve and Childbirth in Early Judaism* (diss. Dallas Theological Seminary 2006).

The study is primarily a monograph on Jewish views concerning Eve and childbirth as they relate to 1 Tim 2:13–15. Chapter three examines selected passages from a wide range of Jewish sources, including the writings of Philo. (DTR; based on author's summary in DA)

N. G. COHEN, 'La dimensión judía del judaísmo de Filón. Una elucidación de *De Spec. Leg.* IV 132–150,' *Revista Bíblica* 68 (2006) 215–240.

Spanish translation of an article first published in English; see RRS 8722. (JPM)

N. G. COHEN, 'Philo's *Cher.* 40–52, Zohar III 31a, and BT Hag. 16a 1, 2,' *Journal of Jewish Studies* 57 (2006) 191–209.

The author argues that Philo's exceptional reference to the book of Jeremiah in *Cher.* 49 can be explained on the assumption that he used an esoteric commentary by 'Jeremiah'. This commentary is said to have been composed in Greek, as reflected in LXX Jer. 3:4, and also influenced passages in the medieval book of Jewish mysticism, the Zohar, and the Babylonian Talmud, which show, in her view, a general resemblance to Philo's interpretation. In this way the author hopes to give further support to the earlier thesis of Samuel Belkin that there are direct connections between Philo and the Zohar. (MSN)

N. G. COHEN, 'The Prophetic books in Alexandria: the Evidence from Philo Judaeus,' in M. H. FLOYD and R. D. HAAK (eds.), *Prophets, Prophecy, and Prophetic Texts in Second Temple Judaism* (London–New York 2006) 166–193.

Assuming that the prophetic books were widely available in Greek by the time of Philo, the author addresses the problem of why they are so sparsely quoted in Philo's works. She argues that his references echo the liturgical use of the prophets as *Haftarah* in Alexandria. This argument is supported by three separate considerations: (1) reviewing material already published in 1997 (see summary SPhA 2000, p. 152), Cohen lists all the prophetic quotations as well as possible allusions to them and compares them to the *Haftarot* read between 17 of Tammuz and Yom Kippur, which are attested much later in sources from the Land of Israel; (2) on the basis of a close reading of *Conf.* 128–130 she argues for Philo's use of a Hebrew lexical concordance written in Greek; (3) she suggests that Philo's references to 'the friends of Moses' and the school of Moses can be identified as a group of contemporary Alexandrian Jews, who were allegorists and favoured non-Pentateuchal passages. It is from these circles, Cohen suggests, that he received exegesis of passages not included in the Pentateuch. (MSN)

I. COLEMAN, 'Antiphony: Another Look at Philo's *On the Contemplative Life*,' *Studia Liturgica* 36 (2006) 212–230.

Philo's *On the Contemplative Life* presents 'the earliest liturgical use of the term *antiphônos*' (212). One author maintains that Philo's understanding of this term reflects responses to a soloist rather than the alternation of choirs responding to each other; the latter sense combines ancient meanings of the term as 'reply' and 'octave.' Coleman believes, however, that in the context in which Philo uses *antiphônos*—namely, the antiphonal singing of the male and female choirs in imitation of male and female singing at the Red Sea in Exodus 15—the term indeed carries the sense of choirs singing in response to each other. In this learned consideration of Philo's treatise, Coleman suggests that in equating the male and female choirs, the Therapeutae displayed a unique interpretation of Exodus 15, that the Therapeutic musical practices were based on the choral singing in Greek drama, and that Philo's account of Therapeutic liturgical practices influenced later Christian ones. Coleman also argues that the group was probably real rather than imaginary, because it is otherwise difficult to understand Philo's motivation in presenting such a detailed account, the equality of men and women is not characteristic of Philo, and the common Egyptian provenience of the Therapuetae and later Christian monastics may explain the influence of the Therapeutae on later Christian practices. (EB)

C. Deutsch, 'The Therapeutae, Text Work, Ritual, and Mystical Experience,' in A. D. DeConick (ed.), *Paradise Now: Essays on Early Jewish and Christian Mysticism*, Society of Biblical Literature Symposium Series 11 (Atlanta 2006) 287–311.

Philo may have intended his treatise *De Vita Contemplativa* to serve different apologetic functions for Jewish and non-Jewish readers and it may have provided him with an opportunity 'to reflect on his own experience as philosopher and text worker' (287). Central to the life of the Therapeutic community is 'text work,' which includes interpretation of Scripture and composition of hymns and relates to both ritual and mystical experience. Using language evocative of priests and Levites, on one hand, and ascent, vision, and ecstasy, on the other, Philo highlights the community's ritual and mystical aspects. His discussion of space—which moves from the inhabited world through regional and local sites toward the interior of the individual members' dwellings—suggests the interiority of the allegorical meaning of the text as studied by individuals and community alike. Philo's description of the community's simple lifestyle and religious gatherings, in which text study is a focus, similarly emphasizes the ritual and mystical aspects of the group. Although parallels exist between the Therapeutic community and Greek philosophers, mystery religion devotees, and practitioners of Egyptian temple religion, Philo presents the ways of the Therapeutic community as superior. (EB)

S. Di Mattei, 'Moses' *Physiologia* and the Meaning and Use of *Physikôs* in Philo of Alexandria's Exegetical Method,' *The Studia Philonica Annual* 18 (2006) 3–32.

In Philo's exegetical method, φύσις occupies a significant place. The author rejects the view that in Philo φυσιολογία is synonymous with 'allegorical interpretation'. As a philosophical term the adverb φυσικῶς refers to a manner of reasoning that is proper to the study of physics. In Jewish exegetes, φυσικῶς indicates the philosophical rationale behind Moses' words. The scope of physics has expanded and also incorporates metaphysics. In the Greek philosophical tradition, φυσιολογία refers to the examination of the phenomena in heaven and the genesis of the universe. This same meaning is found in Philo, for whom the study of the cosmos leads ultimately to knowledge of God the creator. (ACG)

S. Di Mattei, 'Paul's Allegory of Two Covenants (Gal. 4.21–31) in Light of First-Century Hellenistic Rhetoric and Jewish Hermeneutic,' *New Testament Studies* 52 (2006) 102–122.

Philo's works and views play a relatively minor role in this study. The author considers Philo's allegories to be apologetic rather than expository, and that Paul's usage thus does not square with Philo's apologetic (105). On the other hand, the term ἀλληγορέω is predominately used by both authors in the sense 'to speak allegorically.' In the rest of the study the author argues that Paul's allegory is more reflective of Jewish practices which sought to eschatologize the Torah by reading Gen 16:1 through its *haftarah*, Isa 54:1. (TS)

L. DiPaolo Jr, *'The Appropriated God': Hellenistic Thought and the New Testament Christ Hymns* (diss. Loyola University Chicago 2006).

This study investigates the three main images of Christ in the material normally designated as hymnic in the New Testament (Phil 2:6–11, 1 Cor 8:6, Col 1:15–20, John 1:1–18, Heb 1:3–4, 1 Tim 3:16), specifically the images of Christ the pre-existent divinity, Christ the Creator and Christ the Incarnate god. The author concludes that the closest literary antecedents for the first two images can be found in the literary world of Hellenistic Jewish wisdom speculation, specifically that subset of Hellenistic Jewish wisdom speculation influenced by Middle Platonic thought and exemplified by the works of Philo of Alexandria. The third image, that of Christ the Incarnate god, finds its most compelling literary antecedents in works of Greco-Roman religious thought and philosophy, specifically those myths which deal with gods taking human form and serving as slaves. The image of the god as flesh, a subset of those images which deal with Christ as an incarnate god, however, fails to be easily classified as deriving from either Hellenistic Jewish or Greco-Roman literary images. It is an image which had to have arisen from early Christian kerygma. (DTR; based on author's summary in DA)

L. H. Feldman, *Judaism and Hellenism Reconsidered* (Leiden–Boston 2006).

Part three of this vast collection of reprinted essays is devoted to Philo, but it contains only two articles: 'Philo's Version of the 'Aqedah'' (pp. 255–279, summary in *SPhA* 2005 p. 171); 'Philo, Pseudo-Philo, Josephus and Theodotus on the Rape of Dinah' (p. 281–309, *SPhA* 2007 p. 155). References to Philo in other essays are indexed on p. 922. (DTR)

N. Fernandez-Marcos, 'Rewritten Bible or *Imitatio*? the Vestments of the High-Priest,' in P. W. Flint, E. Tov and J. C. VanderKam (eds.), *Studies in the Hebrew Bible, Qumran, and the Septuagint presented to Eugene Ulrich*, Supplements to Vetus Testamentum 101 (Boston 2006) 321–336.

While the label 'rewritten bible' may describe aspects of ancient Jewish literary activity, some Hellenistic Jewish works may also be understood in relation to the Greco-Roman literary practice of *imitatio*, based on the foremost model of Homer; for Jews, Moses' Pentateuch became such a model. Discussions of the high priestly vestments, based on Exodus 28, reflect the imitation of *ekphrasis*, the vivid description of various phenomena including works of art, whose classic example is Homer's description of Achilles' shield (*Il.* 18.477–617). Imitations of *ekphrasis* can be found in the *Letter of Aristeas* 96–99 and Ben Sira 45:6–13. Ben Sira 50:5–21 on the high priest Simon imitates the encomium. Philo provides examples of allegorical *ekphrasis* in *QE* 2.107–123, *Spec.* 1.84–97, and *Mos.* 2.109–135. Focusing on the last passage, Fernández-Marcos shows how Philo blends Platonic and Stoic thinking to portray the high priestly vestments as symbolic of the universe and the high priest himself as a small universe, or microcosm. In *War* 5.230–237 and *Ant.* 3.159–178, Josephus, who uses different terms for the vestments, shows variations on the symbolic *ekphrasis* found in Philo. All these examples suggest that Hellenistic Jewish writers were very interested in the theme of the high priestly vestments and that the tradition of interpretation of these vestments was fairly widespread. (EB)

E. Filler, *Dialectic in Philo* (diss. Bar-Ilan University, Ramat-Gan 2006).

This dissertation seeks to examine whether, besides the known and extensive influence of such Platonic writings as the *Timaeus* on Philo's writings and thought, we can also detect traces of the dialectics of the later Platonic dialogues. The result is patently negative. Most of the dissertation is devoted to explaining the lack of such dialectical terminology. Initially, the possibility of Stoic influence is examined and dismissed. Subsequently, the author asks whether Philo may have been attached to a Sophistic movement in Alexandria and what his attitude to such a movement may precisely have been. Analyzing the occurrences of terms connected to 'sophists', the author highlights the wide span of their meanings as well as Philo's ambivalence. As comparative material from Alexandria is missing, it is not clear whether it is Philo's original contribution to contrast the Sophist in this broad way to the true philosopher. Moreover, the author argues that one of Philo's proofs for the harm engendered by sophistic teachings and instruction is that their inner convictions contradict their spoken declarations. They befittingly preach on matters of ethics, but they fail to implement those very splendid concepts. Here Philo raises an idea which might be original. Authentic philosophy must foster full accord between thinking, will and deed. The contrast between speech and deed (λόγος–ἔργον) is common and acceptable within Greek literature, though the concept of will (βούλευσις, βουλεύματα) appears to be derived from the biblical idea of G-d's will and of mans' free will. In adopting philosophical concepts as ancillary to his exposition of the Torah, Philo is not prepared to accept the technical aspects of philosophy, mainly dialectic, since then one begins to appear as a recipient of a science through which truth becomes attainable, when in fact truth has been exclusively encapsulated within Mosaic Law. Be that as it may, logic has its place and can, within limits, even be to human advantage. It should be remembered that one can easily err within it, and mislead by using it, and it is capable of upsetting the understanding of nature, as it may impair the understanding of ethics. It is therefore preferable to avoid dialectic (except for argumentation with the Sophists). The work ends with a biographical assumption, according to which it is possible that Philo himself was harshly castigated in his youth in a debate with one of those very Sophists, or had witnessed the defeat of a person whom he respected. (MSN, based on author's summary)

F. Frazier, 'Le principe d'égalité chez Philon d'Alexandrie,' *Ktèma* 31 (2006) 291–308.

The 74 occurrences of the term ἰσότης which one encounters in Philo's œuvre demonstrates the quantitative but also the qualitative importance that Philo accords to the principle of equality, which occupies a place at all the levels of reality. In order to evaluate the specific elements of his thought on the concept, the author examines in succession the Greek background which Philo inherited, the two passages in his writings that are directly focused on isotês (*Her*. 133–206, *Spec*. 4,231–238), his utlilization of two concepts linked to equality, democracy and isonomia, and the practical problems associated with its application to society. From the viewpoint of the creator, equality is the principle of unity and balance. Within the cosmos it is associated with the democratic model. It enters not so much in political reflection as in the interpretation of the succession of empires, where it establishes an equilibrium throughout the ages, and also in reflection on social relations, where it recalls the original unity of humanity. This is the reason that the concept is dear to the Therapeutae and the Essenes, who are keen to live as closely as possible to the law of nature. (JR)

K. FUGLSETH, 'The Reception of Aristotelian Features in Philo and the Authorship Problem of Philo's *De Aeternitate Mundi*,' in D. BRAKKE, A.-C. JACOBSEN and J. ULRICH (eds.), *Beyond Reception. Mutual Influences between Antique Religion, Judaism, and Early Christianity*, Early Christianity in the Context of Antiquity 1 (Frankfurt 2006) 57–67.

Fuglseth's paper is in fact a response to a contribution by M. Niehoff in the same volume (see summary below). Arguing that in the treatise *De aeternitate mundi* preserved in the Philonic corpus there are many statements that are clearly non-Philonic, he wishes to review the question of authorship. According to him, 'substantial divergences between *De aeternitate mundi* and other Philonic writings argue in favour of either a non-Philonic origin or that he is paraphrasing and/or quoting other authors.' In the main part of his article, he to a large extent presents and supports some of the main problems pertaining to a Philonic authorship as set forth in a Norwegian 1987 PhD dissertation, written in Norwegian, by Roald Skarsten, who argued that Philo did not write *Aet.* (see RRS 8795). (TS)

M. E. FULLER, *The Restoration of Israel: Israel's Re-gathering and the Fate of the Nations in Early Jewish Literature and Luke-Acts*, Beihefte zur Zeitschrift für die neutestamentliche Wissenschaft und die Kunde der älteren Kirche 138 (Berlin 2006), esp. 82–102.

This book examines, first, how early Jewish literature interprets Israel's exile and restoration and the fate of other nations at the time of this restoration and, second, how Luke-Acts uses or modifies these interpretations. Fuller discerns several patterns in early Jewish literature that include a literal understanding of Jewish return to the land of Israel; an inter-Jewish understanding, whereby a subset of Israel is given prominence among the wider Jewish community; an emphasis on the re-gathering of the twelve tribes; and a spiritualized interpretation, in which the literal meaning of restoration disappears or diminishes greatly. Differing emphases are placed upon divine intervention and the role of the messiah. The fate of the nations may be viewed locally with respect to the land or cosmically with respect to the eschaton; and some sources see a positive role for the nations. Drawing upon some of these motifs, Luke-Acts emphasizes Jesus as the Davidic messiah in Israel, later enthroned in heaven; the twelve Apostles as leaders of eschatological Israel; and incorporation of other nations and enemies who also remain bound to the land of Israel. Paul goes beyond the restoration of Israel to proclaim God's kingdom in the Roman Empire and ultimately in Paradise. Philo sees the role of the Jews in the Diaspora positively as colonizers rather than exiles. Based on the important distinction between his use of 'Israel' and 'Jews,' Fuller claims that Philo understands restoration symbolically as a return of all virtuous people to wisdom or God and that the physical aspect is less important than the spiritual or allegorical one. (EB)

G. GÄBEL, *Die Kulttheologie des Hebräerbriefes. Eine exegetisch-religionsgeschichtliche Studie*, Wissenschaftliche Untersuchungen zum Neuen Testament 2.212 (Tübingen 2006), esp. 112–127.

Philo's understanding of the τύποι of the Holy tent and the tent itself revealed to Moses differs greatly from the one in Hebrews. This is the reason that the specific form of the archetype-image relation in Hebrews cannot be deduced from contemporary Greek thought, i.e. Middle Platonism. Philo only refers once, in *Spec.* 3.205ff., to the meaning of the cleansing of the sanctuary (Num 19). However, the discussion about cleansing water is found several times. Even if Philo is aware of such claims and rituals for the ordinary domestic sphere, his focus lies on the explanation of the sprinkling of cleansing water as a precondition for the admission to the temple and for participation in the cult. At the same time, extrinsic and inner cleansing—denoting ethical and spiritual purification—and forgiveness of sins are inextricably linked together. (GS)

A. C. GELJON, 'Philo en de kerkvaders,' *Schrift* no. 223 (2006) 26–30.

Short presentation of some examples of Philo's influence on the Church fathers Origen, Clement, and Gregory of Nyssa. Both Clement and Origen take over, for example, Philo's allegorical exegesis of Hagar and Sarah. Gregory of Nyssa stands in the same tradition of negative theology as Philo. This is evidenced by their common interpretation of the darkness in Ex 20:21 as referring to God's incomprehensibility. (ACG)

A. C. GELJON, 'Philo of Alexandria and Gregory of Nyssa on Moses at the Burning Bush,' in G. H. VAN KOOTEN (ed.), *The Revelation of the Name YHWH to Moses*, Themes in Biblical Narrative 9 (Leiden–Boston 2006) 225–236.

The author discusses Philo's interpretation of God's appearance to Moses in the burning bush (Ex 3). God's words 'I am He-who-is' indicates that God's essence consists in being, and that his nature cannot be expressed in words. God is thus unnameable and incomprehensible. In his description of the burning bush Gregory of Nyssa makes use of Philo's narrative. According to his interpretation the words 'I am He-who-is' are spoken by God the Son. For him both God the Father and God's Logos, Christ, can be called ὁ ὤν. In this way he differs from Philo, who regards God's Logos as standing on a lower ontological level than God and as subordinated to God. (ACG)

M. HADAS-LEBEL, *פילון האלכסנדרוני. בין יהדות להלניזם* [= *Philo of Alexandria. Between Judaism and Hellenism*], translated by A. GILADI (Tel Aviv 2006).

This monograph is a Hebrew translation of *Philon d'Alexandrie. Penseur en Diaspora* (Librairie Arthème Fayard 2003); see summary in *SPhA* 2006 p. 161). It follows the translation of H. A. Wolfson's *Philo. Foundations of Religious Philosophy in Judaism, Christianity and Islam* (Jerusalem 1970) and marks an important event in Israeli scholarship. The translation of the term 'diaspora' in the title as 'Between Judaism and Hellenism' indicates a disposition to think in terms of unbridgeable dichotomies, which was not implied by the French author. Yet overall the translation is faithful to the original and offers a very useful introduction to Philo in highly readable Hebrew. Israeli students have already greatly benefited from this book, which places Philo into the context of contemporary Hellenistic culture and clearly explains the different genres of his work. (MSN)

H. F. HÄGG, *Clement of Alexandria and the Beginnings of Christian Apophaticism,* Oxford Early Christian Studies (Oxford 2006).

At several places the author discusses Philo as a predecessor of Clement's ideas on God. Clement's distinction between the unknowable God and his Son or dynamis who is knowable can be compared to Philo's distinction between God's unknowable essence and his powers by which he can be known (pp. 238–240). Philo's interpretation of the darkness in Exodus 19 as relating to God's incomprehensibility can be found with some differences in Clement, Origen, and Gregory Nazianzus (pp. 256–258).

B. HAM, 'L'interprétation allégorique de l'arche de Noé chez Philon d'Alexandrie,' *Graphè* (2006) 63–77.

The author examines the allegorical interpretation of the ark of Noah that Philo presents in *QG* 2.1–7. The key to all the themes that Philo develops is the identification of the ark with the human body. The article concludes with the quotation of *QG* 2.34, which helps the reader understand better the importance of physical allegory in facilitating the discovery of the higher truths as they relate both to the human microcosm and to the macrocosm. These truths bear witness to the existence and the wisdom of the true author, God the creator. (JR)

G. HATA, *Nottoraretta Seisho* [*The Bible taken over by Christians*] (Kyoto 2006), esp. 128–134.

Brief remarks on how Philo illustrates the use of the Greek Bible. (DTR; based on author's summary)

P. HEGER, 'Sabbath Offerings according to the Damascus Document—Scholarly Opinions and a New Hypothesis,' *Zeitschrift für die Alttestamentliche Wissenschaft* 118 (2006) 62–81.

The author discusses Philo's explanation of the Sabbath offerings (*Spec.* 1.168–170), of the New Moon (177–180) and of the Passover offerings (181–185) in the context of the interpretation of the offerings of the Sabbath (Num. 28–29) in the Damascus Document. According to Philo, the Sabbath offering is instead of the weekly Tamid offering. Heger concludes that according to the Damascus Document, the weekday offering should not be offered on Sabbath, being replaced by the particular Sabbath offerings. (ACG)

J. L. HILTON, 'Apuleius, *Florida* 23 and Popular Moral Philosophy,' *Acta Classica (South Africa)* 49 (2006) 137–144.

Apuleius, *Flor.* 23, Philo, *Prov.* 2.22 and popular philosophical ideas in the work of Seneca *De Providentia* all use the metaphors of a rich man whose wealth matters little in comparison with his health, and a ship whose costly fittings are useless in a storm. Similar material is also to found in *Flor.* 14, 22, and 23. It is suggested that these themes were drawn from a text which discussed the views of competing schools on such questions. (DTR)

P. W. van der Horst, *Jews and Christians in their Graeco-Roman context. Selected Essays on Early Judaism, Samaritanism, Hellenism, and Christianity*, Wissenschaftliche Untersuchungen zum Neuen Testament 196 (Tübingen 2006).

This volume, marking the author's sixtieth birthday, reprints three articles: 'Philo's *In Flaccum* and the Book of Acts' (pp. 98–107, see summary *SPhA* 2007 p. 158); 'Common Prayer in Philo's *In Flaccum* 121–124' (pp. 108–113, *SPhA* 2006, p. 162); 'Philo and the Rabbis on Genesis: Similar Questions, Different Answers' (pp. 114–127, *SPhA* 2007 p. 160). The fourth article on Philo is translated from the Dutch original and appears here in English for the first time; see separate listing. (DTR)

P. W. van der Horst, 'Philo of Alexandria on the Wrath of God,' in Idem (ed.), *Jews and Christians in Their Graeco-Roman Context. Selected Essays on Early Judaism, Samaritanism, Hellenism, and Christianity*, Wissenschaftliche Untersuchungen zum Neuen Testament 196 (Tübingen 2006) 128–133.

English translation of an article originally published in Dutch in 1993 and summarized in *SPhA* 1996 p. 130 (= RRS 9344). (DTR)

P. W. van der Horst, 'Two Short Notes on Philo,' *The Studia Philonica Annual* 18 (2006) 49–55.

In this brief article the author responds to two articles in the 2005 volume of *The Studia Philonica Annual*. In the first section he points out that Frank Shaw in his article on Caligula's use of the name of the God of the Jews (see summary *SPhA* 2008 p. 186) could have strengthened his conclusion by observing the grammatical structure of the key sentence in *Legat*. 353. In the second section he focuses on Alan Kerkeslager's article (see *SPhA* 2008 p. 176) which argues that the three Greeks, Dionysius, Lampo and Isidorus, were not involved in the events of 38 c.e. in Alexandria because they were absent from the city. He agrees that Kerkeslager makes a good case that they were not directly involved. Nevertheless the argument has various weaknesses that should be pointed out. For example, even though they may have been physically absent, their influence was most likely still very strong. (DTR)

S. Inowlocki, *Eusebius and the Jewish Authors: His Citation Technique in an Apologetic Context*, Ancient Judaism and Early Christianity 64 (Leiden–Boston 2006).

Slightly revised English translation of the author's dissertation, submitted to the University of Brussels in 2003 and summarized in *SPhA* 2006 p. 164. It represents a landmark study of the way the Church father and apologist Eusebius made use of Jewish writings in his writings, examining his methods from both a philosophical/theological and a philological point of view. It revises the traditional perception of Eusebius as above all a compiler and faithful citer of earlier sources. His method of citing Philonic texts is studied in great detail, esp. in chapter five, with particular attention devoted to the way he extracts the cited passages from their contexts and sometimes modifies the actual text. (DTR)

A. P. Johnson, 'Philonic Allusions in Eusebius, *PE* 7.7–8,' *CQ* N. S. 56 (2006) 239–248.

Eusebius' *Praeparatio evangelica* has been extensively studied for its wealth of material quoted from earlier, especially Middle Platonic, authors. Its literary allusions, however, have gone largely unnoticed. The article focuses on Book 7 in which the lives of the ancient Hebrews is studied. Here Philo of Alexandria's *De Abrahamo*, although never named by Eusebius, provided a model for chaps. 7–8. The author discusses various allusions and notes two divergences between Eusebius and his model: his emphasis is historical rather than allegorical, and he manipulates the narrative to separate his own position, together with that of the ancient Hebrews, from the Jews and Judaism. (DTR)

H. M. Keizer, 'Philo en het Nieuwe Testament,' *Schrift* no. 223 (2006) 21–25.

Article in Dutch for a non-specialist public on the possible relationship between Philo and the New Testament, in particular sketching similarities and differences between Philo (*Opif.* 134, 146; *Leg.* 1.31, 39) and Paul (1 Cor 15:44–49), Philo (*Leg.* 3.96, 102) and the Epistle to the Hebrews (Hebr 1:2–3, 8:5–6), and Philo (*Opif.* 24–25, 31; *Deus* 31–32) and the Prologue of John (Joh. 1:1–4, 14). (HMK)

A. Kerkeslager, 'Agrippa and the Mourning Rites for Drusilla in Alexandria,' *Journal for the Study of Judaism* 37 (2006) 367–400.

The author reconstructs the chronology of the events in 38 C.E. in Alexandria and concludes that Agrippa's visit to the city took place during the mourning rites for Drusilla, the sister of the Roman emperor Gaius. During these rites the Jews resist the installation of images (most probably images of Drusilla) in the synagogues. This was seen as treasonable impiety and as an implicit denial of the legitimacy of rule by the Julio-Claudian dynasty. The edict issued by Flaccus was an appropriate response from the standpoint of Roman policy and the violence to which it led was meant to be punitive. The entire sequence of events was fully in harmony with normal Roman legal and administrative policies. (ACG)

A. Kerkeslager, 'Jews in Egypt and Cyrenaica 66–c. 235 CE,' in S. T. Katz (ed.), *Cambridge History of Judaism, Volume 4: The Late Roman Period* (Cambridge 2006) 53–68.

Philo is cited as evidence of the period before the revolt in Egypt in 116–117 C.E. The topic of most significance for Philonic studies is the argument that neither Jews in Egypt nor their Gentile Christian sympathizers could have survived the revolt to pass on the works and ideas of Philo to the later Christian communities in Egypt. From this and various sources dating to after the revolt in 116–117 it is argued that the copies of Philo's works and related Philonic ideas that circulated in Egypt after the revolt were most likely introduced by Christians who imported them from other regions in which Philo's works already had been circulating before the revolt. There are no direct continuities between Philonic Jewish groups in Egypt before the revolt and the later Philonizing Christian groups in Egypt after the revolt. (DTR, based on author's summary)

H. C. KIM, 'A Marriage in the Qumran community,' in IDEM, *Nuzi, Women's Rights, and Hurrian Ethnicity, and Other Academic Essays*, Hermit Kingdom Studies in Identity and Society 1 (Cheltenham Pa. 2006).

Based primarily on the presentation of 'On the Life of Moses' in *The Essential Philo* (ed. Nahum Glatzer), Kim describes Philo's portrayal of Moses' four roles as philosopher-king, legislator, priest, and prophet. Philo emphasizes Moses' virtues and goes so far as to attribute divine qualities to him. Some questions considered and debated by scholars include Philo's audience for the treatises on Moses, Philo's claim about the influence of Moses on Greek culture, Philo's own borrowing from Greek culture in his portrayal of Moses and Mosaic Law, Philo's fashioning of Moses for his own purposes, the human or divine origin of Moses' powers, and Philo's understanding of prophecy. (EB)

J. KLAWANS, *Purity, Sacrifice, and the Temple: Symbolism and Supersessionism in the Study of Ancient Judaism* (Oxford 2006).

Contemporary religious and cultural biases have led modern scholars to misconstrue or misrepresent ancient Israelite, Jewish, and Christian stances toward the Temple cult. These scholars have separated the study of purity and sacrifice, which belong together, and have understood purity but not sacrifice to have a spiritualized significance for the ancient practitioners. Scholars have also understood sacrifice as a primitive form of worship later replaced by better, more acceptable forms. To point out and counter these scholarly understandings, Klawans examines purity and sacrifice in biblical Israel (Part I) and approaches to the Temple cult in Second Temple literature, rabbinic literature, and the NT (Part II). Ancient Israelites viewed sacrifice as an act of *imitatio Dei* aimed at bringing God's presence into the sanctuary. Philo 'may well present the first truly integrated interpretation of the entire sacrificial process, beginning with ritual and moral purification' (117). His approach to this process—what Klawans terms 'the most sustained and sophisticated analysis of purity and sacrifice in ancient Jewish literature' (123)—is sympathetic and combines symbolic and practical discussions. Some of Philo's views may be unique to him but they also show continuities with earlier views, particularly 'that the temple represents the cosmos and the priests serve as its angelic caretakers' (123). (EB)

D. KONSTAN, 'Philo's *De virtutibus* in the Perspective of Classical Greek Philosophy,' *The Studia Philonica Annual* 18 (2006) 59–72.

The article discusses various themes relating to Philo's analysis of the virtues in his *De virtutibus*, with special emphasis on his treatment of two principal virtues, courage and humanity (φιλανθρωπία). Humanity is a newcomer to the classical list of virtues. Philo gives it a special place in *Virt.*, showing that Moses extends this virtue, which is closely related to gentleness and mildness, not only to human beings but also to animals. Like Plato, Philo defines courage as a kind of knowledge, and following Aristotle he regards it as the middle way between rashness and cowardice. Practisers of wisdom, who are full of proud thoughts, are said to exercise true courage. This kind of connection between wisdom and courage does not occur in Greek philosophy. The same applies to the view that confidence in God's aid as a result of piety can simply be identified with courage. (ACG)

E. KOSKENNIEMI, 'Philo and Classical Drama,' in J. NEUSNER, A. J. AVERY PECK, A. LAATO, R. NURMELA and K.-G. SANDELIN (eds.), *Ancient Israel, Judaism, and Christianity in Contemporary Perspective: Essays in Memory of Karl-Johan Illman* (Lanham, MD 2006) 137–151.

The author presents and briefly discusses Philo's references to persons in classical drama. He finds that Philo mentions several dramas, and although he seldom names the plays or the author, almost all of his references can be identified as belonging to dramas from which we have at least fragments. Philo mentions Sophocles once (*Prob.* 19); quotes Ion once (*Prob.* 143); mentions Aeschylus twice (*Prob.* 143, *Aet.* 49); and Euripides often. Menander is quoted, but not mentioned by name. In addition, Philo several times also reveals his knowledge about theatres. Koskenniemi's conclusion is that Philo was deeply committed to the world of the theatre, that he quoted from memory, and that he often used the dramatists to underscore points in his expositions of the Torah. (TS)

A. LE BOULLUEC, *Alexandrie antique et chrétienne. Clément et Origène*, Collections des Études Augustiniennes Série Antiquité 178 (Paris 2006).

Frequent references to Philo, indexed on p. 465, in this important collection of studies by the distinguished French scholar on early Christianity in Alexandria, with particular emphasis on the writings and intellectual milieu of Clement and Origen. (DTR)

J. R. LEVISON, 'Philo's Personal Experience and the Persistence of Prophecy,' in M. H. FLOYD and R. D. HAAK (eds.), *Prophets, Prophecy, and Prophetic Texts in Second Temple Judaism* (London–New York 2006) 194–209.

Despite a recent consensus that Jews in antiquity believed that prophecy had ceased with the prophets Haggai, Zechariah, and Malachi, several Jewish texts from the Second Temple period suggest that such a belief was not universal. While some modern writers try to distinguish between biblical prophecy and later prophetic experiences, Philo's autobiographical accounts of his own experience of inspiration when he is interpreting Scripture are quite similar to his accounts of prophetic inspiration and even of Moses' prophetic experience. Similarities between Philo's description of prophetic experience and of his own experience include sudden inspiration, loss of awareness of one's surroundings, and extraordinary insight. Similarities between Philo's description of Moses' experience as a prophet and of Philo's own experiences as an exegete include two forms of inspiration, through divine possession and an inner prompting of the soul. In contrast to the earlier consensus, then, Philo is an invaluable witness to the notion 'that prophecy has not ceased, that the divine spirit has not withdrawn from Israel' (209). (EB)

C. LÉVY, 'Philon et les passions,' in L. CICCOLINI (ed.), *Receptions antiques: Etudes de littérature ancienne* (Paris 2006) 27–41.

Having shown that many contradictory points of view have been stated on the subject of the passions in Philo, the author focuses on four points: the different Philonic conceptions of the soul; the typologies and representations of passiòn; the problem of therapy; and finally what appears to be the Philonic paradox *par excellence*, passion transcended by folly. It appears that Philo expresses himself sometimes in Platonic terms, sometimes in

Stoic terms, depending on the text on which he is commenting, but also depending on convictions that never coincide, so to speak, with specific philosophical doctrines. (JR)

A. Lieber, 'Jewish and Christian Heavenly Meal Traditions,' in A. D. DeConick (ed.), *Paradise Now: Essays on Early Jewish and Christian Mysticism,* Society of Biblical Literature Symposium Series 11 (Atlanta 2006) 313–339.

Cultic sacrificial meals and eschatological or heavenly banquets reflect both community boundaries and divine–human boundaries. The author considers various representations of these meals in Philo, Epistle to the Hebrews, Luke, John, and rabbinic literature. According to Philo's interpretations of Exod 24:11—especially in *QE*—Moses, Aaron, and the 70 elders ascend to an immortal, divine place; the food is spiritual rather than physical; and the vision of the divine unifies Israel, a nation that also partakes of the spiritual food of manna. Philo similarly assigns spiritual meaning to sacrificial practices, in which seeing God becomes 'the culminating moment of the rite' (321). Even while the Temple is standing Philo turns sacrifice into an internal, spiritual rite and thereby legitimates a pious life away from this Temple. In NT sources, accounts of Jesus and meal symbolism point to 'a collapsing of the boundaries that had formerly structured humanity's relationship to the divine; and [by contrast] in rabbinic sources, the eschatological meal provides a model for the divine-human encounter that necessitates the maintenance of the very boundaries that are challenged in the emergent Christian tradition' (339). (EB)

J. N. Lightstone, *The Commerce of the Sacred: Mediation of the Divine among Jews in the Greco-Roman World,* new edition (New York 2006).

This republished edition of the author's earlier book (published in 1984; see RRS a8465) includes a new foreword by Willi Braun and an updated bibliography by H. W. Basser. Generally speaking, Lightstone takes issue with scholarly categories used to describe Judaism in the Greco-Roman period and scholarly use of the past 'to validate or invalidate present preferences' (p. x). As in the first edition, the Appendix is devoted to questioning Goodenough's interpretation of Philo as the proponent of an actual mystery religion and to arguing that Philo should not be held as representative of Hellenistic Judaism but rather as 'a particular type of Jewish Holy Man in the Greco-Roman world' (129). (EB)

P. J. Lindqvist, *Sin at Sinai: Early Judaism Encounters Exodus 32* (diss. Åbo Akademi, Finland 2006).

The study focuses on the early Jewish history of reception of one of the narrative climaxes of the Hebrew Bible/Old Testament, the story of the worship of the golden calf image described in Ex 32. Because of the controversial nature of the story, it played an interesting role in religious debates in the early centuries of our era, which can be followed in some detail. Several textual corpora are studied, the most important of which are firstly the Hellenistic-Jewish authors Philo and Josephus and the pseudepigraphic Pseudo-Philo, all of them from the first century C.E., secondly the Aramaic translations of the Pentateuch (targums) and thirdly the vast rabbinic corpus from Mishna until the final redaction the Babylonian Talmud, including the numerous midrashic works. The study may thus be categorized as a contribution to the field of the study of midrash, broadly speaking, and secondarily as a study in the religious confrontation of the early centuries. (DTR; based on author's abstract)

P. LINDQUIST, 'Sin at Sinai: Three First Century Versions,' in J. NEUSNER, A. J. AVERY PECK, A. LAATO, R. NURMELA and K.-G. SANDELIN (eds.), *Ancient Israel, Judaism, and Christianity in Contemporary Perspective: Essays in Memory of Karl-Johan Illman* (Lanham, MD 2006) 225–246.

Lindquist here discusses three different authors' versions of the so-called 'golden calf episode.' The authors dealt with are Philo, Josephus and Pseudo-Philo (*Biblical Antiquities*). According to Lindquist these authors represent two different perspectives: Philo and Josephus deal with Judaism in contact and conflict with foreign cults, culture and civilization; Pseudo-Philo represents a kind of introvert Judaism, without traces of intercultural encounters. He then deals extensively with the more literal exposition in Philo's *Mos.* 2.159–173, but comments rather briefly on the more allegorical treatments of *Ebr.* 66–70, 95–105, *Post.* 162–169, *Sacr.* 128–130 and *Fug.* 90–102. He finds that Philo presents Moses in line with the aretalogies of Hellenistic literature, and that his noble character, as well as the exemplary victory of the Levites over the wrong, are the focal points of this episode. (TS)

P. LUISIER, 'De Philon d'Alexandrie a la Protennoia trimorphe: variations sur un theme de grammaire grecque,' in L. PAINCHAUD and P.-H. POIRIER (eds.), *Coptica—gnostica—manichaica* (Quebec–Paris 2006) 535–555.

In his discussion of the coptic treatise of Nag Hammadi, Prôtennoia trimorphê, which is a translation of a Greek original, the author investigates a number of Greek terms which are concealed behind Coptic expressions, namely ἠχώ φωνή λόγος. In attempting to determine how this triad could be used in the context of the history of salvation, the author states that it is necessary to find an author who explains how one can move from the literal to the figurative sense of the words. This leads one to an author who gladly makes use of allegory, such as Philo. A reading of Philo's allegorical treatises makes clear that the triad sound–voice–speech, which has its origin in Stoic grammatical analysis, has been utilized by the Alexandrian for the purposes of his exegesis. (JR)

F. MANNS, 'Il matrimonio nel giudaismo antico,' in *Dizionario di Spiritualità Biblico-Patristica*, vol. 42 *Il matrimonio nella Bibbia* (Roma 2006), esp. 144–145.

This volume on marriage in the Bible (OT and NT) and in Judaism devotes a brief section to Philo, listing Philonic views and statements on sexual morality, virginity (male as well as female), with 27 references to Philonic treatises. (HMK)

A. M. MAZZANTI, 'Il lessico dei 'misteri' in Filone di Alessandria. Un'analisi semantica,' in A. M. MAZZANTI (ed.), *Il volto mistero. Mistero e rivelazione nella cultura religiosa tardoantica* (Castel Bolognese (Ravenna) 2006) 21–34.

The article offers an analysis of Philo's use and interpretation of terms related to the mystery cults, notably μυστήριον, ὄργια and τελετή, starting with a brief survey of the *status questionis*. While Philo's judgement of the mysteries as idolatrous and immoral rituals based on mythical fictions and falsehoods is nothing but negative, this does not preclude his using mystery terms with reference to the Judaic religion. While Judaism for Philo represented the only authentic religion, with rites of universalistic significance, this study argues that the mysteries, inasmuch as their aim was divine illumination, in the eyes of Philo allowed for a positive interpretation in philosophical terms, i.e. symbolizing initiation of the soul into the noetic realm. (HMK)

M. McDowell, *Prayers of Jewish Women. Studies of Patterns of Prayer in the Second Temple Period,* Wissenschafliche Untersuchungen zum Neuem Testament 2.211 (Tübingen 2006), esp. 139–153.

This study examines how women at prayer are presented in the literature of the Second Temple period. A section is devoted to Philo's writings in which several prayers spoken by women alone are analysed, namely the prayers of Rachel, Sarah, Rebecca, Hagar, Miriam and the women's choir, the Theraputae, and women offering prayers at the Temple. The author concludes that these prayers in Philo show patterns similar to prayers in other writings. Although the theology of Philo's works is different from the other documents, the prayers demonstrate similar patterns in content, form, and social location. (ACG)

S. Morlet, 'L'Écriture, image des vertus: la transformation d'un thème philonien dans l'apologétique d'Eusèbe de Césarée,' in F. Young, M. J. Edwards and P. Parvis (eds.), *Studia Patristica: Papers presented to the Fourteenth International Conference on Patristic Studies held in Oxford 2003*, 5 vols. (Leuven–Paris–Dudley Mass. 2006) 42.187–192.

The author discerns Philo's influence in Eusebius' notion of the patriarchs as images of virtue and models for a virtuous life. But in contrast to Philo the Church father does not explain their lives allegorically. The lives are just illustrations of virtue and Eusebius' reading remains on a literal level. Furthermore the term 'image' has also the connotation of 'example', which is absent in Philo. (ACG)

N. Neumann, 'Wenn Lukas liest... : Ansätze hellenistischer Allegorese im dritten Evangelium,' *Biblische Zeitschrift* N. F. 50 (2006) 161–173.

Besides Aristobulus and Aristeas, Philo is mentioned as an example of Jewish-Hellenistic interpretation of the Bible, esp. *Opif., Leg.* and *Mos*. The common ground of the method of allegoric interpretation is that below the surface of the text a hidden meaning exists, which can be worked out by extensive remuneration. In this sense Philo, for example, interprets the two trees in the Garden of Eden (Gen 2) in an ethical way (*Opif.* 154). In addition, linguistic parallels in the technique of queries and interpretation exist, as well as the notion that Homer as well as Moses allude to various philosophical ideas (see Luke 20:17). In this way the author gives support to his thesis that Luke uses the technical terminology pertaining to Hellenistiic allegoresis in interpreting his Bible (see Luke 20:37). This shows that he is in accordance with the tradition represented in particular by Philo. (GS)

M. R. Niehoff, 'Philo's Contribution to Contemporary Alexandrian Metaphysics,' in D. Brakke, A.-C. Jacobsen and J. Ulrich (eds.), *Beyond Reception. Mutual Influences between Antique Religion, Judaism, and Early Christianity,* Early Christianity in the Context of Antiquity 1 (Frankfurt 2006) 35–55.

The author argues that in *Aet.* Philo made a significant contribution to the contemporary Alexandrian discourse by stressing the literal meaning of Plato's *Timaeus*, which had since Aristotle predominantly been understood metaphorically. For this purpose Philo adduced Aristotle's witness in *De Caelo* and quoted some other, probably Alexandrian interpretations of the *Timaeus*. His position in *Aet.* significantly correlates with his exegesis in *Opif.* (MSN)

C. O'BRIEN, 'Platonism and the Tools of God,' *Trinity College Dublin Journal of Postgraduate Research* 6 (2006) 60–72.

Although Philo's name is not mentioned in the title, most of the article focuses on his thoughts on the instrumental role of the divine Logos in the process of creating and structuring the cosmos. The analogy is with tools used by a craftsman or an architect. The main theme examined is the 'Logos-cutter' in *Her.*, which, it is concluded, is a distinctively Philonic concept effectively combining elements from Platonist and Judaic sources. There are also some remarks on the agricultural imagery applied to the cosmos in *Plant.* In Neoplatonism the ideas of divine tools were replaced by the notion of procession. In Gnostic thought, too, divine hypostases are not generally regarded as instruments, but rather as aspects of God. (DTR)

J. PELÁEZ, 'El judaísmo helenístico, en especial el alejandrino,' in A. PIÑERO (ed.), *Biblia y Helenismo. El pensamiento griego y la formación del cristianismo* (Córdoba 2006) 103–127.

This extensive and well documented study examines Christianity from the perspective of its origins, with the history of the encounter between Hellenism and Bible forming the central perspective. Within this context the author presents a brief description of the thought and development of the Jewish community in Alexandria with special reference to Philo. (JPM)

L. PERNOT, 'La vie exceptionnelle de Joseph d'après Philon d'Alexandrie, *De Iosepho*,' in M. FARTZOFF, É. GENY and É. SMADJA (eds.), *Signes et destins d'élection dans l'Antiquité* (Besançon 2006) 147–165.

After briefly recalling the exceptional traits of Joseph as presented in Gen 37–50, the author argues that Philo's Joseph is not a monolithic figure fixed in his biblical perfection and the subject of unvarying general admiration. On the contrary, he is a figure who is adapted, explicated, discussed and transmitted. In his treatise *De Iosepho*, Philo makes use of and adapts literary language. He applies a certain number of literary forms which were current in the Greek world of his time: biography, encomium, the novel. He also wants to interpret his life. His interpretation takes the form of an exegetical explication on two levels, the literal and the allegorical. Through various manipulations, the personage of Joseph is transformed in order to serve as an expression of contemporary political ideals. (JR)

P. K. POHJALA, *Similarities of Redaction of the Gospel according to Matthew with Texts of Philo of Alexandrinus* (Liskeard, Cornwall 2006).

This monograph-length study argues that several texts and details in the Gospel of Matthew closely resemble discussions in the writings of Philo. On the basis of detailed examination of texts it is concluded that Matthew was acquainted with Philo's writings when redactionally formulating 5:13–16, 6:19–24 and 12:43–45, and also when writing his own material 20:1–16. In order to focus the study, the examination is restricted to these four texts. The first chapter introduces the topic, discusses secondary literature and explains the method used, which is described (p. 18) as 'explicit empiristic reading of extant material'. The second chapter looks at the historical background. The extensive Hellenization of Palestine and lively cultural connections with Alexandria meant that it is quite plausible that the Gospel author should have knowledge of Philo's writings. Chapter three examines Matt 5:13–16. It is argued that its redaction is grounded in a specific tradition of prayers of thanksgiving listing individual parts of creation such as are found in Philo, particularly in *Spec.* Book 1. Chapter four presents *Sacr.* 11–49 as the clear Philonic parallel for Matt 20:1–16 and in particular its main theme of reward for labour. Various aspects of this text are discussed, including Matthew's use of numerals. Chapter five turns to 12:43–45 and its theme of the entry of vice in the place vacated by good, for which an astonishing number of Philonic parallels can be given. Chapter six examines Philonic parallels for Matt 6:19–24 and in particular the use of the Greek term *oxus* for the keenness of vision and the mind. The final two chapters present the conclusions of the study and a full-length summary. There is no general bibliography, but extensive lists of literature are presented at the end of each chapter. (DTR)

J. Pollard and H. Reid, *The Rise and Fall of Alexandria: Birthplace of the Modern Mind* (New York 2006), esp. 192–200.

Although Athens and Rome were the leading cities in the classical world, Alexandria, a city with 'a unique soul' (xv) greatly deserves recognition for its impressive contributions, preserved in writing, to many fields of knowledge. Declaring Alexandria to be 'the greatest mental crucible the world has ever known' (xix), the authors bring the ancient city to life in their vivid account of people, events, and ideas from the founding of the city in 331 B.C.E. to the Muslim conquest in 646 C.E. Philo's writings offer a flavor of the city and its political turbulence under Rome. Philo himself was devoted to comparing Jewish and Greek tradition, and he saw Moses as 'the original perceiver of divine wisdom' (194), whose teachings underlay Greek philosophy. Philo's efforts, and especially his concept of the Logos, inadvertently provided the philosophical foundation of Christianity; and the Essenes and Therapeutae, whom he described, may have been models for early Christian monastic groups. While one should appreciate the authors' great enthusiasm for their subject, readers may notice that the section on Philo contains mistaken references and some assertions that should have been stated more tentatively. (EB)

B. Pouderon, 'Pharos et Cumes: deux lieux de pèlerinage judéo-hellénistiques à l'époque de Constantin?: enquête sur le témoignage de la «Cohortatio ad Graecos» restituée à Marcel d'Ancyre,' in B. Caseau, J.-C. Cheynet and V. Déroche (eds.), *Pèlerinages et lieux saints dans l'Antiquité et le Moyen âge: mélanges offerts à Pierre Maraval* (Paris 2006) 395–415.

Analysis of the twin descriptions made by the author of the Cohortatio attributed to Justin of Pharos, a definite Jewish 'place of memory' and of the cave of the Sibyl at Cumae, of which the religious links are more problematic. Connections are made with the *Letter of Aristeas* and Philo for the former site, and with the *Theosophy of Tübingen*, the *Sybilline*

Oracles and a scholion on Plato *Phdr.* 244b for the latter. (DTR; based on a summary in APh)

R. Radice, 'A proposito del rapporto fra Filone e gli stoici,' *Fortunatae* 17 (2006) 127–149.

This study on the relationship between Philo and the Stoics leads to the conclusion that Philo cannot be considered a 'neutral' source for Stoic thought, given the fact that the texts on which he draws undergo both an exegetical and a philosophical adaptation: exegetical inasmuch as Philo is bound to take into consideration the biblical narrative; philosophical inasmuch as Philo's perspective is of a transcendent, Platonic nature. Once aware of this 'deformation', and having made the necessary corrections of perspective, we can conclude, however, that in none of the examined passages (*Opif.* 8, *Sacr.* 68, *Leg.* 2.22, *Opif.* 26, *Migr.* 180, *Opif.* 66f., *Conf.* 156, *Spec.* 1.32) does Philo violate the Stoic substance of his sources. This is because the foundation of Philo's allegorical method is essentially Stoic (e.g. the unity and 'many ways of being' of God, cf. the theory of the *dunameis*). (HMK, based on the author's summary)

J. Riaud, 'Pâque et sabbat dans les fragments I et V d'Aristobule,' in C. Grappe and J.-C. Ingelaere (eds.), *Le Temps et les temps dans les littératures juives et chrétiennes au tournant de notre ère* (Leiden–Boston 2006), esp. 112–113, 118–120.

In the treatment of the fragment treating the date of Passover, the Philonic texts on the subject are faithfully summarized. Like Aristobulus, Philo uses the term τὰ διαβατήρια in order to designate the crossing of the borders of Egypt by Israel. In commenting on the fragment on the Sabbath the author mentions various Philonic texts which are close to the thought of Aristobulus. (JR)

D. G. Robertson, 'Mind and Language in Philo,' *Journal of the History of Ideas* 67 (2006) 423–442.

Wide-ranging article which analyses and problematizes Philo's pronouncements on mind and language against the background of contemporary Platonist and Stoic doctrine. Particular emphasis is placed on the interplay of immateriality and materiality in Philo's concept of the human logos. The two kinds of logos in human beings are paralleled by a distinction in the cosmic realm, in which there is a higher, divine logos and also logos as cosmic principle. Robertson is struck by a new emphasis on divine speech in Philo which has biblical roots. Turning to the theme of essence and nature of mind, he notes the stubborn tendency shown by Philo to view the connection of thought and language in terms of a contrast between the physical and the immaterial, the logos being seen as an intermediary between the two. The difficulty then arises of the interface between the two, for example in how corporeal speech carries incorporeal meaning. In this view spoken language comes to be regarded as inferior, but Philo likes the idea that the inferior part of something can be joined together with the superior part, i.e. audible word and intelligible thought. The background of these ideas might be thought to be Stoic (esp. the doctrine of 'sayables'), but there are several points at which Philo introduces Platonist ideas, and he appears to anticipate the later Neoplatonic distinction between discursive and non-discursive thought. (DTR)

J. R. ROYSE, 'The Text of Philo's *De virtutibus*,' *The Studia Philonica Annual* 18 (2006) 73–101.

As part of a seminar on the treatise *De virtutibus*, Royse examines the textual basis of the work as presented in the critical edition of C-W, building on earlier work done by Hilgert (RRS 1406) and Runia (RRS 9171). The treatise is clearly a kind of appendix to the four books of *Spec.*, but it seems that Philo himself did not make the organization of the various sub-treatises very clear and this is reflected in their transmission. A discussion follows on the original title of work and the arrangement of its various parts. Fortunately the order as found in the Seldenianus manuscript (S) is confirmed by the early evidence of Clement of Alexandria. Another problem raised by our evidence is whether there may have been a lost section of the work entitled Περὶ εὐσεβείας (*De pietate*). Royse offers arguments that we should take the evidence of the *Sacra parallela* seriously on this point. In addition there is some intriguing evidence about this postulated lost work in the Oxyrhynchus papyrus, which is discussed at some length. Royse then turns to some of the fascinating deviant readings furnished by ms. S which can be explained by various kinds of scribal intervention. Recently a further witness for the text has been discovered in the form of a Vienna papyrus, but its evidence is very limited. Finally brief remarks are devoted to the question of whether Philo's works were revised by a Jewish-Rabbinic scribe. Royse briefly discussed the biblical text quoted at *Virt.* 184 and concludes that there is little doubt that the text here is influenced by Aquila's translation of the Hebrew Bible. (DTR)

D. T. RUNIA, 'Philo – een introductie,' *Schrift* no. 223 (2006) 3–11.

A lightly revised reprinting of the introductory article in Dutch on Philo first published in 1989 (RRS 8953) and also published in an English version (RRS 9059). It focuses on Philo's attitude to the problems of acculturation in the predominantly Hellenic cultural milieu of Alexandria. (DTR)

D. T. RUNIA, E. BIRNBAUM, K. A. FOX, A. C. GELJON, H. M. KEIZER, J. P. MARTÍN, R. RADICE, J. RIAUD, D. SATRAN, G. SCHIMANOWSKI and T. SELAND, 'Philo of Alexandria: an Annotated Bibliography 2003,' *The Studia Philonica Annual* 18 (2006) 143–204.

The yearly annotated bibliography of Philonic studies prepared by the members of the International Philo Bibliography Project covers the year 2003 (131 items), with addenda for the years 1999–2002 (7 items), and provisional lists for the years 2004–06. (DTR)

D. T. RUNIA and G. E. STERLING (eds.), *The Studia Philonica Annual*, Vol. 18 (Atlanta 2006).

This volume in the journal dedicated to the thought of Philo contains three general articles, a special section entitled on Philo's *De virtutibus* with an introduction and three articles, one review article, the usual bibliography section (see summary above), and nine book reviews, followed by the annual News and Notes section and Notes on contributors. The various articles are summarized elsewhere in this bibliography. This volume is the first in the series to be published by the Society of Biblical Literature in Atlanta. Its cover has been renewed and shows a picture of Ezra reading the Law from the wall painting in the Synagogue of Dura Europus. (DTR)

K. O. Sandnes, 'Markus: en allegorisk biografi?,' *Dansk-teologisk-tidsskrift* 69 (2006) 275–297.

H. Tronier recently addressed the question of genre in Mark's Gospel (see *SPhA* 2007 p. 187). He claimed that Mark was written in a way similar to how Philo interpreted the biblical narratives about the lives and journeys of Moses and Abraham, arguing that Philo's biographies are allegorical presentations of the identity of the Jewish people, and that Mark is an allegory of a similar kind. The present article questions Tronier's interpretation of Philo, e.g. by urging a distinction between the biography of Moses and those of Abraham. Furthermore, the author argues that Mark's Gospel is narrative and not expository like Philo's *Abr.* and *Migr.* (TS)

G. Schimanowski, *Juden und Nichtjuden in Alexandrien: Koexistenz und Konflikte bis zum Pogrom unter Trajan (117 n. Chr.)*, Münsteraner Judaistische Studien 18 (Berlin 2006), esp. 117–139.

In this survey of religious, cultural and ethnic conflicts in Ancient Alexandria, Philo is used throughout as a source for much information about the city. In addition, an entire chapter deals with Philo as a Jew, Alexandrian and Roman; this chapter has already been published in a different form elsewhere (see *SPhA* 2005, p. 190). In addition the two 'historical' books *Flacc.* and *Legat.* play an important role in the chapter about the first pogroms against Jews in the city. The same also pertains to the outline of the intellectual and religious co-existence of Jews and non-Jews mentioned occasionally in his exegetical writings as well (*Mos.* 1.278, *Ios.* 255). Apart from his well-known negative attitudes towards Egypt, more benign views are represented forth, for example in *Ios.* (GS)

B. Schliesser, *Abraham's Faith in Romans 4: Genesis 15:6 and its History of Reception in Second Temple Judaism and Paul. A Contribution to the Pauline Concept of Faith* (diss. Fuller Theological Seminary 2006).

Philo is one of the Jewish inter-testamental sources examined for the reception history of Abraham's faith described in Gen 15:6. Just like Paul in Romans, these texts are witness to the hermeneutical effort to adapt an authoritative text to the present time and its needs. The study has now been published in the series Wissenschafliche Untersuchungen zum Neuen Testament, 2nd series (2007). (DTR; based on author's abstract)

G. Schöllgen (ed.), *Reallexikon für Antike und Christentum*, Vol. 21 (Stuttgart 2006).

H. O. Maier, art. Kleidung II (Bedeutung), 1–60, esp. 29–30 (Clothing II, meaning); A. Faivre, art. Kleros (κλῆρος), 65–96, esp. 75–76 (lot, inheritance); M. Becker, art. Klugheit, 98–175, esp. 140–144 (cleverness, practical intelligence); A. Lumpe, art. Königsweg, 217–222, esp. 218–219 (Royal highway); L. Fladerer and D. Börner–Klein, art. Kommentar, 274–329, esp. 300–302 (Commentary; section on Philo by D.B.–K.); A. Lumpe, art. Kontemplation, 485–498, esp. 490–492 (Contemplation; includes section on Therapeutae); W. Speyer, art. Kopf, 509–535, esp. 524–525 (Head); D. Wyrwa, art. Kosmos, 614–761, esp. 652–661 (Cosmos). (DTR)

T. SELAND, 'Philo, Magic and Balaam: Neglected Aspects of Philo's Exposition of the Balaam Story,' in J. FOTOPOULOS (ed.), *The New Testament and Early Christian Literature in Greco-Roman Context: Studies in Honor of David E. Aune*, Novum Testamentum Supplements 122 (Leiden–Boston 2006) 333–346.

After presenting a brief review of much discussed issues relating to magic, religion and society, the author makes a comparison of the Philonic and Septuagintal vocabulary of magic. Then he deals more explicitly with Philo's picture of Balaam as a magician. He finds that Philo's picture of Balaam is complex. On the one hand, Philo has to cope with the biblical and related traditions about the great prophecies of Balaam. On the other hand, once he is released from his prophetic possession, Balaam is and remains for Philo a magical diviner. (TS)

P. D. STEIGER, *Theological Anthropology in the Commentary 'On Genesis' by Didymus the Blind (Egypt)* (diss. Catholic University of America 2006).

This dissertation places Didymus' Commentary *On Genesis* in the context of fourth century Alexandria. Didymus' exegetical method shows him to be an heir of Philo, Clement and Origen, but his theological anthropology bears the impress of Antony and Athanasius. The first chapter places Didymus in his theological context by tracing the development of Christianity in Egypt and the Alexandrian Catechetical School. (DTR, based on author's summary)

G. E. STERLING, ''The Queen of the Virtues': Piety in Philo of Alexandria,' *The Studia Philonica Annual* 18 (2006) 103–123.

In Philo's thought piety, (εὐσέβεια) holds a prominent place. In De Virtutibus it receives separate treatment. It has become the cardinal virtue and he calls it 'the queen of virtues' and the 'leading' and 'greatest virtue'. It refers to the human response to and perception of God. Piety has an intellectual component and Philo uses it in the context of the human understanding of God. Unlike Hellenistic philosophers who subordinate piety to justice (δικαιοσύνη) or another virtue, Philo regards piety as a source for all other virtues. The reason for this prominent place can be found in Philo's theism. Just as God is the supreme source of all that exists, so is piety the source of the virtues. Philo is led to this understanding by his attempt to view his ancestral religion as a form of philosophy. (ACG)

G. J. STEYN, 'Torah Quotations Common to Philo, Hebrews, Clemens Romanus and Justin Martyr: What is the Common Denominator?,' in C. BREYTENBACH, J. C. THOM and J. PUNT (eds.), *The New Testament Interpreted: Essays in Honour of Bernard C. Lategan*, Supplements to Novum Testamentum 124 (Leiden–Boston 2006) 135–151.

Certain Torah quotations are common to Philo, to the unknown author of Hebrews and to some of the early Church Fathers. These quotations represent a similar reading in the different groups of literature, which in some instances jointly differ from the reading in the LXX. One is thus confronted with the question: what is the common denominator? The possibilities explored in this paper include (a) the common Hellenistic milieu, (b) literary interdependence upon each other, (c) independent use of a 'testimony book', (d) sharing the same oral tradition, (e) independent use of a common *Vorlage* in the literary tradition, (f) the role of a Christian editorial hand, and (g) geographical proximity of the authors. It is argued that the answer to this question is probably to be found not in any single possibility, but rather in a combination of some of these. With regard to the Torah quotations it is suggested that the author of Hebrews wrote from Alexandria to Christians in Rome and, being familiar with the works of Philo, made use of Philo's Torah tradition. Clement of Rome and Justin Martyr both wrote later from Rome and, being familar with the work of Hebrews, made use of his tradition in turn. (DTR, based on author's summary)

T. TAGO, 'On *kosmos noetos* in *De Opificio Mundi* of Philo of Alexandria' [Japanese], *Patristica: Proceedings of the Colloequia of the Japanese Society for Patristic Studies (Tokyo)* 10 (2006) 29–44.

The purpose of the article is to examine the meaning of the *kosmos noêtos* (the intelligible world) in *Opif.* In Philo's exegesis of the Creation, a scheme of the intelligible world as model and the sensible world as its copy plays an important part. He places the intelligible world in the divine Logos as the creative power of God, and by regarding the intelligible world as contents of God's thought he gives it an ontologically lower status than God. This seems a result of Philo's reading of *Timaeus* from his own point of view. Although his interpretation of the creation of human beings is not coherent, Philo makes clear that their status derives from being the image of God on account of the human intellect and suggests the possibility of ascending from the sensible world to the intelligible world and ultimately to God. (DTR; based on the author's summary)

J. E. TAYLOR, 'Pontius Pilate and the Imperial Cult in Roman Judaea,' *New Testament Studies* 52 (2006) 555–582.

While Pontius Pilate is often seen as agnostic, in modern terms, the material evidence of his coinage and the Pilate inscription from Caesarea indicate a prefect determined to promote a form of Roman religion in Judaea. Unlike his predecessors, in the coinage Pilate used peculiarly Roman iconographic elements appropriate to the imperial cult. In the inscription Pilate was evidently responsible for dedicating a Tiberieum to the Dis Augustis. This material evidence may be placed alongside the report in Philo *Legat.* 299–305 where Pilate sets up shields, an action that is likewise associated with the Roman imperial cult-honouring Tiberius in Jerusalem. (DTR, based on author's summary)

C. TERMINI, 'The Historical Part of the Pentateuch According to Philo of Alexandria: Biography, Genealogy, and the Philosophical Meaning of the Patriarchal Lives,' in N. CALDUCH-BENAGES and J. LIESEN (eds.), *Deuterocanonical and Cognate Literature Yearbook* (Berlin 2006) 265–297.

According to Philo, the historical parts of the Pentateuch (in particular Genesis) constitute a kind of Jewish ἀρχαιολογία. From the literary point of view, this ancient history belongs to the genre of βίος and γενεαλογικὴ ἱστορία, including models of virtue and iniquity set in a retributive framework (*Praem.* 1–3, *Mos.* 2.46–7). But from a deeper, synchronic point of view, this ancient history must be considered an integral part of the Mosaic law. The creation account serves as the beginning (ἀρχή) of the law, indicating the consonance between the latter and the cosmic order (*Opif.* 1–3). The patriarchs, then, are 'living laws', archetypes who by following nature have fullfilled the Mosaic legislation even before its formulation in writing (*Abr.* 3–6). The point of intersection between the law of nature and the Mosaic precepts is formed by the virtues. Piety (εὐσέβεια) and justice (δικαιοσύνη) are at the basis of Abraham's biography (*Abr.* 60–207, 208–261), and they parallel the two tables of the Decalogue, which in turn provide the taxonomy for the special laws. Thus Philo extends the validity of the Torah from Sinai back to creation, a tendency present in writings from Middle-Judaism. By his original reformulation of Biblical ancient history in light of the philosophical concept of natural law (νόμος φύσεως), Philo accomplished for the Hellenistic Jewish world a project comparable with Cicero's achievement in *De legibus*. (HMK, based on author's conclusion)

H. P. Thyssen, 'Philosophical Christology in the New Testament,' *Numen International Review for the History of Religions* 53 (2006) 133–176.

The idea of this article is to determine the sense of the Logos in the Prologue of John's Gospel by making use of the subsequent Christian doctrinal tradition. As an introduction, the general influence of Hellenistic Judaism on early Christian speculative theology and exegesis is illustrated by examples from Philo and Justin. Further, it is argued that Justin's scriptural argument shows that the traditional derivation of the Logos of the Prologue from the word of creation of Genesis I did not exist at that early stage, since if it did, that derivation ought to have appeared in Justin. Since no other derivation of a Logos in the cosmological sense from the Bible is possible, the presence of this idea in John can only be explained as the result of influence from the eclectic philosophy of Jewish Hellenism as witnessed by Philo. (TS; based on author's abstract)

E. C. Tibbs, *'Now concerning Spiritism': Communication with the Spirit World as Religious Experience in First Corinthians 12 and 14* (diss. The Catholic University of America 2006).

In this investigation of the religious experience portrayed by Paul in I Corinthians 12 and 14 texts from Plutarch, Josephus, Philo, and Pseudo-Philo serve as historical witnesses contemporary with Paul to the activities of good spirits possessing persons and speaking through them by use of the vocal chords. The study has now been published in a revised version in the series Wissenschaftliche Untersuchungen zum Neuen Testament 2nd Series (2007) under the title *Religious Experience of the Pneuma: Communication with the Spirit World in 1 Corinthians 12 and 14*. (DTR; based on author's summary)

J. L. Tinklenberg de Vega, *'A Man Who Fears God': Constructions of Masculinity in Hellenistic Jewish Interpretations of the Story of Joseph* (diss. Florida State University 2006).

Hellenistic Jewish interpreters of the Bible often restructured and modified biblical texts in an effort to further their own ideological perspectives. Among the many adaptations they made, these exegetes often sought to transform the familiar stories to better fit or express their own constructs of gender identity. The study attempts to uncover the ideologies of masculinity in the depiction of Joseph in three First Century Hellenistic Jewish texts: *The Jewish Antiquities* of Josephus, Philo's *De Somniis*, and the anonymous *Joseph and Aseneth*. The texts are studied by means of a close reading of each author's rhetorical structures, particularly noting the ways terminology and literary structures describing maleness are held in opposition to femaleness, on the assumption that gender was a culturally constructed (rather than innate or essential) category. In the course of the study a variety of constructions are confirmed: masculinity as dominance over the self (Josephus), as sexual propriety and non-violence (*Joseph and Aseneth*), and as avoidance of eunuchism, feminine company, and violating establish hierarchies (Philo). (DTR, based on author's summary)

T. H. TOBIN S.J., 'The World of Thought in the Philippians Hymn (Philippians 2:6–11),' in J. FOTOPOULOS (ed.), *The New Testament and Early Christian Literature in Greco-Roman Context. Studies in Honor of David E. Aune*, Novum Testamentum Supplements 122 (Leiden–Boston 2006) 91–104.

Compared with other hymns in the New Testament which recognize three states of existence of Christ (John 1:1–18; Col 1:1–15; Heb 1:3f.), Phil 2:6–11 is different because the text does not ascribe a cosmological role to the preexistent one, even though he is represented as a figure who thinks and makes decisions. In giving to him personal or human-like characteristics the author may be influenced by the figure of the Heavenly Man in Philo. Even if the hymn writer may not have been familiar with Philo's writings, it is likely that he was aware of theological speculation similar to what is found there. It should be noted that Tobin presupposes his own analysis of Philo's interpretation of the creation narrative which distinguishes different stages in which the Logos was only gradually assimilated to the Heavenly Man. (DTR)

H. TRONIER, 'Markus: en allegorisk komposition om Jesu vej: Replik til Karl Olav Sandnes,' *Dansk-teologisk-tidsskrift* 69 (2006) 298–306.

This article is a response to Karl Olav Sandnes' critical response to a study by Tronier in 2005 on biographical aspects in the Gospel of Mark in the light of Philo's biographies. According to Tronier, Mark does not belong to the conventional genre of biography: it is an allegorical composition about Jesus' way, led by the heavenly spirit, not about his whole life. (TS)

G. VELTRI, *Libraries, Translations, and 'Canonic' Texts: The Septuagint, Aquila and Ben Sira in the Jewish and Christian Traditions*, Supplements to the Journal for the Study of Judaism 109 (Leiden–Boston 2006).

To understand the development of an authoritative, canonical body of texts, one must also consider how works that once held canonical status later lost this status. Veltri considers three examples: the canonization of the Septuagint in Jewish-Hellenistic and Christian tradition and its decanonization in rabbinic literature; patristic and rabbinic use of Aquila's Greek translation of the Bible and Babylonian rabbinic replacement of Aquila's translation by Targum Onkelos; and the Book of Ben Sira from the perspective of its Greek prologue and of rabbinic literature. Contrary to accepted opinion, the rise and fall of books among rabbinic Jews and Christians does not have to do with their opponents' use of these books, but rather with inner dynamics within each community such as change in the primary language used by the community and the disappearance of the Alexandrian Jewish community. Among other sources, Philo is used to illuminate the process of canonization of the Greek Bible in Alexandria. (EB)

U. VOLP, *Die Würde des Menschen. Ein Beitrag zur Anthropologie in der Alten Kirche*, Supplements to Vigiliae Christianae 81 (Leiden–Boston 2006), esp. 77–81.

In this habilitation thesis of the Friedrich-Wilhelm University Bonn brief remarks are made on Philo's anthropology as part of the Jewish-Christian tradition until the 2nd cent. C.E. Philo particularly values the doctrine of the εἰκὼν θεοῦ. The human being in the likeness of God is on the borderline (μεθόριος) of the eternal and non-eternal nature, partaking in both in equal measure: the human body in the non-eternal, the human rationality in the divine nature (see *Opif.* 46). Philo's line of argument ends in his ethical call to be aware of oneself as an image of God. These Philonic themes can be observed in the anthropology of the early church fathers. (GS)

A. WASSERSTEIN and D. J. WASSERSTEIN, *The Legend of the Septuagint From Classical Antiquity to Today* (Cambridge 2006), esp. 35–45.

This book traces how the legend about the translation of the Hebrew Bible into Greek evolved over two millennia and how Jews, Christians, Muslims, and pagans adapted this legend for their own purposes, most often to buttress the authority of the Greek text on which they relied. Besides an Introduction and Conclusion, chapters include: *The Letter of Aristeas*; The Hellenistic Jewish Tradition; The Rabbis and the Greek Bible; The Ptolemaic Changes; The Church Fathers and the Translation of the Septuagint; Among the Christians in the Orient; The Muslims and the Septuagint; Josippon and the Story of the Seventy; Karaites, Samaritans and Rabbanite Jews in the Middle Ages; and The Septuagint in the Renaissance and the Modern World. The section on Philo presents his account in *Mos.* 2.25–44 and carefully compares it with the *Letter of Aristeas*. Aspects of Philo's account that differ from the *Letter* include Philo's combination of the figures of high priest and king into one, emphasis on divine involvement, description of details related to the island, account of an annual celebration, omission of particulars related to the translation and the Library, added emphasis on the interest of the king, and, especially, 'the recognition that translation of Scripture needs a special vocabulary and that that special vocabulary is useful and valuable in direct proportion to its uniformity' (45). (EB)

R. VAN DE WATER, 'Michael or Yhwh? Toward Identifying Melchizedek in 11q13,' *Journal for the Study of the Pseudepigrapha* 16 (2006) 75–86.

Scholars have debated whether Melchizedek in 11Q13 is an angel or Yhwh himself. A way of understanding this ambiguity is provided by the rabbinic doctrine of 'two powers in Heaven,' a concept similar to Philo's portrayal of the divine Logos and to beliefs ascribed to the 'Magharians,' a later name given to a first-century Jewish sect. The varied images for Melchizedek in 11Q13 as both Yhwh himself and his intermediary are also drawn from various biblical passages and can thus be seen as 'a natural development of their seminal overlapping in biblical tradition' (86). (EB)

M. WOLTER, 'Der Reichtum Gottes,' *Jahrbuch für biblische Theologie* 21 (2006) 145–160.

The semantic contours of the concept of the 'richness of God' as it occurs in about ten Philonic texts can be summarized as follows: (1) God is immeasurable and the quality of his richness marks his being God in clear differentiation from human beings and their richness. (2) God is not rich only for himself but also in order to do good things for others, because his richness has the intrinsic property to be transmitted to another in a universal sense. In this transmission God acts in caring for and preserving his whole creation. (3) Because God is God his richness is immeasurable and in this way his action towards his creation in the described manner is the reason for his being God. Many texts underline this Philonic background, which in turn illustrates the New Testament discourse on the 'richness of God' as a tradition shared between Hellenistic Judaism and Christianity. (GS)

B. G. WRIGHT, 'Translation as Scripture: The Septuagint in Aristeas and Philo,' in W. KRAUS and R. G. WOODEN (eds.), *Septuagint Research: Issues and Challenges in the Study of the Greek Jewish Scriptures*, Society of Biblical Literature Septuagint and Cognate Studies 53 (Atlanta 2006) 47–61.

Based on ideas propounded by G. Toury, A. Pietersma has posited an interlinear model of the Septuagint according to which the Greek translation is understood as originally meant to have been used together with the Hebrew. In two accounts of the origins of the LXX—the *Letter of Aristeas* and Philo—however, the LXX stands independent of the original Hebrew. These accounts thus go beyond the interlinear model and reflect circumstances contemporary to the later authors. The *Letter of Aristeas* likely served as 'a foundational myth of origins for the Septuagint's transformed position/function as an independent, scriptural authority' (54). Taking this position of the LXX as a given, Philo argues for the precision of the Greek translation in relation to the Hebrew, probably to underscore its divine origins and to justify Philo's own exegetical approach which relied so closely upon the translation's exact wording. (EB)

Xuefu ZHANG, *Feiluo sixiang daolun I: liangxi wenming shiyezhong de youtai zhexue* [*An Introduction to the Thought of Philo I: Jewish Philosophy in the Context of the Hebrew and Hellenistic Civilizations*] (Beijing 2006).

This is vol. 1 of a two-volume treatment of the thought of Philo in Chinese. Vol. 2 was published in 2008. According to the cover the aim is to study Philo from the perspective of Hellenistic Judaism. Vol. 1 consists of four chapters. The first places Philo in his Alexandrian and Jewish context. There then follows a chapter on Allegorical interpretation, asking whether it is based on free association or on structured hermeneutics and arguing for its cosmological foundation and a link to ecstatic experience. Chapter three focuses on ontology, including discussions of the two worlds, God and the Logos. Chapter four is entitled Soul, Free Will, Virtue. Various lists and indices complete the volume. (DTR, based on a table of contents supplied by Sze-Kar Wan)

Extra items from before 2006

D. H. AKENSON, *Surpassing Wonder: The Invention of the Bible and the Talmuds* (Montreal–Kingston 1998), esp. 128–132.

The author considers the Bible and later literature based on it as inventions of three sets of texts and their faiths: ancient YHWH faith, or 'Judahism'; the modern Jewish faith, also called Rabbinic or Talmudic Judaism; and the Christian faith, which developed out of Jesus-faith. The texts of these faiths resulted from events in which the 'chief idol' of each was destroyed—first Solomon's Temple and then Herod's Temple. Thus Judaism and Christianity are each understood as inventing a religion of the Temple in which they established the Temple not 'on this earth, but in their hearts, in the heavens, and in each home' (409). Philo is included in a survey of the richly diverse manifestations of Judahism in the Second Temple period. Although, according to Akenson, Philo is relatively—and unjustly—ignored in discussions of the pre-70 C.E. period, he provides an excellent example of 'a highly-devout diaspora Judahist' (128), fully conversant with the contemporary Greek philosophical writings, who points in several ways to elements in future Jewish and Christian religions. In this regard, Akenson finds especially significant the question–and–answer form used by Philo and found in later rabbinic literature; Philo's allegorization of the Temple, which showed the later religions that 'the Temple could continue to exist, independent of the vagaries of the physical world'; the Logos concept, reflected later in the Gospel of John; Philo's emphasis on Moses as mediator between the Logos and God's people, a theme later transformed by Christian apologists who substituted Jesus for Moses; and, finally, Philo's thinking in 'types,' an approach used by later Christians (131–132). (EB)

J. ÁLVAREZ MAESTRO, 'San Agustín y el pensamiento hebreo,' *Augustinus* 50 (2005) 11–27.

The author affirms with confidence that Augustine read both the Septuagint and Philo as importance sources for the history of salvation and the history of the Jewish people. (JPM)

M. AMERISE, 'Costantino il « Nuovo Mosè »,' *Salesianum* 67 (2005) 671–700.

In this well-documented study, the author elaborates the many correspondences that can be found between Eusebius' *Life of Constantine* and Philo's *Life of Moses*. Constantine—just like Moses—is presented by Eusebius as king, priest, legislator, liberator, and as excelling in virtue, faith, study of the Scriptures and prayer. The *Life of Constantine* clearly has hagiographic characteristics, just as Philo's *Life of Moses* has been recognized as one of the example texts for Christian hagiography. (HMK)

R. D. AUS, *Imagery of Triumph and Rebellion in 2 Corinthians 2:14–17 and elsewhere in the Epistle: an Example of the Combination of Greco-Roman and Judaic Tradition in the Apostle Paul*, Studies in Judaism (Lanham, MD 2005).

The author contends that the imagery of 2 Cor. 2:14–17 must be understood against the dual background of Greco-Roman triumph and Jewish portrayals of rebellion. Particularly relevant are the three-day triumphal procession of the Roman consul and general Paulus following his victory over Macedonia in 168 B.C.E. and Jewish interpretations of Korah's rebellion in Numbers 17:6–15. Philo (57–58) is among the Jewish sources surveyed, which also include the Masoretic Text, the Septuagint, the Wisdom of Solomon 18:20–25, 4 Macc. 7:11, Targums, and rabbinic writings. Philo's allegorical interpretations of the Numbers passage in *Her*. 201–202 and *Somn*. 2.234–236 shed light upon Paul's metaphorical uses of life and death imagery in 2 Cor. 2:15–16. (EB)

D. BRADSHAW, *Aristotle East and West: Metaphysics and the Division of Christendom* (Cambridge 2004), esp. 59–64.

The study's title does not make very clear that its main subject is the development of the Aristotelian concept of *energeia* in western and eastern Christian theology. A brief but instructive section is devoted to Philo's contribution. It is surprising to learn (p. 60) that the 'quaint interpretation of Adam's love for Eve' in *Leg*. 2.40 is 'the first appearance since the Lyceum of the characteristic Aristotelian contrast between *energeia* and *dunamis*.' Philo's chief contribution is to interpret the *energeia* of God in terms of his activity and not his actuality (as in Aristotle). He only makes the distinction between God's *ousia* and his *energeia* in one passage, but in a larger sense this contrast runs throughout his statements on human knowledge of God. Bradshaw concludes (p. 64): 'what we find in Philo ... is not a direct anticipation of later developments, but a suggestive and highly original mélange of ideas, many of which will find a home in other contexts'. (DTR)

Y. COHEN-YASHAR, ''I am that I am' (Exodus 3, 14) as a Basis for a Philosophical Ontology according to Philo Alexandrinus,' in *Proceedings of the Twelth World Congress of Jewish Studies: Division A – The Bible and its World* (Jerusalem 1999) 185–194.

The author addresses a problem, which occurred in the translation of Philo's writings into Hebrew, namely the rendition of the expression 'I am who I am'. After reviewing the different meanings of the verb 'to be' in Greek and Hebrew, the author shows that, parallel to Maimonides, Philo has chosen the ontological meaning, stressing that God is essentially unknowable to man. (MSN)

J. J. COLLINS, 'Anti-Semitism in Antiquity? The Case of Alexandria,' *Archiv für religionsgeschichte* 7 (2005) 86–101.

See the summary of another version of the same article in *SPhA* 2008, p. 170. (DTR)

C. A. EVANS, *Ancient texts for New Testament Studies: a Guide to the Background Literature* (Peabody MA 2005), esp. 167–173.

This is an introduction to various bodies of literature that pertain to biblical—and especially NT—scholarship. After an Introduction, chapters are devoted to OT Apocrypha and Pseudepigrapha, Dead Sea Scrolls, versions of the OT, Philo and Josephus, Targums, rabbinic literature, NT Apocrypha and Pseudepigrapha, early Church Fathers, Gnostic Writings, other writings (e.g., Greco-Roman, Samaritan), and examples of NT exegesis. The section on Philo (167–173) lists his treatises in the Loeb edition, highlights aspects of his work particularly relevant to NT studies—such as his allegorical approach, relationship to rabbinic writings, and concepts of the Logos, perfect man, and shadow and substance—, and provides bibliographic information for each subsection as well as a general bibliography. (EB)

S. Hylen, *Allusion and Meaning in John 6*, Beihefte zur Zeitschrift für die neutestamentliche Wissenschaft und die Kunde der älteren Kirche 137 (Berlin–New York 2005), esp. 102–117.

In John 6 allusions are found to the story of the manna in the wilderness (Ex 16:14–15), and Jesus says 'I am the bread of life'. These words are often seen as forming a contrast with the manna story. Hylen poses the question 'what if the characters and actions of John 6 were read as interpreting the story of the Exodus instead of as a departure from this story?' (p. 2). Within this framework the author examines allusions to Exodus in ancient Jewish writings, focusing on Ezekiel, Jubilees, Wisdom and Philo. Philo identifies manna with heavenly wisdom, which is associated with learning that comes without labour. It is food for the soul. The manna is also equated with God's Logos. Philo uses details from the manna story to describe the Logos. Hylen suggests that John's interpretation of Exodus may be shaped by other readings. The study is a reworked version of an Emory University dissertation completed in 2004. (ACG)

G. N. Khairallah, 'L'herméneutique dans la penseé de Philon d'Alexandrie,' in R. G. Khoury and J. Halfwassen (eds.), *Platonismus im Orient und Okzident* (Heidelberg 2005) 41–48.

In Philo's day two schools were well known in philosophical circles in Alexandria, Aristotelianism and Platonism. At this time a significant event occurred in the history of philosophy, the meeting of hellenized philosophy and oriental thought, particularly in the form of Jewish religious thought which had moved to Alexandria. This is the context for the emergence and development of Philo's thought, a meeting point of philosophy and religion. Philo's allegorical hermeneutic can be seen as a syncretistic attempt to mediate between Greek, Jewish, and—later—Christian thought. (JR)

M. Merino Rodriguez, *Clemente de Alejandría: Stromata VI–VIII, Vida intelectual y religiosa del cristianismo, Introducción, traducción y notas*, Fuentes Patrísticas 17 (Madrid 2005).

Merino edits and translates the last three books of Clement of Alexandria' *Stromata*. He quotes nearly a hundred passages of the corpus Philonicum, following in general the previous study of A. van den Hoek (RRS 8834). Merino emphasizes Philo's role as predecessor especially in the treatment of arithmology in *Str*. 6.84–86 and in the presentation of the Decalogue in *Str*. 6.139–145. The use of 18 verses of Solon on the topic of the ages of man, *Str*. 6.144, coincides completely with the text of Philo, *Opif*. 104. (JPM)

R. Radice, G. Reale, C. Kraus Reggiani and C. Mazzarelli, *Filone di Alessandria: Tutti i trattati del Commentario Allegorico alla Bibbia*. 2nd ed, I Classici del Pensiero: sezione I Filosofia classica e tardo-antica (Milan 2005).

Reprint (by publisher Bompiani, Milan) of the 1994 edition (by publisher Rusconi, Milan) for which see RRS 2407, now with the useful addition of Cohn-Wendland's Greek text. The latter in its turn was the result of merging five separate volumes dating from 1981 to 1988 (for which see R-R 2402–06) into one single collection of the 19 treatises together forming the Allegorical Commentary (incl. *Opif.*). The rich 'Monografia Introduttiva' by Giovanni Reale and Roberto Radice introducing the 19 treatises is taken over from the 1987 publication. Each treatise (Greek text and Italian translation) is preceded by a schematic presentation of its structure and an analytic summary of its contents, and followed by explanatory notes. The massive volume (clx + 1946 pages due to the addition of the Greek text), when compared to the 1994 edition, has a more extensive bibliography, which however does not go beyond the 1980s apart from referring to RRS and *SPhA*. (HMK)

G. ROSKAM, *On the Path to Virtue: The Stoic Doctrine of Moral Progress and its Reception in (Middle-)Platonism* (Leuven 2005), esp. 146–219.

This monograph deals with the problem of moral progress in ancient Stoicism. In Part II the views of Philo and Plutarch are discussed. In Philo's philosophical interpretation of Scripture the theme of moral progress takes an important place. In Scripture he finds several examples of προκόπτοντες (Aaron, Noah) and various symbols of προκοπή. On the road to virtue the προκόπτων is somewhere between total wickedness and perfection, the former represented by a totally bad person such as Cain, the latter by the few people able to attain wisdom and to become σόφος like Abraham. Roskam concludes that Philo is acquainted with the Stoic doctrine of moral progress but the Stoic view is not his basic frame. He does not, as the Stoics do, regard the προκόπτων as fundamentally bad. Rather, he is inclined to the Peripatetic-Platonic view in which progress is seen as a separate third phase different from both virtue and vice. Although Philo uses several Stoic notions, he is not a Stoic philosopher. (ACG)

C. SCHLUND, *'Kein Knochen soll gebrochen werden': Studien zu Bedeutung und Funktion des Pesachfests in Texten des frühen Judentums und im Johannes-evangelium*, Wissenschaftliche Monographien zum Alten und Neuen Testament 107 (Neukirchen-Vluyn 2005).

In the lightly revised edition of her dissertation (Humboldt University, Berlin 2004) the research assistant of the German Septuaginta translation project deals with the meaning and function of Passover in Early Judaism and the Gospel of John. Philo has a particular importance for Hellenistic Judaism. Methodically, Schlund operates with the classification developed from the research of P. Borgen and F. Siegert. Two themes should be distinguished from each other in the interpretation of Passover. On the one hand there is the allegorical explanation: the estrangement of the soul from the passions (= Egypt) and the acceptance of the pure wisdom and truth (= Land of Canaan); this explanation (διάβασις) is unique to Philo's works. On the other hand Philo stresses the importance of the (high)–priestly intervention on behalf of the entire (Jewish) people. In this way Passover is first and foremost a feast of thanks and enjoyment through the deliverance from slavery in Egypt, uniting all the people in a congregation of worship (συναγωγή). The slaughter of the sacrificial animal without any participation of cultic staff reminds thereof. Except for the sacrifice by all the Israelites, the Passover animal and its blood does not play any part. It is striking that neither in the historical nor in the allegorical interpretation is there any mention of the protection or sparing of the Israelites by God. It seems that this aspect (especially of the LXX) does not carry any weight for Philo, although his texts do pick up specific Septuagintal terminology rather frequently. (GS)

J. Woyke, *Götter, 'Götzen', Götterbilder. Aspekte einer paulinischen 'Theologie der Religionen'*, Beihefte zur Zeitschrift für die neutestamentliche Wissenschaft 132 (Berlin–New York 2005).

Discussions on aspects of Philo's theology occur at various points in this Tübingen dissertation. On pp. 90–94 there is an extensive excursus on the terminology used for foreign gods, in which Philo's use of the terms εἴδωλα, θεοπλαστεῖν and θεοί is also investigated. It is only against the background of a Platonic world-view that the term εἴδωλον can have the double signification of 'a divine image' and 'phantom'. The designation of the stars as θεοὶ αἰσθητοί, however, is conventional and does not imply veneration. On pp. 123–126 Philo's concept of faith is outlined: it comprises knowledge of God, trust in God, and conversion as well. On pp. 133–138 F. Siegert's thesis that *QE* 2.2 betrays the existence of polytheistic sympathizers of the Hellenistic synagogue is contested. Jethro, however, could be the symbol of such an exterior circle of adherents. Further references to Philo's doctrine of monotheism are found on pp. 174–176 and 397–401. The author observes a tendency to abstract from God's activity in history; in contrast to Stoicism, Philo confines the knowledge of a Creator's existence to the intellectual inference of philosophers. (GS)

The Studia Philonica Annual 21 (2009) 109–123

SUPPLEMENT

A Provisional Bibliography 2007–2009

The user of this supplemental Bibliography of the most recent articles on Philo is reminded that it will doubtless contain inaccuracies and red herrings because it is not in all cases based on autopsy. It is merely meant as a service to the reader. Scholars who are disappointed by omissions or are keen to have their own work on Philo listed are strongly encouraged to contact the Bibliography's compilers (addresses in the section Notes on Contributors).

2007

Aa.vv., *Lun Moxi de sheng ping [On the Life of Moses]* (Beijing 2007).

T. Alekniene, 'L'enigme de la 'patrie' dans le Traite 1 de Plotin: heritage de l'exégèse philonienne?,' *Recherches augustiniennes et patristiques* 35 (2007) 1–46.

M. Alesso, 'Qué es una madre judía según Filón,' *Circe* 11 (2007) 11–25.

M. Alexandre, 'Les études philoniennes et le renouveau patristique,' in Y.-M. Blanchard *et al.* (eds.), *'De commencement en commencement.' Le renouveau patristique dans la théologie contemporaine* (Paris 2007) 141–179.

A. Angel, 'From Wild Men to Wise and Wicked Women: an Investigation into Male Heterosexuality in Second Temple Interpretations of the Ladies Wisdom and Folly,' in D. W. Rooke (ed.), *A Question of Sex? Gender and Difference in the Hebrew Bible and Beyond*, Hebrew Bible Monographs 14 (Sheffield 2007) 145–161.

S. Badilita, *Recherches sur la prophétie chez Philon d'Alexandrie* (diss. Université de Paris IV–Sorbonne 2007).

J. M. G. Barclay, *Flavius Josephus: Translation and Commentary, Volume 10 Against Apion: Translation and Commentary* (Leiden–Boston 2007).

C. T. Begg, 'Balaam's Talking Ass (Num 22,21–35): Three Retellings of Her Story Compared,' *Annali di Storia dell'Esegesi* 24 (2007) 207–228.

C. T. Begg, 'Israel's Confrontation with Edom (Num 20,14–21) according to Josephus and Philo,' *Revista Catalana de Teología* 32 (2007) 1–18.

C. T. Begg, 'Josephus' and Philo's Retelling of Numbers 31 Compared,' *Ephemerides theologicae Lovanienses* 83 (2007) 81–106.

C. T. Begg, 'The Rephidim Episode according to Josephus and Philo,' *Ephemerides theologicae Lovanienses* 83 (2007) 367–383.

C. T. BEGG, 'Two Ancient Rewritings of Numbers 11,' *Revista Catalana de Teología* 32 (2007) 299–317.

P. J. BEKKEN, *The Word is Near You. A Study of Deuteronomy 30:12–14 in Paul's Letter to the Romans in a Jewish Context*, Beihefte zur Zeitschrift für die neutestamentliche Wissenschaft und die Kunde der älteren Kirche 144 (Berlin–New York 2007).

K. BERTHELOT, 'Philo of Alexandria and the Conquest of Canaan,' *Journal for the study of Judaism in the Persian, Hellenistic and Roman period* 38 (2007) 39–56.

K. BERTHELOT, 'Zeal for God and Divine Law in Philo and the Dead Sea Scrolls,' *The Studia Philonica Annual* 19 (2007) 113–129.

P. BILDE, 'Filon som polemiker og politisk apologet,' in A. K. PETERSEN and K. S. FUGLSETH (eds.), *Perspektiver på jødisk apologetik*, Antikken og kristendommen 4 (København 2007) 155–180.

E. BONA, 'Echi di Filone nella Vita Syncleticae (BHG 1694)?' *Revista de Filologia e di Istruzione Classica* 135 (2007) 220–230.

M. BONAZZI, C. LÉVY and C. STEEL, *A Platonic Pythagoras. Platonism and Pythagoreanism in the Imperial Age*, Monothéismes et Philosophie 10 (Turnhout 2007).

A. P. BOS, 'Is God 'Maker' of 'Vader' van de kosmos? Het debat tussen Plato en Aristoteles en de voortzetting ervan bij Philo,' in K. SPRONK and R. ROUKEMA (eds.), *Over God* (Zoetermeer, Netherlands 2007) 47–71, 188–191.

D. BOYARIN, 'Philo, Origen, and the Rabbis on Divine Speech and Interpretation,' in J. E. GOEHRING and J. TIMBIE (eds.), *The World of Early Egyptian Christianity: Language, Literature, and Social Context: Essays in Honor of David W. Johnson* (Washington DC 2007).

F. CALABI, 'Tra Atene e Gerusalemme: Anima e parola in Filone di Alessandria,' in R. BRUSCHI (ed.), *Gli irraggiungibili confini. Percorsi della psyche nell'età della Grecia classica* (Pisa 2007) 217–236.

F. CALABI, 'Filone di Alessandria e Ecfanto. Un confronto possible,' in M. BONAZZI, C. LÉVY and C. STEEL (eds.), *A Platonic Pythagoras. Platonism and Pythagoreanism in the Imperial Age*, Monothéismes et Philosophie 10 (Turnhout 2007) 11–28.

J. CHERIAN, *Toward a Commonwealth of Grace: A Plutocritical Reading of Grace and Equality in Second Corinthians 8:1–15* (diss. Princeton Theological Seminary 2007).

H. CLIFFORD, 'Moses as Philosopher-sage in Philo,' in A. GRAUPNER and M. WOLTER (eds.), *Moses in Biblical and Extra-Biblical Traditions* (Berlin–New York 2007) 151–167.

N. G. COHEN, *Philo's Scriptures: Citations from the Prophets and Writings: Evidence for a Haftarah Cycle in Second Temple Judaism*, Supplements to the Journal for the Study of Judaism 123 (Leiden–Boston 2007).

J. J. COLLINS, 'Philo and the Dead Sea Scrolls: Introduction,' *The Studia Philonica Annual* 19 (2007) 81–83.

R. COX, *By the Same Word: Creation and Salvation in Hellenistic Judaism and Early Christianity*, Beihefte zur Zeitschrift für die neutestamentliche Wissenschaft und die Kunde der älteren Kirche 145 (Berlin–New York 2007).

M. R. D'ANGELO, 'Gender and Geopolitics in the Work of Philo of Alexandria: Jewish Piety and Imperial Family Values,' in T. PENNER and C. VANDER STICHELE (eds.), *Mapping Gender in Ancient Religious Discourses*, Biblical Interpretation Series 84 (Leiden–Boston 2007) 63–88.

S. DI MATTEI, 'Quelques précisions sur la φυσιολογία et l'emploi de φυσικῶς dans la méthode exégétique de Philon d'Alexandrie,' *Revue des Études Juives* 166 (2007) 45–74.

A. DINAN, 'The Mystery of Play: Clement of Alexandria's Appropriation of Philo in the *Paedagogus* (1.5.21.3–22.1),' *The Studia Philonica Annual* 19 (2007) 59–80.

T. L. DONALDSON, *Judaism and the Gentiles: Jewish Patterns of Universalism (to 135 CE)* (Waco TX 2007), esp. 217–278.

M. EBNER, 'Mahl und Gruppenidentität. Philos Schrift De Vita Contemplativa als Paradigma,' in M. EBNER (ed.), *Herrenmahl und Gruppenidentität*, Quaestiones disputatae 221 (Freiburg 2007) 64–90.

C. ESCUDÉ, *La Guerra de los Dioses: los Mandatos Bíblicos frente a la Política Mundial* (Buenos Aires 2007), esp. 91–96.

L. H. FELDMAN, 'Moses the General and the Battle Against Midian in Philo,' *Jewish Studies Quarterly* 14 (2007) 1–18.

L. H. FELDMAN, *Philo's Portrayal of Moses in the Context of Ancient Judaism* (Notre Dame IN 2007).

L. H. FELDMAN, 'The Case of the Blasphemer (Lev. 24:10–16) according to Philo and Josephus,' in L. LIDONNICI and A. LIEBER (eds.), *Heavenly Tablets: Interpretation, Identity and Tradition in Ancient Judaism*, Supplements to the Journal for the Study of Judaism 119 (Leiden 2007) 213–226.

P. FRICK, 'Johannine Soteriology and Aristotelian Philosophy: a Hermeneutical Suggestion on Reading John 3,16 and 1 John 4,9,' *Biblica* 88 (2007) 415–421.

P. FRICK, 'The Means and Mode of Salvation: A Hermeneutical Proposal for Clarifying Pauline Soteriology,' *Horizons in Biblical Theology* 29 (2007) 203–222.

E. FRÜCHTEL, 'Philon und die Vorbereitung der christlichen Paideia und Seelenleitung,' in F. R. PROSTMEIER (ed.), *Frühchristentum und Kultur*, Kommentar zu frühchristlichen Apologeten. Ergänzungsband 2 (Freiburg 2007) 19–33.

K. S. FUGLSETH, 'Filons forhold til tempelet i Jerusalem i eit apologetisk perspektiv,' in A. Klostergaard PETERSEN *et al.* (eds.), *Perspektiver på jødisk apologetik*, Antikken og kristendommen 4 (København 2007) 263–82.

S. GAMBETTI, 'A Brief Note on Agrippa I's Trip to Alexandria in the Summer of 38 CE,' *Journal of Jewish Studies* 58 (2007) 33–38.

F. GARCÍA MARTÍNEZ, 'Divine Sonship at Qumran and in Philo,' *The Studia Philonica Annual* 19 (2007) 85–99.

A. C. GELJON, 'Didymus the Blind's Use of Philo in his Exegesis of Cain and Abel,' *Vigiliae Christianae* 61 (2007) 282–312.

A. C. GELJON, 'God in de duisternis: een Alexandijnse uitleg van Exodus 20:21,' *Hermeneus* 79 (2007) 184–190.

M. E. GORDLEY, *The Colossian Hymn in Context: An Exegesis in Light of Jewish and Greco-Roman Hymnic and Epistolary Conventions*, Wissenschaftliche Untersuchungen zum Neuen Testament 2.Reihe 228 (Tübingen 2007), esp. 105–108.

J. P. Hering, *The Colossian and Ephesian Haustafeln in Theological Context: an Analysis of their Origins, Relationship, and Message*, American University Studies Series 7, Theology and Religion 260 (New York etc. 2007).

G. HOLTZ, *Damit Gott sei alles in allem: Studien zum paulinischen und frühjüdischen Universalismus* (Berlin–New York 2007), esp. 139–167.

R. A. HORSLEY, *Wisdom and Spiritual Transcendence at Corinth: Studies in First Corinthians* (Eugene 2007).

J. HYLDAHL, 'Mellem ny og gammel kultur: Allegori i apologetisk perspektiv i aleksandrinsk jødedom,' in A. KLOSTERGAARD PETERSEN *et al.* (eds.), *Perspektiver på Jødisk Apologetik*, Antikken og kristendommen 4 (København 2007) 181–206.

O. KAISER, *Des Menschen Glück und Gottes Gerechtigkeit. Studien zur biblischen Überlieferung im Kontext hellenistischer Philosophie* (Tübingen 2007), esp. 209ff.

M. B. KARTZOW, *Gossip and Gender: Othering of Speech in the Pastoral Epistles* (diss. University of Oslo 2007), esp. 112–114.

S. W. KEOUGH, *Exegesis Worthy of God: the Development of Biblical Interpretation in Alexandria* (diss. University of Toronto 2007), esp. chap. 3.

A. KOVELMAN, 'Jeremiah 9:22–23 in Philo and Paul,' *Review of Rabbinic Judaism* 10 (2007) 162–175.

S. KRAUTER, 'Die Beteiligung von Nicht-juden am Jerusalemer Tempelkult,' in J. FREY, D. R. SCHWARTZ and S. GRIPENTROG (eds.), *Jewish Identity in the Greco-Roman World,* Ancient Judaism and Early Christianity 71 (Leiden–Boston 2007) 55–74.

M. LANDFESTER and B. EGGER (eds.), *Geschichte der antiken Texte. Autoren– und Werklexicon,* Der Neue Pauly Supplemente Band 2 (Stuttgart 2007), esp. 456–459.

P. LANFRANCHI, 'Reminiscences of Ezekiel's *Exagoge* in Philo's *De vita Mosis,*' in A. GRAUPNER and M. WOLTER (eds.), *Moses in Biblical and Extra-Biblical Traditions* (Berlin–New York 2007) 144–150.

K. D. LAVERY, *Abraham's Dialogue with God over the Destruction of Sodom: Chapters in the History of the Interpretation of Genesis 18* (diss. Harvard University 2007).

J. LEONHARDT-BALZER, 'Jewish Worship and Universal Identity in Philo of Alexandria,' in J. FREY, D. R. SCHWARTZ and S. GRIPENTROG (eds.), *Jewish Identity in the Greco-Roman World,* Ancient Judaism and Early Christianity 71 (Leiden–Boston 2007) 29–54.

C. LÉVY, 'La question de la dyade chez Philon d'Alexandrie,' in M. BONAZZI, C. LÉVY and C. STEEL (eds.), *A Platonic Pythagoras. Platonism and Pythagoreanism in the Imperial Age,* Monothéismes et Philosophie 10 (Turnhout 2007) 11–28.

A. LIEBER, 'Between Motherland and Fatherland: Diaspora, Pilgrimage and Spiritualization of Sacrifice in Philo of Alexandria,' in L. LI DONNICI and A. LIEBER (eds.), *Heavenly Tablets: Interpretation, Identity and Tradition in Ancient Judaism,* Supplements to the Journal for the Study of Judaism 119 (Leiden 2007) 193–210.

N. E. LIVESEY, *Circumcision as a Malleable Symbol: Treatments of Circumcision in Philo, Paul, and Justin Martyr* (diss. Southern Methodist University 2007).

J. P. LOTZ, *Ignatius and Concord: the Background and Use of the Language of Concord in the Letters of Ignatius of Antioch,* Patristic Studies 8 (New York 2007).

A. LOUTH, *The Origins of the Christian Mystical Tradition: from Plato to Denys,* 2nd ed (Oxford 2007).

S. D. MACKIE, *Eschatology and Exhortation in the Epistle to the Hebrews,* Wissenschaftliche Untersuchungen zum Neuen Testament 2. Reihe 223 (Tübingen 2007), esp. 108–111, 117–122.

J. MAIER, 'Bezeugung der Bibel,' in A. GRABNER-HAIDER (ed.), *Kulturgeschichte der Bibel* (Göttingen 2007) 181–211.

J. P. MARTÍN, 'Il primo convegno italiano su Filone di Alessandria,' *Adamantius* 13 (2007) 276–281.

A. M. MAZZANTI, 'Filone di Alssandria,' in U. MATTIOLI, A. CACCIARI and V. NERI (eds.), *Senectus. La vecchiaia nell'antichità ebraica e cristiana. Vol. III Ebraismo e cristianesimo* (Bologna 2007) 99–109.

A. M. MBUVI, *Temple, Exile, and Identity in 1 Peter*, Library of New Testament Studies 345 (London etc. 2007).

L. H. MILLS, *Zaratoustra, Philo, the Achaemenids and Israel, Part II: Being a Treatise Upon the Antiquity and Influence of the Avesta* (Whitefish MT 2007).

M. MIRA, Art. 'Filone di Alessandria,' in L. F. MATEO-SECO and G. MASPERO (eds.), *Gregorio di Nissa. Dizionario* (Rome 2007) 287–289.

H. NAJMAN, 'Philosophical Contemplation and Revelatory Inspiration in Ancient Judean Traditions,' *The Studia Philonica Annual* 19 (2007) 101–111.

M. R. NIEHOFF, 'Homeric Scholarship and Bible Exegesis in Ancient Alexandria: Evidence from Philo's 'Quarrelsome' Colleagues,' *Classical Quarterly* 57, no. 1 (2007) 166–182.

M. R. NIEHOFF, 'Did the *Timaeus* Create a Textual Community?' *Greek, Roman, and Byzantine Studies* 47 (2007) 161–191, esp. 170–177.

F. OERTELT, 'Vom Nutzen der Musik. Ein Blick auf die Funktion der musikalischen Ausbildung bei Philo von Alexandrien,' in A. STANDHARTINGER, H. SCHWEBEL and F. OERTELT (eds.), *Kunst der Deutung—Deutung der Kunst: Beiträge zu Bibel, Antike und Gegenwartsliteratur. FS Sieghild von Blumenthal* (Münster 2007) 51–62.

M. OSMANSKI, *Filona z Aleksandrii: etyke upodabniania sie do Boga* (Lublin 2007).

S. J. K. PEARCE, *The Land of the Body: Studies in Philo's Representation of Egypt*, Wissenschaftliche Untersuchungen zum Neuem Testament 204 (Tübingen 2007).

S. J. K. PEARCE, 'Philo on the Nile,' in J. FREY, D. R. SCHWARTZ and S. GRIPENTROG (eds.), *Jewish Identity in the Greco-Roman World*, Ancient Judaism and Early Christianity 71 (Leiden–Boston 2007) 137–157.

B. PEARSON, 'Earliest Christianity in Egypt: Further Observations,' in J. E. GOEHRING and J. TIMBIE (eds.), *The World of Early Egyptian Christianity: Language, Literature, and Social Context: Essays in Honor of David W. Johnson* (Washington DC 2007).

A. K. PETERSEN, 'Filon som apologet—en læsning af De migratione Abrahami,' in *Perspektiver på Jødisk Apologetik*, Antikken og kristendommen 4 (København 2007) 233–262.

A. PIÑERO, *Literatura judía de época helenística en lengua griega. Desde la versión de la biblia al griego hasta el Nuevo Testamento* (Madrid 2007).

P. K. Pohjala, *Divination by Bowls in Bible, Septuagint, Qumran Texts, Philo and Matthew 13:1–12: Magnified Visions from Glass Bowls in Bible Interpretation* (London 2007).

E. Regev, *Sectarianism in Qumran: a Cross-Cultural Perspective,* Religion and Society 45 (Berlin 2007).

D. Robertson, *Word and Meaning in Ancient Alexandria: Theories of Language from Philo to Plotinus* (Aldershot 2007).

D. T. Runia, 'Philo in the Reformational Tradition,' in R. Sweetman (ed.), *In the Phrygian Mode: Neocalvinism, Antiquity and the Lamentations of Reformed Philosophy,* Christian Perspectives Today (Lanham MD etc. 2007) 195–212.

D. T. Runia, 'The Rehabilitation of the Jackdaw: Philo of Alexandria and Ancient Philosophy,' in R. Sorabji and R. W. Sharples (eds.), *Greek and Roman Philosophy 100 BC–200 AD* (London 2007) 483–500.

D. T. Runia, E. Birnbaum, K. A. Fox, A. C. Geljon, H. M. Keizer, J. P. Martín, R. Radice, J. Riaud, D. Satran, G. Schimanowski and T. Seland, 'Philo of Alexandria: an Annotated Bibliography 2004,' *The Studia Philonica Annual* 19 (2007) 143–204.

D. T. Runia and G. E. Sterling (eds.), *The Studia Philonica Annual,* Vol. 19 (Atlanta 2007).

L. Saudelli, 'La *hodos anô kai katô* d'Héraclite (Fragment 22 B 60 DK/33 M) dans le *De Aeternitate Mundi* de Philon d'Alexandrie,' *The Studia Philonica Annual* 19 (2007) 29–58.

G. Schöllgen (ed.), *Reallexikon für Antike und Christentum Lieferungen 170* (Stuttgart 2007).

M. Simon-Shoshan, 'The Tasks of the Translators: the Rabbis, the Septuagint, and the Cultural Politics of Translation,' *Prooftexts* 27 (2007) 1–39.

G. E. Sterling, 'The First Theologian: The Originality of Philo of Alexandria,' *Princeton Theological Monograph Series* 65 (2007) 145–162.

L. T. Stuckenbruck, 'To What Extent did Philo's Treatment of Enoch and the Giants Presuppose a Knowledge of the Enochic and Other Sources Preserved in the Dead Sea Scrolls?,' *The Studia Philonica Annual* 19 (2007) 131–142.

J. E. Taylor, 'Philo of Alexandria on the Essenes: A Case Study on the Use of Classical Sources in Discussions of the Qumran-Essene Hypothesis,' *The Studia Philonica Annual* 19 (2007) 1–28.

C. Termini, 'Isacco, ovvero la dinamica del riso in Filone di Alessandria,' in C. Mazzucco (ed.), *Riso e comicità nel cristianesimo antico. Atti del convegno di Torino, 14–16 febbraio 2005, e altri studi* (Alessandria 2007) 123–160.

C. Termini, 'La Scrittura nei tre grandi commenti di Filone di Alessandria: forme e metodi esegetici,' *Ricerche Storico-Bibliche* 19 (2007) 47–73.

C. TIBBS, *Religious Experience of the Pneuma: Communication with the Spirit World in 1 Corinthians 12 and 14*, Wissenschaftliche Untersuchungen zum Neuen Testament 2.Reihe 230 (Tübingen 2007), esp. 125–131.

P. J. TOMSON, *Blessing in Disguise: eulogeo and eucharisteo between 'Biblical' and Everyday Greek Usage*, Voces Biblicae (Leuven–Dudley MA 2007).

R. M. VICTOR, *Colonial Education and Class Formation in Early Judaism: A Postcolonial Reading* (diss. Texas Christian University 2007).

D. WINSTON, 'Philo of Alexandria on the Rational and Irrational Emotions,' in J. T. FITZGERALD (ed.), *Passions and Moral Progress in Greco-Roman Thought* (London–New York 2007) 201–220.

S. M. B. Zorzi, *Desiderio della bellezza* (ἔρως τοῦ καλοῦ). *Da Platone a Gregorio di Nissa: tracce di una rifrazione teologico-semantica*, Studia Anselminana 145. Historia theologiae 1 (Rome 2007), esp. 181–199.

2008

F. ALESSE (ed.), *Philo of Alexandria and Post-Aristotelian Philosophy*, Studies on Philo of Alexandria 5 (Leiden–Boston 2008).

J. S. ALLEN, *The Despoliation of Egypt in Pre-Rabbinic, Rabbinic and Patristic Traditions*, Supplements to Vigiliae Christianae 92 (Leiden–Boston 2008), esp. 91–117 and passim.

M. A. BADER, *Tracing the Evidence: Dinah in Post-Hebrew Bible Literature*, Studies in Biblical Literature 162 (New York 2008).

S. BADILITA, 'Retraite au désert et solitude du prophète chez Philon,' *Adamantius* 14 (2008) 43–51.

P. J. BEKKEN, 'The Controversy on Self-Testimony According to John 5:31–40; 8:12–20 and Philo, Legum Allegoriae III.205–208,' in B. HOLMBERG and M. WINNINGE (eds.), *Identity Formation in the New Testament*, Wissenschaftliche Untersuchungen zum Neuen Testament 2.227 (Tübingen 2008) 19–42.

R. M. VAN DEN BERG, *Proclus' Commentary on the Cratylus in Context: Ancient Theories of Language and Naming*, Philosophia Antiqua 112 (Leiden–Boston 2008), esp. 52–56.

M. BOERI, 'Estrategias argumentativas filonianas en *De aeternitate* y *De providentia*,' *Nova Tellus* 26 (2008) 39–65.

M. BONAZZI, 'Towards Transcendence: Philo and the Renewal of Platonism in the Early Imperial Age,' in F. ALESSE (ed.), *Philo of Alexandria and Post-Aristotelian Philosophy*, Studies on Philo of Alexandria 5 (Leiden–Boston 2008) 13–52.

E. BOVO and C. LÉVY, 'Le 'je' de l'être juif chez Philon d'Alexandrie et Lévinas,' *Antiquorum Philosophia* 2 (2008) 137–156.

F. CALABI, '*Eremia*. Il deserto di Filone Alessandrino,' *Adamantius* 14 (2008) 9–23.

F. CALABI, *God's Acting, Man's Acting: Tradition and Philosophy in Philo of Alexandria*, Studies in Philo of Alexandria 4 (Leiden–Boston 2008).

C. CARLIER, *La Cité de Moïse*, Monothéismes et Philosophie 11 (Turnhout 2008).

D. CIARLO, 'De mutatione nominum. L'interpretazione del cambiamento dei nomi biblici da Filone Alessandrino a Giovanni Crisostomo,' *Augustinianum* 48 (2008) 149–204.

J. DILLON, 'Philo and Hellenistic Platonism,' in F. ALESSE (ed.), *Philo of Alexandria and Post-Aristotelian Philosophy*, Studies on Philo of Alexandria 5 (Leiden–Boston 2008) 223–232.

H. DÖRRIE, M. BALTES, C. PIETSCH and M.-L. LAKMANN, *Die philosophische Lehre des Platonismus: Theologia Platonica. Bausteine 182–205: Text, Übersetzung, Kommentar*, Der Platonismus in der Antike 7.1 (Stuttgart-Bad Cannstatt 2008) esp. 108–110, 414–415.

T. R. ELSSNER, *Josua und seine Kriege in jüdischer und christlicher Rezeptionsgeschichte*, Theologie und Frieden 37 (Stuttgart 2008).

L. H. FELDMAN, 'Philo's Interpretation of Korah,' in K. E. POMYKALA (ed.), *Israel in the Wilderness. Interpretations of the Biblical Narratives in Jewish and Christian Traditions*, Themes in Biblical Narrative. Jewish and Christian Traditions 10 (Leiden–Boston 2008) 55–70.

E. FILLER, 'Description of the Creation by Philo in the Light of the Neopythagorean Theory of Numbers [Hebrew],' *Daat* 62 (2008) 5–26.

E. FILLER, 'The Nature of Number Seven in Propensity Towards Number One in Philo [Hebrew],' *Daat* 63 (2008) 5–26.

S. GOLBERG, 'The Two Choruses Become One: The Absence–Presence of Women in Philo's On the Contemplative Life,' *Journal for the Study of Judaism in the Persian, Hellenistic and Roman period* 39 (2008) 459–470.

R. GOUNELLE, and J. M. PRIEUR (eds.), *Le Décalogue au miroir des Pères*, Cahiers de Biblia Patristica 9 (Strasbourg 2008).

M. GRAVER, 'Philo of Alexandria and the Origins of the Stoic ΠΡΟΠΑΘΕΙΑΙ,' in F. ALESSE (ed.), *Philo of Alexandria and Post-Aristotelian Philosophy*, Studies on Philo of Alexandria 5 (Leiden–Boston 2008) 197–221.

L. GUSELLA, 'Il deserto dei Terapeuti a confronto con quello di Esseni e Qumraniei,' *Adamantius* 14 (2008) 52–66.

M. HADAS-LEBEL, 'Le désert lieu de la parole,' *Adamantius* 14 (2008) 39–42.

H. HANAFI, 'Philo of Alexandria: A Contribution to the Greek–Egyptian–Jewish Dialogue,' *Diotima* 36 (2008) 74–78.

J. HERZER, 'Zwischen Loyalität und Machtstreben. Sozialgeschichliche Aspecckte des Pilatusbuldes bei Josephus und im Neuen Testament,' in

C. Böttrich and J. Herzer (eds.), *Josephus und das Neue Testament. Wechselseitige Wahrnehmungen*, WUNT 209 (Tübingen 2008) 429–450.

K. Klun, 'From the Decalogue to Natural Law: from the Philosophy of Philo of Alexandria [Slovenian],' *Phainomena: Journal of Phenomenology and Hermeneutics* 17 (2008) 27–61.

E. Koskenniemi, 'Moses—A Well-Educated Man: A Look at the Educational Idea in Early Judaism,' *Journal for the Study of the Pseudepigrapha* 17 (2008) 281–296.

C. Lévy, *Les Scepticismes*, Bibliographie thématique «Que sais-je» 2829 (Paris 2008), esp. 84–87.

C. Lévy, 'La conversion du scepticisme chez Philon d'Alexandrie,' in F. Alesse (ed.), *Philo of Alexandria and Post-Aristotelian Philosophy*, Studies on Philo of Alexandria 5 (Leiden–Boston 2008) 103–120.

A. A. Long, 'Philo and Stoic Physics,' in F. Alesse (ed.), *Philo of Alexandria and Post-Aristotelian Philosophy*, Studies on Philo of Alexandria 5 (Leiden–Boston 2008) 121–140.

S. Lorenzen, *Das paulinische Eikon-Konzept. Semantische Analysen zur Sapientia Salomonis, zu Philo und den Paulusbriefen*, Wissenschaftliche Untersuchungen zum Neuen Testament 2.250 (Tübingen 2008).

H. Margaritou Andrianesi, 'On Philo's Platonism. The Natural Laws of Consequences in Philo,' *Diotima* 36 (2008) 52–73.

M. W. Martin, 'Progymnastic Topic Lists: A Compositional Template for Luke and Other Bioi,' *New Testament Studies* 54 (2008) 18–41.

E. F. Mason, *'You are a Priest Forever': Second Temple Jewish Messianism and the Priestly Christology of the Epistle to the Hebrews*, Studies on the Texts of the Desert of Judah 74 (Leiden–Boston 2008).

A. M. Mazzanti, 'L'Egitto e il deserto: la dispersione e l'aggressione all'anima. Note a *Legum allegoriae* II.84–87,' *Adamantius* 14 (2008) 31–38.

P. Mpungu Muzinga, *La pratique des rituels de Nombres 19 pendant la période hellénistique et romain*, Études bibliques 58 (Pendé 2008).

E. Muehlberger, 'The Representation of Theatricality in Philo's Embassy to Gaius,' *Journal for the Study of Judaism* 39 (2008) 46–67.

J. H. Newman, 'The Composition of Prayers and Songs in Philo's *De vita contemplativa*,' in A. Houtman, A. D. Jong and M. Misset-van de Weg (eds.), *Empsychoi Logoi—Religious Innovations in Antiquity. Studies in Honour of Pieter Willem van der Horst*, Ancient Judaism and Early Christianity 73 (Leiden–Boston 2008) 457–468.

M. R. Niehoff, 'Questions and Answers in Philo and *Genesis Rabbah*,' *Journal for the Study of Judaism* 39 (2008) 337–366.

J. S. O'Leary, 'Japanese Studies of Philo, Clement and Origen,' *Adamantius* 14 (2008) 395–402.

T. E. Phillips, 'Will the Wise Person Get Drunk?'. The Background of the Human Wisdom in Luke 7:35 and Matthew 11:19,' *Journal of Biblical Literature* 127 (2008) 385–396.

R. Radice, 'Philo and Stoic Ethics. Reflections on the Idea of Freedom,' in F. Alesse (ed.), *Philo of Alexandria and Post-Aristotelian Philosophy,* Studies on Philo of Alexandria 5 (Leiden–Boston 2008) 141–167.

I. Ramelli 'Philosophical Allegoresis of Scripture in Philo and Its Legacy in Gregory of Nyssa,' *The Studia Philonica Annual* 20 (2008) 55–100.

G. Ranocchia, 'Moses against the Egyptian: the Anti-Epicurean Polemic in Philo,' in F. Alesse (ed.), *Philo of Alexandria and Post-Aristotelian Philosophy,* Studies on Philo of Alexandria 5 (Leiden–Boston 2008) 75–102.

G. Reydams-Schils, 'Philo of Alexandria on Stoic and Platonist Psycho-Physiology: the Socratic Higher Ground,' in F. Alesse (ed.), *Philo of Alexandria and Post-Aristotelian Philosophy,* Studies on Philo of Alexandria 5 (Leiden–Boston 2008) 169–195.

A. Runesson, D. D. Binder and B. Olsson (eds.), *The Ancient Synagogue from its Origins to 200 C.E.: A Source Book* (Leiden–Boston 2008).

D. T. Runia, 'Worshipping the Visible Gods: Conflict and Accommodation in Hellenism, Hellenistic Judaism and Early Christianity,' in A. Houtman, A. D. Jong and M. Misset-van de Weg (eds.), *Empsychoi Logoi—Religious Innovations in Antiquity. Studies in Honour of Pieter Willem van der Horst,* Ancient Judaism and Early Christianity 73 (Leiden–Boston 2008).

D. T. Runia, 'Philo and Hellenistic Doxography,' in F. Alesse (ed.), *Philo of Alexandria and Post-Aristotelian Philosophy,* Studies on Philo of Alexandria 5 (Leiden–Boston 2008) 13–52.

D. T. Runia, E. Birnbaum, K. A. Fox, A. C. Geljon, H. M. Keizer, J. P. Martín, M. R. Niehoff, J. Riaud, G. Schimanowski and T. Seland, 'Philo of Alexandria: an Annotated Bibliography 2005,' *The Studia Philonica Annual* 20 (2008) 167–209.

D. T. Runia and G. E. Sterling (eds.), *The Studia Philonica Annual,* Vol. 20 (Atlanta 2008).

R. W. Sharples, 'Philo and Post-Aristotelian Peripatetics,' in F. Alesse (ed.), *Philo of Alexandria and Post-Aristotelian Philosophy,* Studies on Philo of Alexandria 5 (Leiden–Boston 2008) 55–73.

P. M. Sprinkle, *Law and Life: the Interpretation of Leviticus 18:5 in Early Judaism and in Paul,* Wissenschaftliche Untersuchungen zum Neuen Testament 2.241 (Tübingen 2008).

E. Starobinski-Safran, 'Le thème du désert dans le Midrach et chez Philon d'Alexandrie,' *Adamantius* 14 (2008) 67–78.

E. WASSERMAN, *The Death of the Soul in Romans 7: Sin, Death, and the Law in Light of Hellenistic Moral Psychology*, Wissenschaftliche Untersuchungen zum Neuen Testament 2.256 (Tübingen 2008).

E. WASSERMAN, 'Paul among the Philosophers: The Case of Sin in Romans 6–8,' *Journal for the Study of the New Testament* 30 (2008) 387–415.

B. G. WOLD, 'Ethics in 4QInstruction and the New Testament,' *Novum Testamentum* 50 (2008) 286–300.

J. WOYKE, 'Nochmals zu den 'schwachen und unfähigen Elementen' (Gal. 4.9): Paulus, Philo und διε στοιχεῖα τοῦ κόσμου,' *New Testament Studies* 54 (2008) 221–234.

D. ZELLER, 'Schöpfungsglaube und fremde Religion bei Philo von Alexandrien,' in L. BORMANN (ed.), *Schöpfung, Monotheismus und fremde Religionen*, Biblisch-Theologische Studien 95 (Neukirchen-Vluyn 2008) 125–148.

X. ZHANG, *Feiluo sixiang daolun II: youtai de lüfa he ziwo de zhiliao [An Introduction to the Thought of Philo (II): The Jewish Law and Self-Therapy]* (Beijing 2008).

2009

F. ALESSE, '*Prohairesis* in Philo of Alexandria,' in B. DECHARNEUX and S. INOWLOCKI (eds.), *Philon d'Alexandrie. Un penseur à l'intersection des cultures gréco-romaine, orientale, juive et chrétienne*, Monothéismes et philosophie (Turnhout 2009).

M. ALEXANDRE, 'Monarchie divine et dieux des nations chez Philon d'Alexandrie,' in B. DECHARNEUX and S. INOWLOCKI (eds.), *Philon d'Alexandrie. Un penseur à l'intersection des cultures gréco-romaine, orientale, juive et chrétienne*, Monothéismes et philosophie (Turnhout 2009).

K. BERTHELOT, 'Grecs, Barbares et Juifs dans l'œuvre de Philon,' in B. DECHARNEUX and S. INOWLOCKI (eds.), *Philon d'Alexandrie. Un penseur à l'intersection des cultures gréco-romaine, orientale, juive et chrétienne*, Monothéismes et philosophie (Turnhout 2009).

E. BIRNBAUM, 'Who Celebrated on Pharos with the Jews? Conflicting Philonic Currents and Their Implications,' in B. DECHARNEUX and S. INOWLOCKI (eds.), *Philon d'Alexandrie. Un penseur à l'intersection des cultures gréco-romaine, orientale, juive et chrétienne*, Monothéismes et philosophie (Turnhout 2009).

A. P. BOS, 'Philo on God as 'arche geneseôs',' *Journal of Jewish Studies* 60 (2009) 1–16.

M. BROZE, 'L'Égypte de Philon d'Alexandrie: approches d'un discours ambigu,' in B. DECHARNEUX and S. INOWLOCKI (eds.), *Philon d'Alexandrie.*

Un penseur à l'intersection des cultures gréco-romaine, orientale, juive et chrétienne, Monothéismes et philosophie (Turnhout 2009).

F. CALABI, 'Le repos de Dieu chez Philon d'Alexandrie,' in B. DECHARNEUX and S. INOWLOCKI (eds.), *Philon d'Alexandrie. Un penseur à l'intersection des cultures gréco-romaine, orientale, juive et chrétienne*, Monothéismes et philosophie (Turnhout 2009).

B. DECHARNEUX, 'Le Logos philonien comme fondation paradoxale de l'Évangile de Jean,' in B. DECHARNEUX and S. INOWLOCKI (eds.), *Philon d'Alexandrie. Un penseur à l'intersection des cultures gréco-romaine, orientale, juive et chrétienne*, Monothéismes et philosophie (Turnhout 2009).

B. DECHARNEUX and S. INOWLOCKI (eds.), *Philon d'Alexandrie. Un penseur à l'intersection des cultures gréco-romaine, orientale, juive et chrétienne*, Monothéismes et philosophie (Turnhout 2009).

A. C. GELJON, 'Philo's influence on Didymus the Blind,' in B. DECHARNEUX and S. INOWLOCKI (eds.), *Philon d'Alexandrie. Un penseur à l'intersection des cultures gréco-romaine, orientale, juive et chrétienne*, Monothéismes et philosophie (Turnhout 2009).

M. GOODMAN, 'Philo as a Philosopher in Rome,' in B. DECHARNEUX and S. INOWLOCKI (eds.), *Philon d'Alexandrie. Un penseur à l'intersection des cultures gréco-romaine, orientale, juive et chrétienne*, Monothéismes et philosophie (Turnhout 2009).

S. INOWLOCKI-MEISTER, 'Relectures apologétiques de Philon par Eusèbe de Césarée: le cas d'Enoch et des Thérapeutes,' in B. DECHARNEUX and S. INOWLOCKI (eds.), *Philon d'Alexandrie. Un penseur à l'intersection des cultures gréco-romaine, orientale, juive et chrétienne*, Monothéismes et philosophie (Turnhout 2009).

A. KAMESAR, 'Biblical Interpretation in Philo,' in A. KAMESAR (ed.), *The Cambridge Companion to Philo* (Cambridge etc. 2009) 65–91.

A. KAMESAR (ed.), *The Cambridge Companion to Philo* (Cambridge etc. 2009).

C. LÉVY, 'La notion de signe chez Philon d'Alexandrie,' in B. DECHARNEUX and S. INOWLOCKI (eds.), *Philon d'Alexandrie. Un penseur à l'intersection des cultures gréco-romaine, orientale, juive et chrétienne*, Monothéismes et philosophie (Turnhout 2009).

C. LÉVY, 'Philo's Ethics,' in A. KAMESAR (ed.), *The Cambridge Companion to Philo* (Cambridge etc. 2009) 146–171.

J. P. MARTÍN (ed.), *Filón de Alejandría Obras Completas*. Vol. 1 (Madrid 2009).

J. MOREAU, 'Entre Écriture sainte et *paideia*: le langage exégétique de Philon d'Alexandrie. Étude sur la pistis d'Abraham dans le *Quis rerum divinarum heres sit* 90–95,' in B. DECHARNEUX and S. INOWLOCKI (eds.), *Philon d'Alexandrie. Un penseur à l'intersection des cultures gréco-romaine, orientale, juive et chrétienne*, Monothéismes et philosophie (Turnhout 2009).

O. Munnich, 'La fugacité de la vie humane (De Josepho § 125–147): la place des motifes traditionnels dans l'élaboration de la pensée philonienne,' in B. Decharneux and S. Inowlocki (eds.), *Philon d'Alexandrie. Un penseur à l'intersection des cultures gréco-romaine, orientale, juive et chrétienne,* Monothéismes et philosophie (Turnhout 2009).

M. R. Niehoff, 'Recherche homérique et exégèse biblique à Alexandrie: un fragment sur la Tour de Babel préservé par Philon,' in B. Decharneux and S. Inowlocki (eds.), *Philon d'Alexandrie. Un penseur à l'intersection des cultures gréco-romaine, orientale, juive et chrétienne,* Monothéismes et philosophie (Turnhout 2009).

F. Nobilio, 'Le chemin de l'Esprit dans l'œuvre de Philon d'Alexandrie en dans l'évangile de Jean,' in B. Decharneux and S. Inowlocki (eds.), *Philon d'Alexandrie. Un penseur à l'intersection des cultures gréco-romaine, orientale, juive et chrétienne,* Monothéismes et philosophie (Turnhout 2009).

R. Radice, 'Philo's Theology and Theory of Creation,' in A. Kamesar (ed.), *The Cambridge Companion to Philo* (Cambridge etc. 2009) 124–145.

J. R. Royse, 'The Works of Philo,' in A. Kamesar (ed.), *The Cambridge Companion to Philo* (Cambridge etc. 2009) 32–64.

D. T. Runia, 'Philo and the Christian Tradition,' in A. Kamesar (ed.), *The Cambridge Companion to Philo* (New York 2009).

D. T. Runia, 'Philo and the Early Christian Fathers,' in A. Kamesar (ed.), *The Cambridge Companion to Philo* (Cambridge etc. 2009) 210–230.

D. T. Runia, 'Why Philo of Alexandria is an Important Writer and Thinker,' in B. Decharneux and S. Inowlocki (eds.), *Philon d'Alexandrie. Un penseur à l'intersection des cultures gréco-romaine, orientale, juive et chrétienne,* Monothéismes et philosophie (Turnhout 2009).

L. Saudelli, 'Les fragments d'Héraclite et leur signification dans le *corpus philonicum*: le cas du fr. 60 DK,' in B. Decharneux and S. Inowlocki (eds.), *Philon d'Alexandrie. Un penseur à l'intersection des cultures gréco-romaine, orientale, juive et chrétienne,* Monothéismes et philosophie (Turnhout 2009).

D. R. Schwartz, 'Philo, his Family, and his Times,' in A. Kamesar (ed.), *The Cambridge Companion to Philo* (Cambridge etc. 2009) 9–31.

F. Siegert, 'Philo and the New Testament,' in A. Kamesar (ed.), *The Cambridge Companion to Philo* (Cambridge etc. 2009) 175–209.

F. Siegert, 'Philon et la philologie alexandrine. Aux origines du fondamentalisme chrétien,' in B. Decharneux and S. Inowlocki (eds.), *Philon d'Alexandrie. Un penseur à l'intersection des cultures gréco-romaine, orientale, juive et chrétienne,* Monothéismes et philosophie (Turnhout 2009).

C. TERMINI, 'Philo's Thought within the Context of Middle Judaism,' in A. KAMESAR (ed.), *The Cambridge Companion to Philo* (Cambridge etc. 2009) 95–123.

P. J. TOMSON, 'Le temple céleste: pensée platonisante et orientation apocalyptique dans l'Épître aux Hébreux,' in B. DECHARNEUX and S. INOWLOCKI (eds.), *Philon d'Alexandrie. Un penseur à l'intersection des cultures gréco-romaine, orientale, juive et chrétienne,* Monothéismes et philosophie (Turnhout 2009).

J. WEINBERG, 'La quête de Philon dans l'historiographie juive du XVIe s.,' in B. DECHARNEUX and S. INOWLOCKI (eds.), *Philon d'Alexandrie. Un penseur à l'intersection des cultures gréco-romaine, orientale, juive et chrétienne,* Monothéismes et philosophie (Turnhout 2009).

S. WEISSER, 'La figure du προκόπτων (progressant) ou la proximité de la sagesse,' in B. DECHARNEUX and S. INOWLOCKI (eds.), *Philon d'Alexandrie. Un penseur à l'intersection des cultures gréco-romaine, orientale, juive et chrétienne,* Monothéismes et philosophie (Turnhout 2009).

D. WINSTON, 'Philo and the Rabbinic Literature,' in A. KAMESAR (ed.), *The Cambridge Companion to Philo* (Cambridge etc. 2009) 231–253.

The Studia Philonica Annual 21 (2009) 125–144

BOOK REVIEW SECTION

LOUIS H. FELDMAN, *Philo's Portrayal of Moses in the Context of Ancient Judaism*. Christianity and Judaism in Antiquity Series 15. Notre Dame, Ind.: University of Notre Dame Press, 2007. 542 pages. ISBN 978-0-268-02900-5. Price $80.

Louis Feldman, Abraham Wouk Family Professor of Classics and Literature at Yeshiva University, is a well-known scholar who has published a great number of studies in which he compares Philo's portrait of biblical figures with the treatment by other writers, such as Josephus and Pseudo-Philo. He also wrote a commentary on Josephus' *Judean Antiquities*.

In Feldman's lengthy monograph, *Philo's Portrayal of Moses in the Context of Ancient Judaism*, published in 2007, he places Philo's presentation of the figure of Moses within the broader context of ancient Judaism. In Part I the author discusses some general questions concerning Philo's *De vita Moysis*. He argues that this treatise is a kind of official biography of the most important figure in Judaism and is directed to a non-Jewish audience. The absence of complicated allegorical exegesis is, among other things, indicative. Another important issue in the discussion of *Mos.* is its place within the entire Philonic corpus and the kind of genre to which it belongs. Feldman classifies the treatise as an aretology, i.e. a work in which a hero's excellence and virtues are praised. Examples can be found in Diogenes Laertius, but the example *par excellence* is Socrates, as he is presented in the writings of Plato. Feldman also refers to *Mos.* as an encomium, which enhances Moses' qualities. Aretology and encomium, the characteristics of which are listed by Feldman, overlap each other partly, and their relationship is not clear to me. If they are the same, why does Feldman use both terms? If they are different, Feldman has to explain the difference. Significant is that in *Mos.* Philo never mentions the names of Moses' parents, wife and sons, so that the focus is solely on the figure of Moses. Another characteristic of Philo's presentation of Moses' life is that the miracles told in the biblical account are explained rationally, as is the case with the ten plagues, which Philo tries to explain scientifically in order not to offend intellectual readers.

In Part II Feldman discusses Philo's portrait of Moses' life from his birth until his death. Moses' life is divided into short episodes and in each episode Feldman analyses Philo's description, notes differences with the biblical narrative, refers to other authors and explains why Philo presents Moses in the way he does. The focus is primarily on *Mos.*, but other treatises are also involved. Feldman refers not only to Greco-Jewish authors like Eupolemus, Aristobulus, Artapanus, Josephus, and Ezekiel Tragicus, but also to rabbinic sources and the Samaritan tradition. The Pseudepigrapha, Apocrypha, and the Dead Sea Scrolls are also involved in the discussion, and the author notices parallels between Moses and Jesus, too. Furthermore, Feldman quotes Greek and Latin writers who mention Moses, such as Hecataeus, Galen, and Quintilian.

Part III is devoted to an examination of the virtues which Philo ascribes to Moses. Moses represents the epitome of virtue: he not only possesses the four cardinal virtues—wisdom, courage, temperance, and justice—but also the virtue which Philo calls the queen of virtues, piety. It is through piety that Moses gains the offices of king, lawgiver, prophet, and high priest. Feldman extensively discusses the important question whether Philo presents Moses as a god. He argues that Philo strongly rejects the view that a human being can be deified. Philo refers to Moses as second to God, as God's friend, as co-ruler with God, but he opposes the Samaritan tradition, in which Moses is nearly deified, and the Roman divinization of the emperor.

In his conclusion Feldman states that Philo's Moses is the Jewish equivalent of Plato's philosopher-king, who is also the greatest legislator, and a model high priest. As a prophet he has a unique relationship with God. By way of contrast, Pseudo-Philo's Moses is only an intercessor with God, whereas Josephus, basing himself on Thucydides' portrait of Pericles, presents the Jewish leader as an excellent general. There is also a difference between Philo's portrait in *Mos.* and in his other treatises. *Mos.* is intended for non-Jews in order to show the greatness of the Jewish leader and legislator. For this reason in this treatise Philo avoids complicated allegorical and philosophical exegesis. Generally, he remains loyal to the biblical account with a few exceptions. Moses' education, for instance, is not mentioned in Exodus. It is, among other things, through his education that Moses becomes the philosopher-king, who sees the Platonic world of ideas on Mount Sinai. Philo's presentation of Moses as philosopher-king is a Jewish answer to Plato's *Republic*.

The book contains useful indices: of ancient texts, of names and subjects, of Greek, Latin, and Hebrew words, and of modern scholars, all of which make it easier to consult the rich material that Feldman presents. This monograph is a great achievement. Thanks to Feldman's profound knowledge not only of a great number of Greek and Latin writers, but also of the rabbinic tradition, it offers a mine of information of the figure of Moses, who was so very important for Philo's thought. It is a must for every Philonic scholar.

Albert C. Geljon
Utrecht

ALEX GRAUPNER and MICHAEL WOLTER, eds. *Moses in Biblical and Extra-Biblical Traditions*. BZAW 372. Berlin/New York: Walter de Gruyter, 2007. Pp. viii + 277. Price $123. ISBN 978-3-11-019460-9.

This collection of sixteen essays is the result of a conference held on January 5–7, 2006 at Bonn, in which members of the faculties of Leiden, Oxford, and Bonn participated. The essays explore specific issues about Moses in Jewish and Christian literature from the Hebrew Bible through the early Church. The sixteen essays fall into six large literature groupings: the Torah, the later parts of the Hebrew Bible and LXX, the Dead Sea Scrolls, Philo, the New Testament, and the Early Church.

The first three essays explore various issues within the Torah. Mark J. Harris, "How did Moses part the Red Sea? Science as salvation in the Exodus tradition," tackles the issue of the miraculous by contrasting the naturalistic and miraculous explanations of the event at the Sea. He provides a useful summary of the basic naturalistic explanations. He suggests that biblical scholars prefer mundane explanations while scientists prefer the more spectacular but rational explanations. He concludes that critical interpretation works best when a plurality of views are held in creative tension. While polyvalency is a good principle, it should not be used as a means of avoiding coming to grips with a significant literary and conceptual issue. Axel Graupner, "'Ihr sollt mir ein Königreich von Priestern und ein heiliges Volk sein': Erwägungen zur Funktion von Ex 19,3b–8 innerhalb der Sinaiperikope," analyzes the narrative role of Exod 19:3b–8. He understands the expression ממלכת כהנים to be a subjective genitive and translates it as "ein Königreich, das von Priestern regiert wird." He thinks that the text is a parenthetical insertion that is connected both with 24:3–8 and with Gen 17. It serves as a proem to introduce the Sinai pericope. The text emphasizes Israel's special status by tying status with obedience to the covenant. Udo Rüterswörden, "Moses' Last Day," uses a form of reader response criticism to argue that the fourteen speeches of Moses across the Jordan present Moses as a law-interpreter, not a law-giver. The task of Deuteronomy is to replicate the situation of the readers in the exile for the implied reader of the book. The entry into the land is thus paradigmatic not only for the original exilic readers, but for the implied reader. It is a creative reading of Deuteronomy.

The next three essays explore the place of Moses in other biblical texts. Sebastian Grätz, "'Einen Propheten wie mich wird dir der Herr, dein Gott, erwecken.' Der Berufungsbericht Jeremias und seine Rückbindung an das Amt des Mose," analyzes the relationship of Jeremiah to Moses. He notes that Jer 1:4–10 offers a key theological perspective for the prophetic book. He makes three observations based on a comparison of this text to the Moses traditions: only a prophet may be in succession to Moses (Deut 18:18//Jer 1:9), the call narratives share four common elements as a result of Deuteronomistic influence (Exod 3:9-12//Judg 6:14–21//Jer 1:5–9), and Jer 1:5 builds not only on Deut 18:15 but also on Ps 2:7 and Isa 49:1, 5 to emphasize succession. Johannes Schnocks, "Mose in Psalter," surveys the eight references to Moses in the Psalter (77:21; 90:1; 99:6; 103:7; 105:26; 106:16, 23, 32). He notes that they are basically in Book 4 (Ps 90–106) and suggests that there are three movements within Book 4 that respond to the portrait of David in Ps 89: Ps 90–92, 102–103 offer Moses as an alternative to David; Ps 93–100 present the kingdom of Yahweh as it is grounded in creation and the temple with Moses as a priest (99:6); and Ps 104–106 promote Moses as a national figure. Arie van der Kooij, "Moses and the Septuagint of the Pentateuch," explores some of the texts in the Septuagintal translation of the Pentateuch to determine how they understood Moses. He points out that Lev 26:46 translates the Hebrew התורת with the singular ὁ νόμος, referring to the entire book of Leviticus. He understands the use of πυξίον rather than πλάξ in Exod 24:12 to be a reference to Deuteronomy. This leads him to τὸ δευτερονόμιον in Deut 17:18 that he understands to refer to a "second law" in contrast to Exodus–Numbers; however, he thinks that the second law is the civil law rather than the priestly law based on the distinction between priestly rule and the *gerousia* as the Jewish community was structured in the Hellenistic world. The essay is a good example of how the LXX can be read against its own setting rather than as a literal translation of the Hebrew text.

The next three contributions examine the role of Moses at Qumran, focusing heavily on 4Q377. Wido van Peursen, "Who was standing on the mountain? The portrait of Moses in 4Q377," argues correctly—in my opinion—that God was standing before the people in l. 8, not Moses; Moses is only human, not divine. Phoebe Makiello, "Was Moses considered to be an angel by those at Qumran?," argues against C. Fletcher-Louis who maintained that the covenanters considered Moses divine. She concentrates on 4Q374 frg ii ll. 6–10 and 4Q377 frg 1. Moses is compared to an angel (4Q377 frg 1 ll. 10–12); however, she notes that the comparison does not give him divine status since it does not equate him with an angel. Heinz-Josef Fabry, "Mose, der 'Gesalbte JHWHs'. Messianische Aspekte der Mose-Interpretation in Qumran," draws a similar conclusion based on an overview of the texts at Qumran that mention Moses. The key text is, once again, 4Q377. Fabry contends that it presents Moses in a prophetic role, but distinguishes between Moses as the beginning of the prophetic movement and an eschatological prophet who will announce the Messiah. There is a remarkable convergence of opinion in these three essays in rejecting claims of divine status for Moses at Qumran. While there are Second Temple texts that appear to give Moses a divine status, 4Q374 and 377 do not appear to be among their number.

The next two contributions consider Philo's portrait of Moses. Pierluigi Lanfranchi, "Remininscences of Ezekiel's *Exagoge* in Philo's *De vita Mosis*," correctly maintains that Philo knew the Hellenistic tragedy of Ezekiel. He works through a number of lexical and exegetical parallels to demonstrate this. He suggests that this gave a theatrical dimension to Philo's own presentation. Unfortunately the opening of the initial section of Lanfranchi's essay is missing (pp. 144–45): a page has obviously fallen out in the process of publication. While others have noted the similarities between the two texts previously, Lanfranchi's analysis is the most comprehensive to date. The implication that he drew from this evidence, that Philo learned his theatrical dimension from Ezekiel, overstates the case since Philo frequented theaters (*Ebr.* 177; *Prob.* 141) and undoubtedly read other tragedies, especially Euripides, e.g., he cites Aeschylus in *Prob.* 143, Sophocles in *Prob.* 19 and Euripides in *Leg.* 1.7; 3.202; *Ios.* 78 and *Prob.* 25, 99; *Spec.* 4.47; *Prob.* 101–104, 116, 141, 146, 152(?); and *Aet.* 5, 30, 144. Hywel Clifford, "Moses as Philosopher-Sage in Philo," examines Philo's portrait of Moses as a philosopher, a sage, and a philosopher-sage. He provides a solid treatment of the topic, although he does not break new ground. Readers might want to consult Louis Feldman's *Philo's Portrayal of Moses in the Context of Ancient Judaism* (Notre Dame: University of Notre Dame Press, 2007), that appeared after Clifford presented his paper (see the review elsewhere in this Annual).

The next two essays explore aspects of the place of Moses in the New Testament. John Muddiman, "The Assumption of Moses and the Epistle of Jude," is a defense of the traditional reconstruction of the *Assumption of Moses* and Jude's use of it. He sets this against the recent reconstruction of Richard Bauckham. Muddiman defends the presence of an assumption at the end of the text and argues that the text refers to Michael's restraint in his dispute with the Devil over Moses' body rather than the devil's slander against Moses for having murdered the Egyptian. It is an impressive critique. Stefan Schapdick, "Religious authority re-evaluated: the character of Moses in the Fourth Gospel," surveys the twelve occurrences of Moses in the Fourth Gospel. All of the references appear in the Book of Signs (chapters 1–12). He concludes that the law is valid, but must be evaluated in light of the soteriological significance of Christ. Moses is a witness to Christ and is more than the author of the law: he has life-saving events in his life. However, there is now a conflict between followers of Christ and Judaism for whom Moses is the supreme religious authority. Johannes Tromp, "Jannes and Jambres (2 Timothy 3, 8–9)," argues that the reference to Jannes and Jambres in the Pastorals does not draw from *The Apocryphon of Jannes and Jambres*, but from a tradition that is also attested in CD5.17–19 that, like the reference in the Pastorals, attributes stupidity to those who leave the faith.

The final two essays explore Moses in early Christian literature. Christopher M. Tuckett, "Moses in Gnostic Writings," points out that Moses is seldom referred to in Gnostic writings and when he or his writings are mentioned, it is to offer an alternative reading to the creation stories. He therefore challenges the view that Gnosticism had its roots in Judaism and suggests that we should rather look in the direction of "some kind of radicalized Platonism" (p. 240). While this issue would require a much larger analysis, the essay is provocative. In a perceptive essay, Sabrina Inowlocki, "Eusebius' Appropriation of Moses in an Apologetic Context," asks why Eusebius elected to portray Constantine as a new Moses. She points out that Eusebius glorified Moses as a Hebrew in *PE* when he was addressing a pagan-Christian debate, but was less enthusiastic in *DE* when he dealt with Christianity's relationship to Judaism. Moses was thus an ideal exemplum for Constantine who was neither a bishop nor an apostle. He was like Moses a man *de l'entre deux*.

Most collections of essays are uneven in quality. This is no exception. There are some fine essays that break new ground and there are others that are solid treatments of established positions but are not particularly creative or new. The strength of the collection is that it provides treatments of some of the key texts that have emerged in recent scholarship. The collection as a whole provides snapshots of how Moses was handled in important texts but does not attempt to offer a systematic presentation of the portraits of Moses or how the figure of Moses developed diachronically, although the scope of the treatments permits the reader to do this. The volume is thus useful both for those who are interested in the specific texts as well as for those who want to understand how Moses was treated in diverse settings from the exile of Judah to Eusebius.

Gregory E. Sterling
University of Notre Dame

ANDERS RUNESSON, DONALD D. BINDER and BIRGER OLSSON, eds. *The Ancient Synagogue from its Origins to 200 C.E.: A Source Book*. Ancient Judaism and Early Christianity/Arbeiten zur Geschichte des antiken Judentums und des Urchristentums 72. Leiden: Brill, 2008. xii + 322 pages. ISBN 978-90-04-16116-0. Price €139, $206.

Research into the ancient synagogue is perhaps more popular now than ever before. Recent archaeological discoveries, the reassessment of "normative" Judaism in light of the Dead Sea Scrolls and research into the "Jewishness" of early Christianity has primed the market for a number of new works on the ancient synagogue.

Among the hundreds of published studies, none has been as important or as comprehensive as Lee Levine's *The Ancient Synagogue*.[1] First issued in 2000, a revised edition was published just five years later—an indication of the focused interest on synagogue studies during the early part of the current decade. Levine's work, which attempts to cover the first thousand years, remains an essential reference volume on the ancient synagogue. While Levine's work serves as a detailed historical overview of the worship practices and culture of ancient synagogue life, the present volume provides us with the words of the synagogue members themselves. In this respect, one may read the sourcebook under review as a companion to Levine's survey, filling in the gaps where necessary.

The editors of the present work have each found his own niche within synagogue studies. Anders Runesson is co-editor of an important socio-historical study.[2] Donald Binder's published dissertation attempts to compile all of the primary sources, and thus serves as a proto-collection to the present volume.[3] Finally, Birger Olsson organized the research project at Lund University (1997–2001) which gave birth to the volume under review.

The current work attempts to compile all of the published archaeological, inscriptional, papyrological, legal, and literary sources relating to the ancient synagogue up to 200 C.E. with English translation and commentary. Students of Hellenistic Judaism will already be familiar with the

[1] *The Ancient Synagogue: The First Thousand Years* (2nd ed.; New Haven, Conn.: Yale University Press, 2005).

[2] Anders Runesson and Kari Syreeni, eds. *The Origins of the Synagogue: A Socio-Historical Study* (Stockholm: Aimquiest & Wiksell, 2001).

[3] *Into the Temple Courts: The Place of the Synagogues in the Second Temple Period* (SBLDS 169; Atlanta: Society of Bibilical Literature, 1999).

various sourcebooks, such as Horbury and Noy (inscriptions),[4] Tcherikover (papyri)[5] and Stern (archaeological).[6] But the literary sources from the New Testament, Philo, Josephus, and the Mishnah are collected for the first time in the present volume.

After a nineteen-page introductory essay, the book is divided into materials from the land of Israel (pp. 20–177) and those from the Diaspora (pp. 118–294). The nature of these materials is further categorized as archaeological, inscriptional, papyrus text and literary, along with a suggested date for each entry. Where archaeological evidence is concerned, pictures and/or artists' renderings with schematic plans are included. In addition to Greek, Latin and Hebrew texts, the authors provide brief bibliography, English translation and commentary for each entry. A full, sixteen-page bibliography follows at the end of the book, which cites sources dating from the seventeenth century to the current decade. A fold-out map is also included which marks synagogue sites and the nature of their materials.

Fresh English translations are provided by the editors for most papyri and inscriptions as well as for Josephus. The New Testament entries are taken primarily from the New Revised Standard Version. Among the works of Philo, translations are taken from Smallwood (for *Legat.*),[7] van der Horst (for *Flacc.*),[8] Runia (for *Opif.*)[9] and Colson (LCL), respectively. Entries taken from the Mishnah reprint Philip Blackman's translation.[10] However, it should be noted that the editors, even where they print translations from other sources, frequently alter them to better reflect synagogue terminology. Key words such as *synagōgē* and *proseuchē* are consistently bracketed in the translation to point the reader to the original language. The Greek, Latin and Hebrew texts are printed above the translations, but in the commentary all Greek and Hebrew words are transliterated, which serves those who may not read Greek or Hebrew.

[4] William Horbury and David Noy, *Jewish Inscriptions of Greco-Roman Egypt* (Cambridge: Cambridge University Press, 1992).

[5] Victor Tcherikover, Alexander Fuks and Menahem Stern, *Corpus Papyrorum Judaicarum* (3 vols.; Cambridge: Harvard University Press, 1957–64).

[6] Ephraim Stern, *The New Encyclopedia of Archaeological Excavations in the Holy Land* (4 vols.; Jerusalem: Carta, 1993).

[7] Mary Smallwood, *Philonis Alexandrini Legatio ad Gaium: Edited with an Introduction, Translation and Commentary* (Leiden: Brill, 1961).

[8] Pieter Willem van der Horst, *Philo's Flaccus. The First Pogrom: Introduction, Translation and Commentary* (Leiden: Brill, 2003).

[9] David Runia, *On the Creation of the Cosmos according to Moses: Introduction, Translation and Commentary* (Leiden: Brill, 2001).

[10] Philip Blackman, *Mishnayoth* (7 vols.; 2nd ed.; New York: Judaica, 1963–4).

The volume includes twenty-seven selections from Philo (based on the index), second only to the selections taken from the New Testament. Some of the Philonic materials are perhaps debatable. For example, *Deus* 8–9 (= No. 161) and *Spec.* 3.169–71 (= No. 169) are included because it is assumed that the term "temple" (*hieros*) is equivalent to the term "synagogue."[11] Further, *Decal.* 40–41 (= No. 199) is included because the verb *philosophein* occurs, and Philo frequently associates "philosophizing" with the Sabbath (p. 256). Since the synagogue is a place of gathering on the Sabbath, the editors assume an implicit reference, and include the text. Of course, source books attempt to be comprehensive, and thus the inclusion of some debatable texts is perhaps required.

Despite any criticisms, the present volume provides us with a comprehensive sourcebook for four hundred years of synagogue history in little more than three hundred pages. The commentaries, although speculative and brief at times,[12] are generally reasonable and enlightening. The editors' translations appear to be careful and tailor-made to reflect synagogue terminology. On the whole, this volume is an essential reference guide to anyone interested in pursuing ancient synagogue studies.

Justin M. Rogers
Cincinnati University

[11] To be sure, the editors note the uncertainty of interpreting *hiera* as "synagogues" in the commentary (p. 203).

[12] See No. 2 in which it is assumed that the six *hydriai* in John 2:6 refer to *miqvaoth*, and further that the presence of *miqvaoth* suggests a synagogue setting for the wedding in Cana. One might also wish for further enlightenment on such debated archaeological sites as the Capernaum synagogue (No. 8), which is assumed to date to the first century despite the meager evidence (but see the commentary, pp. 31–32), and the Ostia synagogue (No. 179). The argument between Birger Olsson and L. Michael White is mentioned, but not discussed in great detail (see L. Michael White, "Synagogue and Society in Imperial Ostia: Archaeological and Epigraphic Evidence," *HTR* 90 [1997]: 23–58; see also Olsson's rejoinder: "The Oldest Original Synagogue Building in the Diaspora: A Response to L. Michael White," *HTR* 92 [1999]: 409–33). Of course, the editors must limit the commentary as much as possible to keep the volume at a reasonable length. The bibliographies provide more than enough information for the reader to chase further references.

Eric F. Mason, *'You are a Priest Forever': Second Temple Jewish Messianism and the Priestly Christology of the Epistle to the Hebrews*. Studies on the Text of the Desert of Judah 74. Leiden: Brill, 2008. xiv + 229 pages. ISBN 90-04-14987-8. Price €79, $117.

In a revision of his 2005 Notre Dame doctoral dissertation, Eric F. Mason provides us with a study of Jesus as High Priest, a key motif in Hebrews that Mason argues is best understood against the specific Second Temple Jewish background provided in the Dead Sea Scrolls (DSS). Mason does not suggest any type of direct relationship between Hebrews and the scrolls; rather, he argues that "two elements contributing to Hebrews' presentation of Jesus as priest—the notion of heavenly priesthood and an angelic understanding of Melchizedek—are best paralleled in ideas found in the Dead Sea Scrolls" (203).

Mason first surveys what Hebrews itself has to say about Jesus as Priest. After examining the non-priestly titles the epistle uses for Christ (especially "Son" (υἱός), "pioneer" (ἀρχηγός) and "forerunner" (πρόδρομος)), he succinctly examines the five passages that explicitly refer to Jesus as (high) priest or as having a priestly role: Hebrews 1:1–14; 2:5–18; 4:14–5:10; ch. 7; and chapters 8–10. Mason concludes from this survey that the author's understanding of Jesus as high priest arises from his own "conscious, sustained theological reflection" on Ps 2:7 and 110:1, 4 with most of the affirmations about Jesus' priesthood being clearly based upon "widespread early Christian tenets" and commonplaces in Second Temple Judaism. However, Mason determines that the possible antecedents of one emphasis, Jesus as the *heavenly* high priest, is worth further investigation.

Mason next reviews previous scholarly proposals for the background of this heavenly high priest motif. He dismisses the notion that the motif is original to the author (it seems impossible given Hebrews was not written in a religious-intellectual vacuum); that it is dependent on Early Christian theology/exegesis (such theories have little evidence and are too speculative); that it is dependent on Gnostic mythology (namely Käsemann's theory, which relies on outdated understandings of Gnosticism and its sources and drives too great a wedge between Palestinian and Hellenistic Christianity); and dependent on the thought of Philo of Alexandria. In relation to this last thesis, Mason discuses Celsas Spicq's thesis that the Hebrews author's understanding of Jesus as high priest drew directly from the Alexandrian's view of the Logos as mediator between God and the world and his view that priesthood and kingship operated as mediators of the old covenant. Mason responds to Spicq's claims (which the Frenchman himself later modified in the light of the DSS) by recounting Ronald Williamson's critique that Philo's conception of the Logos is purely philosophical and that he held out no expectation for a personal, earthly messiah, both of which are incompatible with Hebrews' understanding of Jesus. Mason does accept that Hebrews draws on Middle Platonic thought or ideas parallel to Philo's (especially in its conception of the two sanctuaries (heavenly and earthly) in Heb 8–9) but cites Gregory Sterling's thesis that Hebrews also evinces a temporal dimension in its discussion of the sanctuaries that is indebted to eschatological concerns.

Chapter three and four are the heart of *You are a Priest Forever,* investigating messianic priest traditions and then Melchizedek traditions in Second Temple Judaism. After Mason has canvassed what scholars have said previously about the possible parallels and relationships between Hebrews and the DSS in these areas, he then moves to his own examination of the evidence. His analysis assumes that the DSS refer to specific figures as "Messiah" but also have "messianic" expectations for others even though they do not have that title. What is more, this diversity of messianic expectations were "fluid and far from standardized" over the Second Temple period. Among the texts that Mason examines in ch. 3 are the Rule of the Community (1QS IX, 11 suggests at some late stage of the document there was an expectation for three figures—an eschatological prophet, a priestly "messiah of Aaron," and a royal 'messiah of Israel'); the *Damascus Document* (which at a minimum expected a messiah priest); the *War Scroll* (the priest here has a liturgical role, including making atonement, as well as a role of rallying troops in the eschatological war); 4QFlor and 4QCatena[a] (these are probably part of the same text which appears to present a messianic diarchy of priest and king); and 4QTest (which indicates the expectation of at least a messianic priest). Mason concludes that the texts he surveys "clearly demonstrate an expectation of a priestly, eschatological figure who would appear alongside a lay figure, often identified as Davidic," with an eschatological prophet also showing up only very occasionally (111). Mason observes that the DSS texts provide very little exegetical support for a priestly messiah, and so he looks to the *Aramaic Levi Document, Jubilees,* and the *Testament of Levi* as offering evidence for a tradition of Levi's divine appointment, a tradition itself derived from a midrashic reading of Gen 34 by reference to Exod 32:25–29; Num 25:6–15; and Deut 33:8–11. From this, Mason claims "traditions of Levi's divine appointment to an eternal priesthood definitely predate Christianity and almost certainly influenced Qumran's priestly messianism" (133).

After quickly explicating Gen 14:18–20 and Ps 110:4 in the MT and LXX, Mason looks at Melchizedek traditions in non-Qumran Second Temple texts: *Genesis Apocryphon* (which takes away the mysteriousness of Gen with its retelling); *Jubilees* (uses Abraham's tithes to endorse tithing *to support* Levitical priests, in contrast to the reading of Hebrews); Pseudo-Eupolemus (Melchizedek *gives* Abraham gifts); Josephus (*J.W.* 6.438; *Ant.* 1.179–81; in both treatises the name is interpreted as "righteous king" which is taken as referring to the character of the person; in *Ant.* there are details that suggest Josephus may share traditions with *Genesis Apocryphon*); and Philo of Alexandria. With respect to this last, Mason looks at *Abr.* 235 (Philo allegorizes the Gen 14 encounter and shares the frequent interpretation that Melchizedek fed Abraham's whole company), *Congr.* 99 (like *Jubilees*, assumes continuity between Abraham's tithe and tithing to support Levites; shares with Josephus and Hebrews the conviction that Melchizedek was the first priest), and *Leg* 3.79–82 (like Hebrews, Philo here interprets Salem in Gen 14 as "peace"; makes a somewhat similar argument as Hebrews about Melchizedek's lack of genealogy, but without an appeal to Ps 110; identifies Melchizedek as "the righteous king"; and identifies him as the Logos, the mediator between God and humanity). Note that the subtitle on p. 131 erroneously refers to *Legat.* instead of *Leg.*

In the second part of his analysis of Melchizedek traditions, Mason focuses on the evidence from the DSS (much of it considerably fragmented). Treatises examined include *Songs of the Sabbath Sacrifice* (which appears to identify Melchizedek as an angelic priest serving in God's heavenly temple and possibly as head of an angelic priesthood); *Visions of Amram* (which seems to associate Melchizedek with Michael as an angelic opponent of Belial); and, in considerably more detail, 11QMelch. Assuming a number of variables and reconstructions, Mason contends 11QMelch "presents Melchizedek as a heavenly, eschatological figure in the service of God. He will deliver the righteous on God's behalf and will execute judgment on Belial and his lot. Also Melchizedek will make atonement for those of his own lot" (185).

Mason concludes his study by comparing Hebrews with his findings about Priestly and Melchizedek traditions. First, he contends that while Hebrews' Jesus is something other than the "messiah of Aaron" or Levi, these conceptions "along with the broader heavenly temple cult supposed in Jewish apocalyptic texts [...] provided a precedent for the author of Hebrews to conceive of Jesus similarly as a priest making atonement and eternal intercession in the heavenly sanctuary" (199). As for Melchizedek, Mason contends that Hebrews shares Qumran's appreciation of him as an eternal, presumably angelic figure (he defends this correct reading of Heb 7:3 in ch. 1 and again in ch. 5). Melchizedek's heavenly nature does not work against Hebrews' argument about the superiority of Christ but rather strengthens it; Mason suggests (202):

> the author of Hebrews was thinking of the relationship of Jesus and Melchizedek in terms akin to his conception of the sanctuaries, but with one further component. The eternal, divine Son was the model, and the angelic Melchizedek was the copy who encountered Abraham and established a non-Levitical priestly precedent in ancient Israel. This in turn prepared the way for the incarnate Son—both the model for Melchizedek yet now also resembling him—to be comprehended as priest.

Mason is to be commended for his careful yet suggestive reading of several Second Temple texts, especially those from Qumran. The study is conservative in scope and does not attempt to answer all the questions related to Hebrews' depiction of Jesus as high priest. For the most part this restraint seems appropriate. However, given Mason's generally positive descriptions of the similarities between Hebrews and Philo, one would like to see greater discussion of what Mason's thesis about the Qumran parallels with Hebrews means for Sterling's ontology vs. eschatology argument mentioned above. Nevertheless, there is much here to occupy those studying how Second Temple traditions sought to navigate the nexus between heaven and earth.

Ronald R. Cox
Pepperdine University

BIRGER A. PEARSON, *Ancient Gnosticism: Traditions and Literature*. Minneapolis, Minn.: Fortress, 2009. xvi + 362 pages. ISBN 978-0-8006-3258-8. Price $26 (paperback).

Birger Pearson has spent more than forty years researching traditions and literature dealing with Gnosticism, Egyptian Christianity and Coptic texts. In addition to penning numerous studies about these subjects in imperial and late ancient Egypt and the broader Roman Empire, Pearson has also played a significant role in the publication and translation of the Coptic Gnostic Library. Philonists should already be familiar with Pearson's writings (especially his 1990 collection of essays, *Gnosticism, Judaism, and Egyptian Christianity* [Fortress] as well as his study *Philo and the Gnostics on Man and Salvation* [Center for Hermeneutical Studies in Hellenism and Moder Culture, Berkeley, Calif., 1977]). With *Ancient Gnosticism* Pearson deviates from his usual technical and focused studies to provide an introduction to Gnosticism. Pearson attempts to write for non-specialists and eschews footnotes in favor of referrals for recommended readings at the end of the book. Given the esoteric and fragmentary nature of the subject matter and the authority earned by the author, such measures at accessibility do not offset the value of Pearson's work for non-Gnosticism scholars. Indeed, this book is a valuable description of the *status quaestionis* of Gnosticism research as Pearson perceives it.

Pearson begins his introduction by providing his answer to the question of "what is Gnosticism?," a debate that currently engages "Gnosticism" scholars and has led some to argue that the category is too pejorative and value-laden to be of use anymore. After acknowledging the limitations of the scholarly construct "Gnosticism" (to be distinguished from terms actually used in ancient writings like *gnosis* or *gnostikos*), Pearson still opts to retain the term as the best descriptor for the "Gnostic school of thought," the prime example of which is the treatise *Apocryphon of John*, which Pearson says originated in the mid-second century C.E. in either Antioch or Alexandria (and was Christianized in Egypt in the later second or early third century). Pearson contends that in Gnosticism, "saving gnosis comes by revelation from a transcendent realm, mediated by a revealer who has come from that realm in order to awaken people to a knowledge of God and a knowledge of the true [divine] nature of the human self" (12). This gnosis is chiefly mediated through the construction and sharing of elaborate myths that reflect upon the divine nature, cosmogony, anthropology and soteriology and which involve similar casts of characters (including a super-noetic, or nearly so, supreme principle, a heavenly realm populated by emanations from that being, an errant but ultimately repentant female figure named Sophia, a malevolent and foolish demiurge responsible for the material universe and human beings as holders of the transcendent divine essence imprisoned in material bodies). The building blocks for Gnostic speculation and mythopoeia are radical reinterpretations of religious (especially biblical and Jewish) and philosophical (especially Platonist) traditions. In both cases, ontological (Platonic) and temporal (Jewish apocalyptic) dualism are appropriated, recast and intensified, rendering as stark as possible the division between the spiritual and material realms and the eschatological goal of the soul's reunification to its divine source. In contrast to early Christian heresiologists and some contemporary scholars, Pearson does not believe that Gnosticism developed out of Christianity but rather only secondarily appropriated Christian characteristics and terminology.

In chapter 2, Pearson describes the evidence for Gnosticism as preserved in Patristic heresiological reports, moving chronologically from the supposed source of the heresy, Simon Magus, through to the "Cainites," a group said to have held Adam's son Cain in honor but which apparently never existed. He not only describes what the different "orthodox" writers said about these heterodox groups but also assesses those reports critically, evincing a *via media* between credulousness and hyper-skepticism. While the Patristic sources are moderately reliable for reconstructing Gnosticism, Pearson suggests it is better to have the Gnostics' own words, which we do (or at least many of them) in the Gnostic Coptic Library, especially the codices found buried near the Egyptian town of Nag Hammadi. Hence, in chapters 3, 5–8 he adds to the Heresiological evidence the primary sources from Sethians ("Classical" Gnostics), Basilideans, Valentinians, Hippolytus' "Three-Principle Systems," and an assortment of "Coptic Gnostic Writings of Unspecified Affiliation." The reader will especially wish to have a translation of the Gnostic Coptic writings ready to hand since Pearson's method is to draw from the literary evidence in describing the different Gnostic "schools." (Fortunately, Pearson provides abundant references to several contemporary translations of the Patristic and primary sources, including the newly released *Nag Hammidi Scriptures*, edited by Marvin Meyer.) His readings of the text are straightforward (Pearson is not a sensationalist), well written if at times a little taxing (he could have used more charts and illustrations to illustrate the different emanations that characterize Gnostic myths), and beneficial to those who wish to work directly with the writings.

The most significant points of interest for students of Philo may be found in chapters 3 and 4. In chapter 3, Pearson discusses the texts related to Sethian, or classical, Gnosticism, the writings he suggests most clearly convey the earliest, pre-Christian form of Gnosticism. Especially helpful is Pearson's detailed description of the contents of the *Apocryphon of John*, including its use of negative theology in describing the transcendent deity (also found in the Sethian tractate *Allogenes*) as well as the reinterpretations of the first several chapters of Genesis. So important is the latter for understanding all of Gnosticism that Pearson sets aside chapter 4 to discuss Gnostic biblical interpretation and how the Hebrew Bible, esp. Genesis, is a main source for Gnostic mythology. Philo looms large in Pearson's discussion here because "the Platonic elements of Gnosticism were mediated by Hellenistic Jewish philosophy, such as was espoused by Philo of Alexandria" through his biblical exegesis (105). While Pearson notes a number of Gnostic interpretations that are similar to Philo's allegorical approach, he also shows that the Gnostic reading of the Bible was rooted in a larger Jewish milieu and has affinities with Pseudepigraphical and Rabbinical traditions. Hence, even though there is a "major departure" from Jewish theology ("split[ting] the Jewish God into two, with creation attributed to a lower deity"), Pearson contends

> that Sethian or Classic Gnosticism developed as a result of the efforts of educated Jews interested in making sense of their traditions. They did this, not

> by rejecting their traditions wholesale, but by applying to them a new hermeneutic, whereby their ancestral traditions were given a radically new meaning. The result was, in effect, the creation of a new religion (32).

Chapters 9 and 10 involve a discussion of two gnosis oriented religious systems, Thomas Christianity and Hermetism, both of which have writings that are present in the Nag Hammadi codices. However, Pearson contends that for all their similar sensitivities, these are not Gnostic systems as they lack the heavenly emanations, Sophia myth, or malevolent demiurge. Still, in the case of Thomas Christianity (which bequeathed to us *Gos. Thom.* among other writings), at its core is the story of the soul trying to get back to its heavenly origin, which Pearson claims is a doctrine rooted in Middle Platonism. Furthermore, *Gos. Thom.* (as we have it in its final, second century C.E. form) also demonstrates a reworking of an earlier, temporal ("horizontal") eschatological orientation to a more mystical ("vertical") orientation, both of which ultimately come from Jewish apocalypticism. In the case of Hermetic religious traditions, there is again the combination of Greco-Roman Egyptian religious speculation with Hellenistic (esp. Platonic and Stoic) philosophy, but without the radical, world demeaning dualism of Gnosticism. Pearson claims that the first tractate of the *Corpus Hermeticum* (*CH*), "Poimandres," which also retells the biblical creation myth, functions for the whole of the corpus in a fashion similar to the role *Ap. John* has for classical Gnosticism (280).

> Like the *Apocryphon of John* it contains a basic myth involving cosmogony, anthropogony, and eschatology, and posits self-knowledge as the basis for salvation. And, like that of the *Apocryphon of John*, the Hermetic myth is indebted to the two great creation texts of the Greco-Roman world, Plato's *Timaeus* and the two creation stories in the book of Genesis. . . . But unlike the *Apocryphon of John*, the Poimandres is not critical of the Genesis story and raises no objections at all to what Moses said.

We might note that Pearson does not adequately discuss here the differences between "Poimandres" and Genesis (which, even though not a reverse reading like *Apoc. John*, is a reworking of the Genesis story and not a simple retelling) or the fact that Genesis and other Jewish traditions present in the *CH* occur in a *non-Jewish, pagan* religiosity, one that is unaware of early Christianity. Such observations help bolster Pearson's contention that it is not necessary to posit a Christian origin for a phenomenon like Gnosticism.

Pearson discusses the most successful form of Gnosticism, Manichaeism, in chapter 11, and its most enduring form, the still existent Mandaeans, in chapter 12. After a brief summary, the book concludes with the aforementioned recommendations for further reading (reflecting current and diverse scholarly views), a general index and an index to "Biblical Passages."

Ancient Gnosticism succeeds both as an introduction to its subject and as a starting place for those who are interested in correlating Philo's philosophical and interpretive tendencies with a curiously similar but radically different set of writings. The benefit will be a greater appreciation for the Alexandrian's intellectual and religious environment as well as for the possible *Nachleben* of the traditions represented in his writings.

Ronald R. Cox
Pepperdine University

PETER STRUCK, *The Birth of the Symbol: Ancient Readers at the Limits of their Texts*. Princeton, N.J.: Princeton University Press, 2004. 316 pages. ISBN: 978-1-4008-2609-4. Price $55.00.

In this broad survey of the development of the literary symbol in Greco-Roman antiquity, Peter Struck has made an exceptional contribution to the study of allegorical readers and their relation to the larger world of literary criticism. Tracing the genealogy of the Greek term *sumbolon* from the classical period until the late Neoplatonic commentators such as Proclus and beyond, Struck has attempted to show the centrality of allegorical modes of thinking to the ancient mind. He is critical of scholars who have considered it an aberration too closely related to theology, philosophy, and divination to be taken seriously in studies of ancient literary criticism. Furthermore, he argues that claims—both ancient and modern—that symbolic readings are inherently external impositions foreign to the text are all too often rash conclusions. While Struck is careful to explain that he is not advocating that modern readers embrace allegorical modes of reading in the manner of the ancients, he insists that a correct understanding of the use of the literary symbol in antiquity raises issues regarding the nature of texts and their meanings which would otherwise go unnoticed.

After an introduction in which he puts his approach in context and discusses past scholarship, Struck explains in his first chapter the ancient debate concerning symbolic modes of reading. Modern accounts of ancient literary criticism tend to focus on Aristotelian and Aristarchan models which were more analytic than interpretive and tended to value clarity instead of obscurity; however, Struck emphasizes allegorical readers such as Porphyry who valued obscurity and argues on the basis of the Derveni Papyrus and its focus on the enigma (*ainigma*) that obscurity as a motive for interpretation may have been the rule rather than the exception in the fifth and fourth centuries B.C.E. Struck also explains that this debate was closely related to philosophical concerns regarding the relationship between language and its referent in the world: "It is a question of an isomorphism between the taxonomy of language and the taxonomy of reality" (58).

In chapter two, Struck undertakes a more strictly chronological approach to his genealogy by examining the early meanings of *sumbolon* prior to 300 B.C.E. In the classical period, he explains that it was primarily used to refer to authentication or proof in the sense of an object broken into two parts in order to indicate an agreement between two parties. However, in the context of divination, it could mean a coincidental meeting which functions as an ominous sign. It is not until the fourth century with Demosthenes (*Against Aristocrates* 83) that *sumbolon* is used to refer to a figurative association of words, and thus by this time it had taken on a meaning more in line with the use of *ainigma* in the Derveni Papyrus. Exploring its association with Pythagorean enigmatic sayings (*puthagoreia sumbola*) and mystery cults, Struck makes the point that a wide variety of uses contributed to the evolution of the term in a literary context.

In chapters three and four, Struck explains how from ca. 300 B.C.E. *sumbolon* gained momentum as a literary term among the Stoics and then continued to be used among various first and second century C.E. authors. Key to the Stoic use of *sumbolon* and allegorical interpretation in general is their universalist ontology which regarded everything a manifestation of *logos* or *pneuma*. In this way, words are naturally connected to their referents and thus it is possible to use poetic texts to uncover deeper philosophical truths. Just as all is *pneuma* in a particular manifestation, so too is every word just a particular manifestation of more general concepts. According to Struck, "We see here developing a notion of what we might call religion as a form of study and intellectual discipline, in which the reading of the poets occupies an important place" (117). Struck then explains how the Stoic use of the literary symbol was carried forth in different ways by three authors flourishing in the first and second centuries C.E.: Cornutus, Heraclitus, and Pseudo-Plutarch. None are philosophers in the strict sense, yet each appropriated Stoic methods of allegorical interpretation. In both Heraclitus and Pseudo-Plutarch, one sees that symbolic modes of reading were closely tied to the rhetorical tradition and this supports Struck's argument that allegory belongs to the world of literary criticism.

In chapter five, Struck steps back to consider the importance of the symbol in the period covered in chapters three and four (300 B.C.E.–200 C.E.) in terms of the various associations of secrecy, chance, mystery cults, and divination which were discussed in chapter two. He argues that just as literary theory in the tradition of Aristotle was associated with rhetorical theory, allegorical interpreters had a great deal in common with practitioners of divination, esoteric philosophy, and cultic language. For example, Struck argues that there is a close association between the ancient concept of the *ainigma* and oracular language. He further discusses ancient authors such as Artemidorus and Macrobius in order to show the strong connection between allegorical interpretation and divination and also emphasizes the importance of Pythagoreanism in relation to the development of allegorical modes of interpretation among the Neoplatonists. Struck ends this chapter with a long passage from Clement of Alexandria (*Strom.* 5.4.21–24) which testifies to the importance of obscure language and symbols in relation simultaneously to oracles, dreams, poets, and philosophy.

In chapters six and seven, Struck turns to the use of the symbol among the Neoplatonists and then in the epilogue which follows, he considers their legacy among later Christian authors and beyond. Struck emphasizes that whereas the Stoic approach to allegorical interpretation rested on their belief that a word has a natural relationship to its referent, the Neoplatonic view emerged from an emanationist ontology which suggested a more direct relationship. In this way, for Neoplatonists such as Iamblichus, a symbolic act or word was actually able to invoke its referent and thus could be considered a talisman. After comparing Iamblichus to Porphyry and mentioning parallels in the Chaldean Oracles, Struck argues that it is the fifth century Neoplatonist Proclus who most fully combines the ideas of the talismanic symbol and literary allegory by creating an intricate ontological map of the cosmos. Most importantly, Proclus completely replaces the mimetic theory of poetry with one that is symbolic.

In his epilogue, Struck shows how the development of the literary symbol which culminated with Proclus had significant implications well beyond antiquity. Beginning with the sixth century Christian Pseudo-Dionysius the Areopagite, Proclus' metaphysics are combined with Christian theology, and for this reason, even the Eucharist could be understood as a theurgic practice which actually invokes divinity. Struck further traces the tradition through John of Damascus (eighth cent.), Dante (twelfth cent.) and even the Romantics. In the short appendix which follows, he reconsiders Chrysippus' interpretation of the mural at Samos in light of his conclusions and posits some intriguing—albeit speculative—possibilities.

Struck's book is particularly remarkable for its simultaneous breadth and attention to detail. It is accessible in its treatment of less familiar authors and at the same time provides close analyses of passages and abundant textual examples. His approach is unique in the way he has combined a philological study of *sumbolon* with a much more far-reaching consideration of allegory and literary theory. In doing so, Struck provides a fascinating *tour de force* of ancient modes of the symbolic and he shows that his conclusions have significant consequences throughout antiquity and beyond. The greatest disappointment to readers of this journal will be that Stuck has only touched on Philo in a couple of chapters.[13] Nonetheless, he has doubtlessly provided an invaluable study for those who wish to better understand the larger Greco-Roman context of Philo's attitude to the Bible as a symbolic medium.

M. Jason Reddoch
University of Cincinnati

[13] Philo is cited six times in chapters two and five: (1) Discussing the use of *sumbolon* in divinatory contexts, Struck explains that this appears early in the classical period and continues throughout later periods. Among other authors, Philo (*Prov.* frag. 2.24) is cited as an example (93–4). (2) Emphasizing the close relationship between Pythagoreanism and the use of enigmatic language, Struck points out the importance of *ainigma* for a number of passages such as Philo's *Prob.* 2 (103). (3) Struck relates the idea of the symbol as a "meaningful coincidence" back to the divinatory associations of *sumbolon* mentioned above in chapter two (171). (4) Struck cites Philo (*Somn.* 2.3–4) to show the close proximity of *ainigma* and prophetic dreaming (177). (5) When Struck examines Artemidorus' use of the language of allegory and the symbol in relation to divination through dreams, he also cites Philo (*Somn.* 2.8) who uses *allegoria* in an onirocritical context (183). (6) Discussing the close connection between allegory, Pythagoreanism, and oracles, Struck cites Philo's *Prob.* 2–4 (201).

The Studia Philonica Annual 21 (2009) 145–149

NEWS AND NOTES*

Philo of Alexandria Group of the Society of Biblical Literature

The Philo of Alexandria Group of the Society of Biblical Literature met for three sessions on November 23–25, 2008 in Boston, Massachusetts, as part of the Annual Meeting of the Society of Biblical Literature.

The first event, a joint session with the Letters of James, Peter, and Jude Section, was devoted to the theme of "The Formation of the Soul in Hellenistic Judaism and James" and was presided over by Stanley Stowers (Brown University). Speakers were Hindy Najman (University of Toronto), "Living in the Soul Alone: Philo of Alexandria on Soul Formation"; Gretchen Reydams-Schils (University of Notre Dame), "Philo of Alexandria on the Contemplative and the Active Lives"; John S. Kloppenborg (University of Toronto), "Stoic Psychagogy and the Letter of James"; Luiz Felipe Ribeiro (University of Toronto), "Self-Mastery, *Apatheia, Metriopatheia,* and Moral Theory in the Epistle of James."

The second session continued the custom of discussing new work on particular Philonic treatises and was presided over by Ellen Birnbaum (Cambridge, Mass.). The focus this year was on *De Vita Contemplativa*. Joan Taylor (London), who is completing work begun by the late David Hay for a new translation and commentary on this treatise for the Philo of Alexandria Commentary Series, began proceedings with very warm tributes to David Hay and a presentation of a sample translation and commentary on *Contempl.* 1–12. Responses were given by Joseph Sievers (Pontifical Biblical Institute, Rome) and Steve Mason (York University, Toronto). Lutz Döring (King's College, London) then spoke on "Philo's Therapeutae and Jewish Law," followed by Ross S. Kraemer (Brown University) who presented a paper on "Philo's Representation of the Therapeutrides Reconsidered." Proceedings finished with a lively exchange of ideas from the floor and panel with equally vigorous and gracious responses from Joan Taylor.

The final session consisted of papers drawn from an open call for papers on any aspect of the work of Philo of Alexandria and was presided over by Sarah Pearce (University of Southampton). Speakers were Katell

* Items of general interest to Philo scholars to be included in this section can be sent to the editor, David Runia (contact details in Notes on Contributors below).

Berthelot (National Center for Scientific Research, France), "Philo's Perception of the Roman Empire"; Tzvi Novick (University of Notre Dame), "Allegory and God: a Study in Philonic Exegesis"; Erin Roberts (Brown University), "Reconsidering the Value of Hope"; George H. van Kooten (University of Groningen), "Philo on Man as God's Likeness and the Platonic Notion of Becoming Like God"; Beth Berkowitz (Jewish Theological Seminary of America), "Clement's Use of Philo and Claims about Jewish-Christian Difference." Following an excellent discussion between speakers and audience, the annual business meeting convened to discuss future plans. Hindy Najman announced that she would be stepping down as co-chair of the Philo of Alexandria Group. Warm tributes were paid to her great efforts and achievements on behalf of the Group in recent years. Sarah Pearce will continue as chair and will be joined by Ellen Birnbaum as co-chair, supported by the Steering Committee (Katell Berthelot, Ron Cox, Martin Goodman, Sabrina Inowlocki Meister, George van Kooten, Hindy Najman, Maren Niehoff, Greg Sterling).

The next meeting of the Philo of Alexandria Group will be at the Annual Meeting of the Society of Biblical Literature in New Orleans, Louisiana on November 21–24, 2009. Two sessions are planned. The first will focus on new work on Philo's *De Agricultura* with presentations by Albert C. Geljon and David Runia and responses to their work by Jim Royse, David Konstan and Sarah Pearce, with Ken Schenck presiding. The second is devoted to the theme of "Philo and the Bible of Alexandria." Speakers include Tessa Rajak, Ben Wright III, Greg Sterling, Maren Niehoff, and Hans Svebakken, with Bob Kraft presiding.

Sarah Pearce
University of Southampton
United Kingdom

In Memoriam David Scholer (1938–2008)

David M. Scholer, Professor of New Testament at Fuller Theological Seminary, died of metastatic colorectal cancer August 22, 2008 in Pasadena, California. David was born in Rochester, Minnesota, July 24, 1938, and after attending public schools in Rochester, he earned degrees at Wheaton College (B.A., major in history; M.A., major in New Testament), Gordon Divinity School (B.D.), Harvard Divinity School (Th.D.). He taught New Testament on the faculties of Gordon-Conwell Theological Seminary (1969–1981), Northern Baptist Theological Seminary at which he also was Dean of the Seminary (1981–1988), North Park College and Theological Seminary (1988–1994), and Fuller Theological Seminary at which from 1996–2006 he also served as Associate Dean of the Center for Advanced Theological Studies (1994–2008). He was ordained to the Christian ministry within the American Baptist Churches/USA in 1966.

In 1993 Hendrickson Publishers published C. D. Yonge's 1854 translation of *The Works of Philo, Complete and Unabridged* in a new and updated version, for which David wrote the foreword and was integrally involved in its preparation, especially with regard to sorting out the textual issues between the Mangey text used by Yonge and the later Cohn-Wendland critical text, as well as keying Yonge's translation to the numbering system of the Loeb Classical Library edition. The Publisher's Preface noted that "[i]t is especially fitting that [David] would have consented to help since the ideas for producing both this edition of Philo's works and our previously published edition of *The Works of Josephus* really grow out of his classroom—having been inspired by his often expressed regret about the lack of an affordable and accessible edition of these important works." Now in its ninth printing, the Hendrickson Yonge volume has surpassed 80,000 copies in circulation.

Although his professional interests in study and teaching were wide-ranging within the fields of New Testament, early church and the Greco-Roman world, the primary emphases of his academic career were the study of gnosticism, especially related to the findings at Nag Hammadi, and the study of women and ministry in the New Testament and the early church. The former interest led to the publication of three volumes of *Nag Hammadi Bibliography*, the first covering 1948–1969 (Leiden: Brill, 1971), the second covering 1970-1994 (Leiden: Brill, 1997), and the final volume covering 1995–2006 (Leiden: Brill, 2008, which came out posthumously), and numerous articles in the area of gnosticism. Out of his latter interest, he developed a course, most recently titled Women, the Bible, and the Church, which he taught thirty times, first offering it at Gordon–Conwell in 1972 and then teaching it in all the seminaries he served, as well as Whitley College in Melbourne. His commitment to the full participation of women as equal partners with men in the ministry of the church led to his speaking on this topic in a multitude of settings and locations over the years and to the publication of numerous articles, pamphlets and a video series. In recognition of his leadership in this cause he was given awards by the Women's Concerns Committee of Fuller (2003), the Evangelical & Ecumenical Women's Caucus (2004), Christians for Biblical Equality (2007), and the Office of Women in Ministry of the American Baptist Churches/USA (2009).

David is survived by his wife of forty-eight years, Jeannette (née Mudgett), and two daughters, Emily Hernandez of Illinois and Abigail Strazzabosco of Pennsylvania, and three grandchildren (of Emily).

Jeanette Scholer
Fuller Theological Seminary
Pasadena, California[1]

Project: Philo of Alexandria in the Origins of Western Culture

A project on Philo of Alexandria in The Origins of Western Culture was started in the Center of Classical Studies, Faculty of Letters of the University of Lisbon, one year ago under the coordination of Manuel Alexandre Jr.

The purpose of this project is to provide an accurate translation of Philo's treatises in Portuguese, each one of them including a general introduction and notes. The first treatises being translated are: *De opificio mundi; Quis rerum divinarum heres; De congressu quaerendae eruditionis gratia; De vita contemplativa; Quod omnis probus liber sit; Legatio ad Gaium* and *In Flaccum*. The last of these is now ready for publishing.

The translation of Philo´s treatises and their publication in bilingual editions will be of considerable interest to areas of knowledge as diverse as ancient philosophy, classical studies, Jewish studies, biblical studies and patristic Studies in the Portuguese–speaking countries.

Manuel Alexandre Jr
University of Lisbon

First volume of Philo Hispanicus published

It will be recalled that in 2003 in the pages of this Journal, José Pablo Martín announced the project that was undertaken to produce the first academically sound Spanish translation of all Philo's writings. I am pleased to report that the first volume has just been published under the title *Filón de Alejandría Obras Completas Volumen I*. The publisher is Editorial Trotta (Madrid) in its series Colección Estructuras y Procesos Serie Religión. The

[1] My warmest thanks to Jeanette for writing this short piece on her late husband and to Donald Hagner (Fuller) for acting as an intermediary. (DTR)

volume contains an extensive introduction to the life, writings, thought and reception of Philo by the general editor, José Pablo Martín (pp. 9–88), followed by a translation of *De opificio mundi* by Francisco Lisi (pp. 95–158) and a translation of *Legum allegoriae* by Marta Alesso (pp. 159–301). The translations are accompanied by their own introductions and notes. The project team is warmly to be congratulated on the publication of this first volume and it is to be hoped that further volumes will soon follow (a total of eight are planned). We hope to provide a fuller review of the first volume in *The Studia Philonica Annual* at a later date.

David T. Runia
Queen's College
The University of Melbourne

The Studia Philonica Annual 21 (2009) 151–153

NOTES ON CONTRIBUTORS

ELLEN BIRNBAUM has taught at several Boston-area institutions, including Boston University, Brandeis, and Harvard. Her postal address is 78 Porter Road, Cambridge, MA 02140, USA; her electronic address is ebirnbaum@comcast.net.

RONALD R. COX is Associate Professor and Seaver Fellow in the Religion Division, Pepperdine University. His postal address is Religion Division, Pepperdine University, Malibu, CA 90263-4352, USA; his electronic address is ronald.cox@pepperdine.edu.

ALBERT C. GELJON teaches classical languages at the Christelijke Gymnasium in Utrecht. His postal address is Gazellestraat 138, 3523 SZ Utrecht, THE NETHERLANDS; his electronic address is geljon@ixs.nl.

HELEEN M. KEIZER is Dean of Academic Affairs at the Istituto Superiore di Osteopatia in Milan, Italy. Her postal address is Via Guerrazzi 3, 20052 Monza (Mi), ITALY; her electronic address is h.m.keizer@virgilio.it.

SCOTT D. MACKIE has taught courses at Loyola Marymount University, Westmont College, and Fuller Theological Seminary. His postal address is 51 Rose Ave. #17, Venice CA 90291, USA; his electronic address is scottdmackie@gmail.com.

JOSÉ PABLO MARTÍN is Professor Consultus at the Universidad Nacional de General Sarmiento, San Miguel, Argentina, and Senior Research fellow of the Argentinian Research Organization (CONICET). His postal address is Azcuenaga 1090, 1663 San Miguel, ARGENTINA; his electronic address is philonis@fastmail.fm.

MAREN S. NIEHOFF is Senior Lecturer in the Department of Jewish Thought at the Hebrew University, Jerusalem. Her postal address is Department of Jewish Thought, Hebrew University, Mt. Scopus, Jerusalem 91905, ISRAEL; her electronic address is msmaren@mscc.huji.ac.il.

TZVI NOVICK is an Assistant Professor in the Department of Theology, University of Notre Dame. His postal address is Department of

Theology, 130 Malloy Hall, University of Notre Dame, Notre Dame, IN 46556, USA; his email address is novick.3@nd.edu.

M. JASON REDDOCH is a graduate student in the Classics Department, University of Cincinnati. His postal address is Classics Department, University of Cincinnati, Cincinnati, OH, USA; his email address is reddocmj@email.uc.edu.

JEAN RIAUD is Professor in the Institut de Lettres et Histoire, Université Catholique de l'Ouest, Angers. His postal address is 24, rue du 8 mai 1945, Saint Barthélemy d'Anjou, FRANCE; his electronic address is jean.riaud@wanadoo.fr.

JUSTIN ROGERS is a graduate student at the Hebrew Union College–Jewish Institute of Religion, Cincinnati. His postal address is 1566 W Loveland Ave, Loveland, OH 45140, USA; his email address is justinrogers35 @hotmail.com.

DAVID T. RUNIA is Master of Queen's College and Professorial Fellow in the School of Historical Studies at the University of Melbourne. His postal address is Queen's College, 1–17 College Crescent, Parkville 3052, AUSTRALIA; his electronic address is runia@queens.unimelb.edu.au.

GOTTFRIED SCHIMANOWSKI is Research Fellow at the Institutum Judaicum Delitzschianum in Münster, Germany. He also works as Schulreferent in the Saarland region of Germany. His postal address is Mittelstaedter Strasse 19, 72124 Pliezhausen, GERMANY; his electronic address is gschimanow@ gmx.de.

TORREY SELAND is Professor of New Testament, School of Missions and Theology, Stavanger, Norway. His postal address is School of Missions and Theology, Misjonsveien 34, 4024 Stavanger, NORWAY; his electronic address is torrey@gmail.com.

GREGORY E. STERLING is Dean of the Graduate School and Professor of New Testament and Christian Origins in the Department of Theology, University of Notre Dame. His postal address is 408 Main Building, University of Notre Dame, Notre Dame IN 46556, USA; his electronic address is sterling.1@nd.edu.

THOMAS H. TOBIN, S.J. is Professor of New Testament and Early Christianity at Loyola University Chicago. His postal address is Department of Theology, Loyola University Chicago, 6525 N. Sheridan Road, Chicago, IL 60626, USA; his electronic address is ttobin@luc.edu.

DAVID WINSTON is Emeritus Professor of Hellenistic and Jewish Studies, Graduate Theological Union, Berkeley. His postal address is 1220 Grizzly Peak, Berkeley, CA 94708, USA; his electronic address is davidswinston@comcast.net.

The Studia Philonica Annual 21 (2009) 155–161

INSTRUCTIONS TO CONTRIBUTORS

Articles and Book reviews can only be considered for publication in *The Studia Philonica Annual* if they rigorously conform to the guidelines established by the editorial board. For further information see also the website of the Annual:

http://www.nd.edu/~philojud

1. *The Studia Philonica Annual* accepts articles for publication in the area of Hellenistic Judaism, with special emphasis on Philo and his *Umwelt*. Articles on Josephus will be given consideration if they focus on his relation to Judaism and classical culture (and not on primarily historical subjects). The languages in which the articles may be published are English, French and German. Translations from Italian or Dutch into English can be arranged at a modest cost to the author.

2. Articles and reviews are to be sent to the editors in electronic form as email attachments. The preferred word processor is Microsoft Word. Users of other word processors are requested to submit a copy exported in a format compatible with Word, e.g. in RTF format. Manuscripts should be double-spaced, including the notes. Words should be italicized when required, not underlined. Quotes five lines or longer should be indented and may be single-spaced. For foreign languages, including Greek and Hebrew, unicode systems are strongly to be encouraged for ease of conversion. In all cases it is **imperative** that authors give **full details** about the word processor (if it is not Word) and foreign language fonts used. Moreover, if the manuscript contains Greek or Hebrew material, a PDF version of the document must be sent together with the word processing file. If this proves difficult, a hard copy can be sent by mail or by fax. No handwritten Greek or Hebrew can be accepted. Authors are requested not to vocalize their Hebrew (except when necessary) and to keep their use of this language to a reasonable minimum. It should always be borne in mind that not all readers of the Annual can be expected to read Greek or Hebrew. Transliteration is encouraged for incidental terms.

3. Authors are encouraged to use inclusive language wherever possible, avoiding terms such as "man" and "mankind" when referring to humanity in general.

4. For the preparation of articles and book reviews the Annual follows the guidelines of *The SBL Handbook of Style for Ancient Near Eastern, Biblical, and Early Christian Studies*, Hendrickson: Peabody Mass., 1999. A downloadable PDF version of this guide is available on the SBL website, www.sbl-site.org. Here are examples of how a monograph, a monograph in a series, an edited volume, an article in an edited volume and a journal article are to be cited in notes (different conventions apply for bibliographies):

Joan E. Taylor, *Jewish Women Philosophers of First-Century Alexandria—Philo's 'Therapeutae' Reconsidered* (Oxford: Oxford University Press, 2003), 123.

Ellen Birnbaum, *The Place of Judaism in Philo's Thought: Israel, Jews, and Proselytes* (BJS 290; SPhM 2; Atlanta: Scholars Press, 1996), 134.

Gerard P. Luttikhuizen, ed., *Eve's Children: The Biblical Stories Retold and Interpreted in Jewish and Christian Traditions* (Themes in Biblical Narrative 5; Leiden: Brill, 2003), 145.

Gregory E. Sterling, "The Bond of Humanity: Friendship in Philo of Alexandria," in *Greco-Roman Perspectives on Friendship*, (ed. John T. Fitzgerald; SBLRBS 34; Atlanta: Scholars Press, 1997), 203–23.

James R. Royse, "Jeremiah Markland's Contribution to the Textual Criticism of Philo." *SPhA* 16 (2004): 50–60. (Note that abbreviations are used in the notes, but not in a bibliography.)

Note that, when joining up numbers in all textual and bibliographical references the n-dash should be used and not the hyphen, i.e. 50–60, not 50-60. For publishing houses only the first location is given. Submissions which do not conform to these guidelines will be returned to the authors for re-submission.

5. The following abbreviations are to be used in both articles and book reviews.

(a) Philonic treatises are to be abbreviated according to the following list. Numbering follows the edition of Cohn and Wendland, using Arabic numbers only and full stops rather than colons (e.g. *Spec.* 4.123). Note that *De Providentia* should be cited according to Aucher's edition, and not the LCL translation of the fragments by F. H. Colson.

Abr.	*De Abrahamo*
Aet.	*De aeternitate mundi*
Agr.	*De agricultura*
Anim.	*De animalibus*
Cher.	*De Cherubim*
Contempl.	*De vita contemplativa*
Conf.	*De confusione linguarum*
Congr.	*De congressu eruditionis gratia*
Decal.	*De Decalogo*
Deo	*De Deo*
Det.	*Quod deterius potiori insidiari soleat*

Deus	*Quod Deus sit immutabilis*
Ebr.	*De ebrietate*
Flacc.	*In Flaccum*
Fug.	*De fuga et inventione*
Gig.	*De gigantibus*
Her.	*Quis rerum divinarum heres sit*
Hypoth.	*Hypothetica*
Ios.	*De Iosepho*
Leg. 1–3	*Legum allegoriae* I, II, III
Legat.	*Legatio ad Gaium*
Migr.	*De migratione Abrahami*
Mos. 1–2	*De vita Moysis* I, II
Mut.	*De mutatione nominum*
Opif.	*De opificio mundi*
Plant.	*De plantatione*
Post.	*De posteritate Caini*
Praem.	*De praemiis et poenis, De exsecrationibus*
Prob.	*Quod omnis probus liber sit*
Prov. 1–2	*De Providentia* I, II
QE 1–2	*Quaestiones et solutiones in Exodum* I, II
QG 1–4	*Quaestiones et solutiones in Genesim* I, II, III, IV
Sacr.	*De sacrificiis Abelis et Caini*
Sobr.	*De sobrietate*
Somn. 1–2	*De somniis* I, II
Spec. 1–4	*De specialibus legibus* I, II, III, IV
Virt.	*De virtutibus*

(b) Standard works of Philonic scholarship are abbreviated as follows:

G-G Howard L. Goodhart and Erwin R. Goodenough, "A General Bibliography of Philo Judaeus." In *The Politics of Philo Judaeus: Practice and Theory* (ed. Erwin R. Goodenough; New Haven: Yale University Press, 1938; repr. Georg Olms: Hildesheim, 1967), 125–321.

PCH *Philo von Alexandria: die Werke in deutscher Übersetzung*, ed. Leopold Cohn, Isaac Heinemann *et al.*, 7 vols. (Breslau: M & H Marcus Verlag, Berlin: Walter de Gruyter, 1909–64).

PCW *Philonis Alexandrini opera quae supersunt*, ed. Leopoldus Cohn, Paulus Wendland et Sigismundus Reiter, 6 vols. (Berlin: Georg Reimer, 1896–1915).

PLCL *Philo in Ten Volumes (and Two Supplementary Volumes)*, English translation by F. H. Colson, G. H. Whitaker (and R. Marcus), 12 vols. (Loeb Classical Library; London: William Heinemann, Cambridge, Mass.: Harvard University Press, 1929–62).

PAPM *Les œuvres de Philon d'Alexandrie*, French translation under the general editorship of Roger Arnaldez, Jean Pouilloux, and Claude Mondésert (Paris: Cerf, 1961–92).

R-R	Roberto Radice and David T. Runia, *Philo of Alexandria: an Annotated Bibliography 1937–1986* (VCSup 8; Leiden etc.: Brill 1988).
RRS	David T. Runia, *Philo of Alexandria: an Annotated Bibliography 1987–1996* (VCSup 57; Leiden etc.: Brill 2000).
SPh	*Studia Philonica*
SPhA	*The Studia Philonica Annual*
SPhM	Studia Philonica Monographs
PACS	Philo of Alexandria Commentary Series

(c) References to biblical authors and texts and to ancient authors and writings are to be abbreviated as recommended in the *SBL Handbook of Style* §8.2–3. Note that biblical books are not italicized and that between chapter and verse a colon is placed (but for non-biblical references colons should not be used). Abbreviations should be used for biblical books when they are followed by chapter or chapter and verse unless the book is the first word in a sentence. Authors writing in German or French should follow their own conventions for biblical citations.

(d) For giving dates the abbreviations B.C.E. and C.E. are preferred and should be printed in small caps.

(e) Journals, monograph series, source collections, and standard reference works are to be be abbreviated in accordance with the recommendations listed in *The SBL Handbook of Style* §8.4. The following list contains a selection of the more important abbreviations, along with a few abbreviations of classical and philosophical journals and standard reference books not furnished in the list.

ABD	*The Anchor Bible Dictionary*, 6 vols. New York etc., 1992
AC	*L'Antiquité Classique*
ACW	Ancient Christian Writers
AGJU	Arbeiten zur Geschichte des antiken Judentums und des Urchristentums
AJPh	*American Journal of Philology*
AJSL	*American Journal of Semitic Languages*
ALGHJ	Arbeiten zur Literatur und Geschichte des hellenistischen Judentums
ANRW	*Aufstieg und Niedergang der römischen Welt*
APh	*L'Année Philologique*
BDAG	Bauer, W., F. W. Danker, W. F. Arndt, and F. W. Gingrich. *A Greek-English Lexicon of the New Testament and Other Early Christian literature.* 3d ed. Chicago: University of Chicago Press, 1999
BibOr	Bibliotheca Orientalis
BJRL	*Bulletin of the John Rylands Library*
BJS	Brown Judaic Studies
BMCR	*Bryn Mawr Classical Review* (electronic)

BZAW	Beihefte zur Zeitschrift für die alttestamentliche Wissenschaft
BZNW	Beihefte zur Zeitschrift für die neutestamentliche Wissenschaft
BZRGG	Beihefte zur Zeitschrift für Religions- und Geistesgeschichte
CBQ	*The Catholic Biblical Quarterly*
CBQMS	The Catholic Biblical Quarterly. Monograph Series
CC	Corpus Christianorum, Turnhout
CIG	*Corpus Inscriptionum Graecarum*. Edited by A. Boeckh, 4 vols. in 8. Berlin, 1828–77
CIJ	*Corpus Inscriptionum Judaicarum*. Edited by J. B. Frey, 2 vols. Rome, 1936–52
CIL	*Corpus Inscriptionum Latinarum*. Berlin, 1862–
CIS	*Corpus Inscriptionum Semiticarum*. Paris, 1881–1962
CPh	*Classical Philology*
CPJ	*Corpus Papyrorum Judaicarum*. Edited by V. Tcherikover and A. Fuks, 3 vols. Cambrige Mass., 1957–64
CQ	*The Classical Quarterly*
CR	*The Classical Review*
CRINT	Compendia Rerum Iudaicarum ad Novum Testamentum
CPG	*Clavis Patrum Graecorum*. Edited by M. Geerard, 5 vols. and suppl. vol. Turnhout, 1974–98
CPL	*Clavis Patrum Latinorum*. Edited by E. Dekkers. 3rd ed. Turnhout, 1995
CSCO	Corpus Scriptorum Christianorum Orientalium
CWS	Classics of Western Spirituality
DA	Dissertation Abstracts
DBSup	*Dictionnaire de la Bible*, Supplément. Paris, 1928–
DPhA	R. Goulet (ed.), *Dictionnaire des philosophes antiques*, Paris, 1989–
DSpir	*Dictionnaire de Spiritualité*, 17 vols. Paris, 1932–95
EncJud	*Encyclopaedia Judaica*, 16 vols. Jerusalem, 1972
EPRO	Études préliminaires aux religions orientales dans l'Empire romain
FrGH	*Fragmente der Griechische Historiker*. Edited by F. Jacoby et al. Leiden, 1954–
GCS	Die griechischen christlichen Schriftsteller, Leipzig
GLAJJ	M. Stern, *Greek and Latin Authors on Jews and Judaism*, 3 vols. Jerusalem, 1974–84
GRBS	*Greek, Roman and Byzantine Studies*
HKNT	Handkommentar zum Neuen Testament, Tübingen
HNT	Handbuch zum Neuen Testament, Tübingen
HR	*History of Religions*
HThR	*Harvard Theological Review*
HUCA	*Hebrew Union College Annual*
JAAR	*Journal of the American Academy of Religion*
JAOS	*Journal of the American Oriental Society*
JAC	*Jahrbuch für Antike und Christentum*
JBL	*Journal of Biblical Literature*
JHI	*Journal of the History of Ideas*
JHS	*The Journal of Hellenic Studies*
JJS	*The Journal of Jewish Studies*
JQR	*The Jewish Quarterly Review*
JR	*The Journal of Religion*
JRS	*The Journal of Roman Studies*
JSHRZ	Jüdische Schriften aus hellenistisch-römischer Zeit

JSJ	*Journal for the Study of Judaism in the Persian, Hellenistic and Roman Periods*
JSJSup	Supplements to the Journal for the Study of Judaism
JSNT	*Journal for the Study of the New Testament*
JSNTSup	Journal for the Study of the New Testament. Supplement Series
JSOT	*Journal for the Study of the Old Testament*
JSOTSup	Journal for the Study of the Old Testament. Supplement Series
JSP	*Journal for the Study of the Pseudepigrapha and Related Literature*
JSSt	*Journal of Semitic Studies*
JThS	*The Journal of Theological Studies*
KBL	L. Koehler and W. Baumgartner, *Lexicon in Veteris Testamenti libros*, 3 vols. 3rd ed. Leiden, 1967–83
KJ	*Kirjath Sepher*
LCL	Loeb Classical Library
LSJ	*A Greek-English Lexicon*. Edited by H. G. Liddell, R. Scott, H. S. Jones. 9th ed. with revised suppl. Oxford, 1996
MGWJ	*Monatsschrift für Geschichte und Wissenschaft des Judentums*
Mnem	*Mnemosyne*
NCE	*New Catholic Encyclopedia*, 15 vols. New York, 1967
NHS	Nag Hammadi Studies
NT	*Novum Testamentum*
NTSup	Supplements to Novum Testamentum
NTA	*New Testament Abstracts*
NTOA	Novum Testamentum et Orbis Antiquus
NTS	*New Testament Studies*
ODJ	*The Oxford Dictionary of Judaism*. Edited by R.J.Z. Werblowsky and G. Wigoder, New York 1997
OGIS	*Orientis Graeci inscriptiones selectae*
OLD	*The Oxford Latin Dictionary*. Edited by P. G. W. Glare. Oxford, 1982
OTP	*The Old Testament Pseudepigrapha*. Edited by J. H. Charlesworth. 2 vols. New York–London, 1983–85
PAAJR	*Proceedings of the American Academy for Jewish Research*
PAL	*Philon d'Alexandrie: Lyon 11–15 Septembre 1966*. Éditions du CNRS, Paris, 1967
PG	Patrologiae cursus completus: series Graeca. Edited by J. P. Migne. 162 vols. Paris, 1857–1912
PGL	*A Patristic Greek Lexicon*. Edited by G. W. H. Lampe. Oxford, 1961
PhilAnt	Philosophia Antiqua
PL	Patrologiae cursus completus: series Latina. Edited by J. P. Migne. 221 vols. Paris, 1844–64
PW	Pauly-Wissowa-Kroll, *Real-Encyclopaedie der classischen Altertumswissenschaft*. 49 vols. Munich, 1980
PWSup	Supplement to PW
RAC	*Reallexikon für Antike und Christentum*
RB	*Revue Biblique*
REA	*Revue des Études Anciennes*
REArm	*Revue des Études Arméniennes*
REAug	*Revue des Études Augustiniennes*
REG	*Revue des Études Grecques*
REJ	*Revue des Études Juives*
REL	*Revue des Études Latines*

RGG	*Die Religion in Geschichte und Gegenwart*, 7 vols. 3rd edition Tübingen, 1957–65
RhM	*Rheinisches Museum für Philologie*
RQ	*Revue de Qumran*
RSR	*Revue des Sciences Religieuses*
Str-B	H. L. Strack and P. Billerbeck, *Kommentar zum Neuen Testament aus Talmud und Midrasch*, 6 vols. Munich, 1922–61
SBLDS	Society of Biblical Literature Dissertation Series
SBLMS	Society of Biblical Literature Monograph Series
SBLSPS	Society of Biblical Literature Seminar Papers Series
SC	Sources Chrétiennes
Sem	*Semitica*
SHJP	E. Schürer, *The History of the Jewish People in the Age of Jesus Christ*. Revised edition, 3 vols. in 4. Edinburgh, 1973–87
SJLA	Studies in Judaism in Late Antiquity
SNTSMS	Society for New Testament Studies. Monograph Series
SR	*Studies in Religion*
SUNT	Studien zur Umwelt des Neuen Testaments
SVF	*Stoicorum veterum fragmenta*. Edited by J. von Arnim. 4 vols. Leipzig, 1903–24
TDNT	*Theological Dictionary of the New Testament*. 10 vols. Grand Rapids, 1964–76
THKNT	Theologischer Handkommentar zum Neuen Testament, Berlin
TRE	*Theologische Realenzyklopädie*, Berlin
TSAJ	Texte und Studien zum Antike Judentum
TU	Texte und Untersuchungen zur Geschichte der altchristlichen Literatur, Berlin
TWNT	*Theologisches Wörterbuch zum Neuen Testament*, 10 vols. Stuttgart 1933–79.
VC	*Vigiliae Christianae*
VCSup	Supplements to Vigiliae Christianae
VT	*Vetus Testamentum*
WMANT	Wissenschaftliche Monographien zum Alten und Neuen Testament
WUNT	Wissenschaftliche Untersuchungen zum Neuen Testament
YJS	*Yale Jewish Studies*
ZAW	*Zeitschrift für die alttestamentliche Wissenschaft*
ZKG	*Zeitschrift für Kirchengeschichte*
ZKTh	*Zeitschrift für Katholische Theologie*
ZNW	*Zeitschrift für die neutestamentliche Wissenschaft*
ZRGG	*Zeitschrift für Religions- und Geistesgeschichte*

www.ingramcontent.com/pod-product-compliance
Lightning Source LLC
Chambersburg PA
CBHW030527100426
42813CB00001B/174
9781589834439